The Causes, Course and Outcomes of World War Two

John Plowright

First published 2007 by
PALGRAVE MACMILLAN
Houndmills, Basingstoke, Hampshire RG21 6XS and
175 Fifth Avenue, New York, N.Y. 10010
Companies and representatives throughout the world

PALGRAVE MACMILLAN is the global academic imprint of the Palgrave
Macmillan division of St. Martin's Press, LLC and of Palgrave Macmillan Ltd.
Macmillan® is a registered trademark in the United States, United Kingdom
and other countries. Palgrave is a registered trademark in the European
Union and other countries.

ISBN-13: 978-0-333-79344-2 hardback
ISBN-10: 0-333-79344-7 hardback
ISBN-13: 978-0-333-79345-9 paperback
ISBN-10: 0-333-79345-5 paperback

This book is printed on paper suitable for recycling and made from fully
managed and sustained forest sources.

A catalogue record for this book is available from the British Library.

A catalog record for this book is available from the Library of Congress.

10   9   8   7   6   5   4   3   2   1
16   15   14   13   12   11   10   09   08   07

Printed in China

To

Alex & James

Two sons – two rays of light

Contents

Acknowledgements

Success is invariably shared while failure is lonely business. Whatever the fate of this book at the hands of the critics and public, its author is happy to acknowledge all its faults as lying with himself and all its virtues as resting on an accumulation of debts – some intellectual, others emotional – but all crucial in making the author what he is and his work what it is.

Special thanks, as always, are due to Sue, Alex and James for their love and toleration.

I would also like to thank all those others who have helped in a variety of ways over the years, particularly my late parents but also Professor Derek Beales, Professor Jeremy Black, Professor David Cannadine, the late Mr Maurice Cowling, Mr Stan Houston, Miss Nela Kashfi, Mr and Mrs Ron Lee, Mrs Gilian Noero, Dr Jonathan Parry, the Reverend William Plowright, Mr Ken Reed, Mr Robin Reeve and all the staff and students – past and present – of Repton School.

JP
Repton

Preface

The origins of this book

In the preface to his *Six Armies in Normandy*, John Keegan writes elegiacally about his childhood during World War Two and the way in which it naturally sparked his interest in that conflict and in military history generally. Having been born in 1956 the present author belongs to a different generation to Keegan's but one which was nevertheless profoundly touched by the events of 1939–45.

My mother served in the Women's Land Army and learnt how to drive a tractor, while my father served in the Royal Air Force Regiment, rising to the rank of Warrant Officer. Many of my childhood 'uncles' and 'aunts', including several with whom I holidayed as a child, had become friends of my parents as a result of their shared wartime experiences. It is difficult to demonstrate but difficult to deny that the events of 1939–45 not only transformed the world map but transformed the lives of those who lived through it and, in consequence, those who came after.

Although the *Beano* and the *Dandy* were my regular comics (supplemented later by second-hand copies of *Look and Learn*), I certainly looked at other comics, if only during regular visits to the barber's, which celebrated British military exploits during the war, and I was entranced as a youth by a German medal in a second-hand shop window en route to the barber's which I took to be an Iron Cross and only several years later learned was a Mother's Cross (awarded to those women who were most prolific in providing offspring for the Third Reich).

My toys were not by any means exclusively the toys of war but I probably derived most pleasure and certainly spent most time lining up Airfix miniature soldiers (sold in packets of 48 for 2/6 or 12.5p), which included the Afrika Korps and the British Eighth Army replete with a figure of Monty. One of the earliest expressions of my historical sensibility was exasperation if anyone suggested I mix soldiers of different periods or from different theatres of war. I still have a D-Day landscape moulded out of plastic, which was a prized present purchased by mail order.

At the age of nine I remember watching the televised scenes of Winston Churchill's state funeral, having already had impressed upon me his claims to greatness and our gratitude. At about this time, if not before, I became an avid watcher of *All Our Yesterdays* (the long-running Granada TV documentary series on the war), as I later became a fan of *The World at War*.

At Stafford Junior school my class was read Ian Serailler's *The Silver Sword* (set against the backdrop of the Nazi occupation of Poland) and a free choice of project at Cavendish Secondary school (before I passed the 13+ and moved on to Eastbourne Grammar School) was devoted to Hitler, with William L. Shirer's 1961 *Rise and Fall of Adolf Hitler* being one of several books relating to World War Two which were repeatedly borrowed from the public library.

As a teenager my pocket money was raised to 3/6 (17.5p per week) specifically in order to enable me to subscribe to Purnell's weekly *History of the Second World War* (published in six – later extended to eight – volumes). At some time later, my interest in history in general and World War Two in particular being by now well established, I was entrusted with some of my parents' wartime memorabilia, including my father's medals and two fascist rings which he had acquired in North Africa or Italy.

Numerous films on television and in the cinema ranging from the 1957 *The Bridge on the River Kwai* to the 1965 *Battle of the Bulge* intensified an interest in the period, and living in Eastbourne meant that the *Battle of Britain* (released 1969) was partly filmed overheard, so as a schoolboy I watched in the playground as Spitfires and Messerschmitts recreated overhead the dogfights of yesteryear.

In all but the last detail my experiences must have been shared in essence by many belonging to my class, time and gender. I do not believe, as some would claim, that it has made my generation obsessed with the Second World War but it has clearly been a longstanding and passionate interest and I was accordingly delighted to be invited to write this volume.

Last but not least, this book is dedicated to my sons Alex and James, in the hope that their generation will never have to live through anything comparable to what is recorded here and that they remember with gratitude everything that their grandparents and all of their time did for subsequent generations.

John Plowright
Repton

Map 1 Germany after World War One, from James and John Plowright.

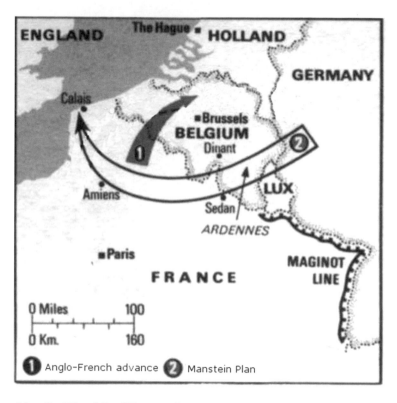

Map 2   The fall of France, from James and John Plowright.

Map 3 The Eastern Front, 1941–42, from James and John Plowright.

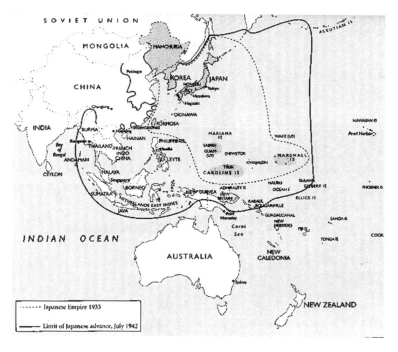

Map 4 The Pacific war, from James and John Plowright.

Map 5 Germany after the Second World War, from James and John Plowright.

Introduction

The nature of this book

A word now on the character, aims and structure of the book. It is intended to offer a synthesis of the most important literature on various aspects of the causes, course and consequences of World War Two. It is obviously impossible in the course of approximately 75,000 words to provide a comprehensive account of the war in all its political, military, diplomatic, social and economic aspects. Instead, the focus is upon those features of the war considered most likely to be studied by those, especially in the United Kingdom and the United States, contemplating or actually embarking upon higher education, without neglecting the needs of the general reader.

Notwithstanding the word limit, it has been thought necessary to range extensively both before and after 1939–45 in order to place that conflict in context, while appreciating the character of the conflict as something more than merely the delayed denouement of the First World War or a prologue to the Cold War.

The individual chapters are meant to be self-contained but a limited amount of repetition between chapters is necessary if this aim is to be fulfilled. The book as a whole, however, will stand or fall on whether, in the opinion of its readers, the author has done anything to illuminate what most would perceive as having been the finest hour of the generation to which his parents belonged.

Some chapters, representing the backbone of the book, will be more analytical than others but in order to appreciate the background and provide an overview of the war, others will be more narrative, and serve the function of cartilage: not mere padding but essential material connecting the constituent parts in a manner designed to ease abrasion and avoid disarticulation.

The structure of the book may be briefly outlined as follows.

Given the view that the period 1914–45 represents a second Thirty Years' War, with 1919–39 representing little more than a suspension of full-scale hostilities, Chapter 1 focuses on the Paris Peace Settlement and asks whether its flawed character rendered a Second World War almost inevitable.

Chapter 2 considers the extent to which World War Two can be characterised as Hitler's war in the course of considering whether Nazi foreign policy followed an ideologically inspired blueprint or whether it should instead be viewed as the inspired improvisation of an opportunistic practitioner of realpolitik.

Chapter 3 focuses upon the British reaction to Hitler's demands, particularly once Neville Chamberlain became the dominant force behind the policy of appeasement, and asks whether the British Prime Minister should be viewed as dim-witted dupe or clear-sighted realist.

The virtual absence of France from Chapter 3 is explained by the fact that the reasons for France's interwar weakness, which led to its following Chamberlain's lead on appeasement, is examined in the course of Chapter 4, when exploring the long- and short-term reasons for the fall of France in the summer of 1940.

Chapter 5 looks at how Britain was able to survive alone in Europe in battling Nazi Germany for the year following the fall of France by examining the Battle of Britain and the Battle of the Atlantic (the section on the latter offering a compressed account of the whole of that campaign).

The Eastern Front is the subject of Chapter 6, explaining how the conflict arose, how Blitzkrieg faltered, and how the Russian steamroller gathered momentum from the time of Stalingrad and gradually pushed the German forces back to Berlin.

The claim that the strategic bombing offensive materially relieved pressure on the Red Army is one of the areas of controversy surrounding the campaign which is examined in Chapter 7.

The alleged barbarism of the Allied bombing of Germany is sometimes compared with the undeniable obscenity of the Holocaust, and Chapter 8 addresses the fundamental questions as to why and when Nazi anti-Semitism became genocidal.

The process whereby the war became truly global is examined in Chapter 9, while Chapter 10 examines how that war segued into the Cold War, with particular reference to the disputes regarding the Second Front and Poland.

The question of what to do with Germany to prevent another war is scrutinised in Chapter 11, which focuses upon two approaches, namely, the post-war division of Germany and the pooling of her sovereignty in what ultimately became the European Union.

Chapters 12 and 13 consider the impact of the Second World War, upon Great Britain and the United States respectively.

1 The Paris peace conference

World War One and the Armistice

Before analysing the Paris Peace Conference, it is first necessary to consider the First World War in general and Wilson's Fourteen Points and the Armistice in particular, because of the role which they together played in fostering the 'stab in the back myth' which legitimated German bitterness and directed it outwards, against the Allied and Associated Powers, rather than inwardly against the conservatives elites in general and the High Command in particular, who actually bore most of the responsibility for starting and then losing the war.

In examining the First World War, the spotlight will be focused upon the Western Front, as that is where the war would be won or lost. It is true that the war escalated from a Balkan crisis to engulf all the European Great Powers and thence the world, but the potential for this arose from the rival network of alliances, which instead of deterring conflict merely ensured that if it came, it would ensnare those with no ostensible interest in the immediate cause of war (Serbia's rejection of Austria–Hungary's ultimatum following the assassination of the Archduke Franz Ferdinand in Sarajevo).

In 1894 France and Russia had become allies, threatening Germany with a war on two fronts. This situation arose because France, humiliated in the Franco-Prussian War of 1870–71, was able to make common cause with Imperial Russia after Germany allowed the Russo-German Reinsurance Treaty to lapse in 1890.

It was to deal with this problem that Count Alfred von Schlieffen, as Chief of the German General Staff, devised the plan which bore his name. This involved defeating France in six weeks and then moving troops eastwards to meet the slower mobilising Russians. To defeat France in six weeks it was considered necessary to attack not at the Franco-German border (which was heavily fortified and where the French forces were massed) but through neutral Belgium and Holland, encircling Paris and then placing French forces in a pincer movement. Helmuth von Moltke (Moltke the Younger) as Chief of the General Staff modified Schlieffen's plans by, for example, respecting Dutch neutrality and reducing the balance of forces on the revolving arc relative to the pivot in Alsace-Lorraine but in essentials it was Schlieffen's plan which was implemented in August 1914.

The invasion of Belgium brought Britain into the war, but this did not unduly worry the Germans as the British Expeditionary Force (BEF) was, in the Kaiser's words, 'contemptibly small', while the Royal Navy's blockade of Germany would not have time to hurt in what was expected to be a short war.

However, the Schlieffen plan began to unravel, as troops had to be dispatched to the Eastern Front (under Hindenburg and Ludendorff) because the Russians mobilised and attacked more quickly than anticipated; Belgian resistance was tougher than expected; and the rapid rifle fire of the highly professional BEF delayed the Germans at Mons.

Most fundamentally, the Germans turned too soon, failed to encircle Paris and allowed a French counteroffensive to be mounted at the River Marne (using troops ferried by taxi-cab from Paris). A failure of nerve on the part of the German High Command resulted in the German forces pulling back, which meant that Paris was safe and the Schlieffen plan had failed.

Both sides then engaged in a 'race to the sea', attempting to outflank one another. They failed, and instead a line of trenches came to be stretched from the Channel to the Swiss frontier, allowing men to take cover from the murderous firepower of modern weapons. Given that the advantage lay with the defender (as a result of barbed wire, entrenchments and machine guns), a situation of deadlock ensued and for most of the next four years warfare on the Western Front was static. Both sides tried but failed to break the deadlock with new tactics (including shock-troops and creeping barrages) and new weapons (including poison gas and the tank).

The first Russian Revolution of 1917, which overthrew the Romanovs, created an opportunity in the East for the Central Powers (Germany, Austria-Hungary, the Ottoman empire and Bulgaria) for although the Provisional Government which replaced Tsarist rule remained committed to the prosecution of the war, it lacked legitimacy, popularity and power, and the German High Command exploited this situation by providing funds and a sealed train to allow Lenin (and other more radical revolutionaries) to return to Russia. Before the year's end the Bolsheviks seized power, committed to making peace with the Central Powers in order to consolidate their revolution.

The USSR (as the Bolsheviks had renamed Russia) made peace with the Central Powers by the March 1918 Treaty of Brest–Litovsk. The end of fighting on the Eastern Front gave the Germans the opportunity to move troops to the Western Front and try to break through before American troops started arriving in large numbers (the United States having entered the war on the Allied side in April 1917). At first Ludendorff's Spring Offensive enjoyed success and the Germans got closer to Paris than at any time since 1914, but the offensive stalled and the Allies counter-attacked and eventually broke through the Hindenburg Line.

By 11 November 1918 the situation for Germany had become so desperate that its representatives signed the Armistice: a cease-fire which was to come into effect at 11 a.m. on the eleventh day of the eleventh month, bringing to an end four years of war.

It is easy to see why Germany signed the Armistice: all its allies had already signed armistices, so it was now fighting alone; the Allied blockade was producing near-starvation conditions; there was disorder on the home front, including naval mutinies, stimulated by intense hardship and partly inspired by Bolshevik propaganda; and the Allies, while not yet on German soil, were steadily advancing and appeared to be unstoppable. The Kaiser had already abdicated in favour of a civilian government and fled to Holland. It was reasoned that further fighting would accomplish no practical end other than hardening the hearts of the enemy, resulting ultimately in even harsher peace terms.

Less immediately comprehensible are the Allies' reasons for agreeing to the Armistice. Pershing (the commander of American forces), for one, urged marching on Berlin. However, the arguments in favour of accepting the Armistice were considered compelling. Firstly, while German forces were in retreat, they were not yet routed. The German army remained a disciplined fighting force capable of inflicting large numbers of casualties in defence of the Fatherland. Secondly, the Kaiser's abdication and replacement by a democratic republic had already satisfied one key war aim. Thirdly, while the United States, having only entered the war in April 1917, had the energy and resources to carry on fighting, the British and French were financially and psychologically exhausted. Moreover, British and French statesmen correctly calculated that the longer the war carried on, the greater would be the role played by American forces, and accordingly the greater would be the role of American politicians at the peace table. Furthermore, the terms of the Armistice satisfied the immediate aims of securing British naval supremacy (the German High Seas fleet sailing under escort to Scapa Flow) and of withdrawing German occupation forces from French and Belgian soil, while also denying Germany the opportunity of renewing the fighting at a later date by obliging it to surrender enormous quantities of war material and to allow Allied forces to occupy the left bank of the Rhine and bridgeheads beyond it. Last but not least in debilitating and disciplining Germany, the Royal Navy's blockade was to remain in force until a peace treaty was signed.

Nevertheless, in several respects the Armistice was fatally flawed. The German High Command had cleverly ducked responsibility for losing the war by passing political control to a civilian government. By concluding the Armistice with that government rather than a military delegation, the Allies were unwitting accomplices in the lie that German politicians rather than the German generals were to be blamed for losing the war.

In short, the Armistice laid the foundations of the 'stab in the back' myth whereby the German people were led to believe that the German army had not been defeated on the battlefield but had been betrayed on the home front by Jewish-Bolshevik defeatists. This myth was immensely appealing because it created a scapegoat for defeat and national humiliation and appeared plausible to many given that the German army remained a disciplined force until the end of the war; Allied troops had not entered German soil when the Armistice was signed; and there had been disturbances on the home front, such as a naval mutiny at Kiel, influenced in part by communist ideas.

The Big Three

The peace conference was held in Paris between January and June 1919. Neither the British nor the Americans had wanted the

French capital to host this event, correctly believing that a neutral city would provide a better backdrop to their deliberations, but they had allowed themselves to be overruled by the French premier. This dispute was the first of many between the 'Big Three': Woodrow Wilson of the United States, Georges Clemenceau of France, and David Lloyd George for Great Britain.

Wilson, the son of a Presbyterian minister and author of the Fourteen Points of January 1918, was idealistic. He was less interested in the precise details of the settlement than in bringing into being a new world order by creating a League of Nations (the fourteenth point) which would prevent future wars by the peaceful resolution of disputes. It was this mission which impelled Wilson to overcome the objections of friends and foes alike to become the first-ever serving president to go to Europe.

Clemenceau, nicknamed 'the Tiger' for his ferocious disposition, wanted a peace settlement which would make France secure by crippling Germany militarily, territorially and economically. Having experienced the hardship and humiliation of the Franco-Prussian War as well as the Great War (in which a quarter of French males aged between 18 and 30 had died and 6000 square miles of France had been devastated), Clemenceau asserted shortly before his death that his 'life hatred has been for Germany because of what she has done to France'.[1] So intense and abiding was his fear of the German threat that he allegedly asked to be buried upright, facing Germany.

In general, Lloyd George occupied an intermediate position between those of Wilson and Clemenceau. He understood very well Clemenceau's desire to 'Make Germany pay' but he also recognised the wisdom of Wilson's view that a harsh treaty would be unlikely to produce a lasting peace if it merely created German resentment. However, such a summary suggests that Lloyd George's position was more consistent and straightforward than was actually the case, or at least than it appeared to contemporaries. So slippery was his performance that, with good reason, he came to be as much distrusted by members within the British delegation as by their American and French counterparts. Thus while Lloyd George's essentially liberal instincts and unerring capacity to see into the minds of most men and the heart of the most complex issues were powerful forces working for moderation, this tended to be undermined by his rather too obvious love of fancy footwork and by his being more wedded to British interests, as he perceived them, than to any framework of moral values.

As the Peace Conference progressed Anglo-American relations improved but those of each country with France deteriorated (Franco-American relations were especially poor). Lloyd George increasingly shared Wilson's concern that the German peace terms were becoming too severe because his own public opinion appeared to be moving in favour of a more moderate peace, his financial and military experts warned him about the dangers of having large forces scattered about the globe, and he was alarmed by labour unrest at home and revolution in Europe (particularly after the news on 21 March 1919 that Bela Kun's communists had seized power in Hungary).

Hence Lloyd George's Fontainebleau Memorandum, in which he argued that the peace should not be so punitive towards Germany that it risked poisoning international relations – which might lead to another war or render Central Europe prey to Bolshevism. However Fontainebleau foundered on the French need for revenge and restitution from Germany combined with reassurances for their security – aims which were simply incompatible with a moderate peace.

The terms of the 1919 Treaty of Versailles represent an uneasy compromise between these disparate views.

The flawed nature of the Treaty of Versailles

The timing and venue of the signing of the Treaty of Versailles were both richly symbolic. The Treaty was signed on 28 June 1919: five years to the day after the event which triggered the conflict, namely, the assassination in Sarajevo of the heir to the Austro-Hungarian throne, the Archduke Franz Ferdinand, by the Serb Gavrilo Princip. The scene of the signing was the Hall of Mirrors in the Palace of Versailles where, 48 years earlier, France had been humiliated at the end of the Franco-Prussian War and the Second Reich had been proclaimed by Bismarck.

The terms of the treaty are best summarised under three headings, namely, territorial clauses, disarmament clauses and war guilt and reparations.

Germany lost all its overseas colonies (to Britain, its Dominions and Japan) and in total lost 12 per cent of its population and

13 per cent of its area (to France, Belgium, Denmark, Poland and League of Nations control). Moreover, in further violation of the principle of national self-determination (on the basis of which the Germans claimed they had signed the Armistice), *Anschluss* (or union) with Austria was explicitly forbidden, and the 3.25 million Sudeten Germans who had formerly been part of the Austro-Hungarian Empire were placed in the new state of Czechoslovakia under the 1919 Treaty of Saint-Germain.

The Rhineland was to be permanently demilitarised and was to be occupied by Allied troops for 15 years, while the German army was limited to a volunteer force of 100,000 men, with no tanks or air force, while the German navy's surface fleet was severely restricted in tonnage and it was banned from the possession of U-boats.

Moreover, having admitted its guilt for starting the war (under Article 231), Germany accepted liability to pay reparations or compensation to the Allies for all its war damages. Although the Treaty of Versailles did not specify the amount to be paid in reparations, it did lay down that for 15 years the coal of the Saar was to go to France.

Not surprisingly the Germans were appalled by what they considered to be the severity of the terms of the Treaty. Firstly, they referred to the Treaty as a *Diktat*, or dictated peace, as German representatives had not had the opportunity to plead their case but were merely invited to sign on the dotted line or reject the Treaty in its entirety and suffer the consequences of a resumption of hostilities which they were plainly in no position to fight.

Originally the Big Four (Vittorio Orlando of Italy being the fourth) had planned to hold a preliminary conference to agree on the terms to be offered, after which it was planned to hold a full-scale conference to negotiate with the enemy. However, as the weeks turned into months what had been intended as a preliminary conference became the actual conference, with the result that a break was made with diplomatic precedent and the Germans never got the opportunity formally to present their case.

This lack of consultation and the alleged harshness of the terms of the Treaty were even more bitterly resented given that Wilson's Fourteen Points had included open diplomacy ('open covenants openly arrived at') and the fact that the Kaiser had abdicated and Germany was now a democratic republic (indeed more democratic than the United States, Great Britain and France insofar as women had been enfranchised and the Weimar Constitution included proportional representation). Just as Louis XVIII had argued that the Bourbon dynasty should not be held answerable for Bonapartist excesses, so Weimar's politicians argued that they should not be punished for the wrongdoing of Wilhelm II.

Having been given no opportunity to negotiate terms, the German delegation in Paris was faced with the stark choice of accepting the Treaty in its entirety or rejecting it and resuming the armed conflict (which Germany was manifestly in no position to do). The Treaty was thus understandably regarded by the Germans and those who sympathised with their cause as a *Diktat*.

Secondly, despite having signed Article 231 they did not really regard themselves as responsible for starting the war and hence liable to pay war damages. Thirdly, the 'stab in the back' myth meant that they did not feel that they had really lost the war, having been betrayed on the home front rather than being defeated on the battlefield. Fourthly, they believed, with a good deal of justification, that the Treaty did not reflect Wilson's Fourteen Points, which they claimed as the basis upon which they had signed the Armistice. As has already been noted Wilson's principle of national self-determination (whereby people of the same nationality reside as citizens in the same sovereign state) was repeatedly ignored, not only with regard to German-speaking parts of the former Austro-Hungarian Empire which were placed under foreign rule (the South Tyrol going to Italy and the Sudetenland becoming part of the new state of Czechoslovakia) but also with regard to areas which had been part of the Second Reich, such as the 'Polish Corridor' (formerly Posen and West Prussia) which was now part of the revived state of Poland and which separated eastern Prussia from the rest of Germany.

The Fourteen Points also spoke of the need to create a League of Nations to prevent future wars. The Covenant (or constitution) of the League was placed in the Treaty of Versailles (as was also true of the treaties of the other defeated powers) but at first Germany was not allowed to become a member because in 1919 it was clearly regarded as morally unfit to participate in international affairs on a par with the victorious powers. This pariah status, which soon helped drive Germany into the arms of the equally leprous Soviet Union, was yet another cause of resentment.

It is true that Wilson had been willing to accept an armistice based upon his Fourteen Points, not least as a means of binding the British and French into accepting his principles. However, they had never been willing to accept the Fourteen Points at face value. Wilson's personal representative, Colonel House, accepted the Allied reservations so that the Fourteen Points were modified to allow for what later came to be called reparations from Germany (which France was particularly keen to secure) and for discussions on freedom of the seas (which the British rejected) at the Peace Conference itself. Nevertheless, the Germans were able, plausibly, to claim that the peace terms which they were offered at Versailles were largely illegitimate because they had accepted the Armistice on the basis that the Fourteen Points would provide the basis for the peace treaty and the Americans had accepted this, only to be overruled by their French and British allies.

Ever since the publication of the Treaty of Versailles in 1919, some have argued that its terms were too harsh. Obviously the Germans had a vested interest in arguing that this was so, but the critics of the Treaty have not been exclusively German. Indeed, Ray Stannard Baker of the American delegation and Harold Nicolson and John Maynard Keynes of the British delegation wrote books claiming that Woodrow Wilson had been outmanoeuvred by Clemenceau and Lloyd George so that the Treaty was both unwise (as it stimulated the German desire for revenge) and unjust.

Keynes resigned from the British delegation in Paris in protest at what he considered to be the unjust impositions made upon Germany, and in 1919 he publicised his beliefs in *The Economic Consequences of the Peace* which argued that the reparations sum proposed would exceed Germany's capacity to pay and would thus not only ruin the German economy but thereby damage the European and world economies and thus undermine future peace.

On learning the terms of the Treaty of Versailles the former Kaiser remarked: 'The war to end war has resulted in a peace to end peace'. This feeling was not restricted to the defeated side. Thus General Smuts wrote to his wife that Versailles was 'not a peace treaty but a war treaty' and Alfred Lord Milner also described it as 'the peace to end peace'. Most presciently Marshal Foch remarked: 'This is not peace; it is an armistice for 20 years'. There is certainly a strong *prima facie* case for regarding the Treaty of Versailles as sowing the seeds of the Second World War.

The peacemakers at Versailles were concerned not just with the threat of a revived Germany but also with the danger posed by the USSR, with its avowed intention of exporting revolution. They thus sought to prevent both the westward expansion of communism from the Soviet Union and any eastward expansion of Germany by creating a string of buffer states in Scandinavia and Central and Eastern Europe out of parts of the former Russian, German and Austro-Hungarian empires. Running from north to south these new or enlarged states included Finland, Estonia, Latvia, Lithuania, Poland, Czechoslovakia, Romania and Yugoslavia.

However, these states were unable to perform this role for several reasons. Firstly, they were not united among themselves but instead quarrelled over disputed lands. Thus both Poland and Czechoslovakia claimed Teschen, for example, and Poland and Hungary both cooperated with Germany in the parcelling out of the Czech 'rump' in March 1939.

Secondly, not only did they face opponents outside their frontiers, they were also often internally divided because they contained substantial minority populations (such as the Sudeten Germans in Czechoslovakia) who were potential fifth columnists.

Thirdly, neither Britain nor France were wholeheartedly committed to supporting these states, particularly when German and Soviet strength revived and they could potentially be 'squeezed' from both directions.

Versailles and the rise of the Nazis

Many problems may be laid at the door of Versailles but the treaty cannot be blamed, except simplistically, for the rise of the Nazis. The allegedly harsh terms of Versailles, and particularly the war guilt and reparations clauses, can be said to have contributed to the political and economic difficulties of the Weimar Republic, undermining popular support for it and contributing towards the revival of aggressive nationalism which (assisted by clever propaganda) helped to transform Nazism from a fringe *völkisch* Bavarian party into a successful mass movement. Hitler never lost an opportunity to condemn 'das Diktat' or 'der Schandvertag' (the shameful treaty). However, Versailles provides neither a necessary nor a sufficient explanation of Hitler's coming to power.

Firstly, the terms of the Treaty of Versailles were not as harsh as was commonly made out. The hyperinflation of 1923, for example, was not the direct consequence of reparations, set at £6600 million or 132 billion gold marks in 1921. Rather it arose out of the German government's strategy of printing more money to wipe out debt and/or discredit reparations. Not having suffered wartime occupation, Germany was actually better placed, in many ways, than France, Belgium or Russia to benefit from the return to peacetime conditions. Reparations did not represent a millstone insofar as American loans under the 1924 Dawes and 1929 Young Plans actually exceeded the amount paid.

Secondly, several of the most onerous features of the Versailles settlement had already been undone before Hitler was appointed Chancellor, including the withdrawal of Allied troops from the Rhineland (in 1930) and the cancellation of reparations (in 1932). Rather it was the Wall Street Crash of October 1929 which fatally undermined the Weimar Republic and gave the National Socialist German Workers' Party (NSDAP) the chance to make significant electoral gains (so that it went from just 12 seats in the Reichstag in 1928 to being the second largest party there with 107 seats after the 1930 election).

Thirdly, if it had not been for the intrigue and miscalculations of the conservative elites then Hitler might never have been appointed Chancellor, as he had never secured a majority in a free vote and NSDAP support had actually fallen between the July and November 1932 Reichstag elections.

Fourthly, it can be argued that the rise of Hitler and the Nazi party was less the result of the humiliating terms of the Versailles treaty than of structural flaws within the Weimar constitution, most notably proportional representation, which gave even extremist parties a public voice and tended to produce weak, unstable coalition governments, and Article 48, which could be abused by a President hostile to the spirit of Weimar, such as Hindenburg.

Most fundamentally, it can be argued that the Treaty of Versailles was not as harsh as commonly alleged at the time and since. It is certainly the case that the Treaty was the result of an uneasy compromise between the views of the 'Big Three'. However, it is worth pointing out that the terms of the Treaty were much less harsh than would have been the case if Wilson and Lloyd George had been unable to exercise a moderating influence upon Clemenceau. If 'the

Tiger' had had his way, Germany would, in addition, have been divided and instead of a demilitarised Rhineland, a separate French-inclined Rhenish state would have come into being.

Germany was certainly weakened but it was not delivered a mortal blow. Germany itself had imposed much more debilitating terms upon Rumania and Russia during the First World War (the latter, for example, losing 25 per cent of its population, arable land and railway network), while its Central Power allies suffered to a far greater extent than Germany did (Hungary, for example, losing 70 per cent of its pre-war territory).

Paradoxically, the weakness of the successor states of the Austro-Hungarian and Russian Empires, added to the exhaustion suffered by France and the pariah status (and hence potential friendship) of the USSR meant that Germany was relatively stronger in Europe after the Paris Peace Conference than it had been in 1914. Thus Germany emerged from Versailles as 'not only the dominant continental power, but potentially more preponderant than in 1914' given the removal of any countervailing power[2] and the failure of the United States, Britain and France to enforce the settlement which they had made in 1919 (although the French did make moves in this direction in the early 1920s, such as their formal treaty of mutual assistance with Poland signed on 19 February 1921, the military convention with Poland of 22 February 1922, and 1923 occupation of the Ruhr).

Furthermore, it is fundamentally misguided to use the Fourteen Points as a yardstick with which to criticise the Treaty of Versailles. The Fourteen Points had been issued by Woodrow Wilson in January 1918, yet Germany did not sign the Armistice until November 1918. In the intervening period there had been a great deal more bloodshed and destruction. It was therefore unreasonable for the Germans to expect that the terms which they had previously rejected would remain unaltered. Moreover, the United States only entered the First World War in April 1917. It therefore only suffered very slightly (especially by January 1918) in comparison with its British and French allies, who had been fighting since August 1914 (hence Pershing's willingness to drive on to Berlin). Moreover, France had been invaded and occupied twice by the Germans in Clemenceau's lifetime (in 1870–71 as well as 1914), and the fighting on the Western Front had laid waste much of France's most valuable farmland and industry. It was therefore naive of the Germans if they really expected the French to accept Wilson's Fourteen Points as the basis of the peace; however, much lip service was paid to its ideals.

It is thus difficult to imagine that allowing the Germans to negotiate at Versailles would have had any significant impact on the terms of the Treaty. The Germans themselves had negotiated with the Bolsheviks but that did not stop them from drawing up the March 1918 Treaty of Brest–Litovsk which was much harsher towards Russia than the Treaty of Versailles was towards Germany.

It is true that the principle of national self-determination was ignored in several respects with regard to Germany, but plebiscites *were* conducted in several areas (including Allenstein and Marienwerder) to take account of the ethnic preferences of the inhabitants. Similarly, although the coal mined in the Saar was to go to France for 15 years as part of Germany's reparations, there would then be a plebiscite to decide whether the region would remain under League control, become part of France or (as proved to be the case in 1935) be returned to Germany. The principle of national self-determination simply had to be overruled on occasion by other, more important considerations such as the need to create states which were economically viable and had defensible frontiers. Hence the inclusion of the Sudetenland in Czechoslovakia.

If the principle of national self-determination had been applied rigorously towards Germany, the absurd result would have been that it would have *expanded* rather than contracted (with the acquisition of Austria and the German-speaking parts of the former Austro-Hungarian Empire) whereas it is the norm for defeated powers to lose territory. Despite losing 12 per cent of its population and 13 per cent of its area, Germany still suffered less proportionately than its defeated allies under the terms of their peace treaties (Saint-Germain with Austria, 1919; Neuilly with Bulgaria, 1919; Trianon with Hungary, 1920; and Sèvres with Turkey, 1920).

As regards the dubious privilege of membership of the League of Nations, Germany only had to wait until 1926, when it was granted not only admission to the League but a permanent seat on its Council.

The reparations issue deserves special consideration, for although the amount was not specified in 1919, the war guilt clause (Article 231) clearly provided the justification for the imposition of massive reparations later: the sum of £6600 million in 1921. Critics of the

Treaty argued that it was historically wrong to attribute the primary blame for starting the First World War on Germany, *either* because the Kaiser was the guilty party and had abdicated *or* because other powers were to blame – notably the Triple Entente in general, for 'encircling' Germany, and Russia in particular, for ordering mobilisation in response to Austria–Hungary's move against Serbia.

Furthermore, critics of the war guilt clause argue that it was economically and politically wrong to impose such a heavy imposition upon Germany as it simply could not afford to pay (having lost 16 per cent of its coal reserves and 48 per cent of its iron production) so that Versailles in general and the reparations bill in particular became a millstone around the neck of the democratic Weimar Republic.

This is not the place to assess Germany's responsibility for starting the First World War, but whoever started it, Germany clearly lost the war, and common sense dictates that it is the defeated powers who pick up the bill.

It has been shown above that the German sense of grievance was aggravated by the 'stab in the back' myth, which appeared superficially plausible, but the failure of Ludendorff's spring 1918 offensive to secure a breakthrough on the Western Front before US troops started arriving in large numbers (despite being reinforced by troops from the Eastern Front released through the Treaty of Brest–Litovsk) meant that Germany was bound to lose the war sooner or later.

In short, Germany had no real choice but to sign both the Armistice and the Treaty of Versailles, whatever their terms, and, as already argued, these terms were not as harsh as commonly claimed. Historians such as Maier, Trachtenberg and Schuker, for example,[3] suggest that notwithstanding all of its losses of territory and resources, Germany still possessed the capacity to pay its reparations bill, especially given help through US loans (under the 1924 Dawes and 1929 Young Plans).

Indeed, insofar as there was a problem with Versailles it was not that it was too harsh but rather that it was too lenient, or rather it would be more accurate to say that the problem was that the terms of Versailles were not enforced rigidly enough. Thus the Allies had the worst of both worlds, with the German people made resentful and embittered, but Germany itself wounded and weakened rather than definitively contained or curbed.

2 Nazi foreign policy

Introduction

Nazi foreign policy is part of the broader intentionalist–structuralist debate about the nature of the Third Reich. Was Nazi foreign policy in essence little more than the product of Hitler's mind or was he not the 'free agent' in shaping policy which he might appear at first sight, given constraints such as the need to take account of the conservative elites (such as the generals and Big Business), public and party opinion, and the state of the economy, to say nothing of international factors? And when we talk about Hitler's mind, should he be viewed as possessing a more or less detailed 'programme' for rearmament and aggression or was he rather an unprincipled opportunist who reacted to changing circumstances? Finally, if Hitler did possess a programme, did his intentions extend further than the conquest of Lebensraum in the East to ultimate world domination?

Mein Kampf as blueprint

The obvious starting point to try to resolve some of these issues is Hitler's *Mein Kampf*, which intentionalists such as Trevor–Roper regard as providing the blueprint for Hitler's foreign policy once he had achieved power. It was dictated to Rudolf Hess in Landsberg prison in 1924, in the course of the nine months which Hitler served, after being sentenced to five years' imprisonment for his part in the abortive 1923 Munich Putsch. It was published in two volumes, in 1925 and 1926, respectively.

In Hitler's view, as expressed in *Mein Kampf*, Wilhelmine Germany had made a costly mistake in needlessly antagonising the British Empire by engaging in a naval arms race, which helped push Britain into the Triple Entente and ultimate entry into the First World War on the side of Germany's enemies. Hitler was not interested in overseas colonies, although he would later feign

17

regret at the loss of Germany's overseas empire through the Treaty of Versailles in order to see what recompense the British government might be willing to offer. Instead, Hitler consistently argued that Britain and Germany had no need to quarrel, as the former was a great maritime and imperial power, while the latter was a continental power whose ambitions lay in the acquisition of living space to the East of the Eurasian land mass. Indeed, Hitler saw alliance between Britain and Germany as natural, as they complemented one another, and desirable, as it would help isolate France – the power which represented the immediate obstacle to Germany achieving its ambitions thanks to the legacy of mistrust arising from the Franco-Prussian and Great wars, and to its self-appointed role as guardian of the Paris Peace settlement. If war with France came, revenge for 1918 would doubtless be sweet but it would not be an end in itself. Rather it would constitute the means to the greater end of securing soil at the expense of Russia, protecting Germany's rear against the threat of another two-front war.

Hitler similarly expressed the desirability of German alliance with Italy in *Mein Kampf*. Italy, like Germany, was dissatisfied with the status quo, despite having sat at the victors' table in Paris. Her acquiescence in Anschluss with Austria – an early part of the programme of creating a Grossdeutschland or Greater Germany – was rightly considered essential by Hitler, and if she could be persuaded to turn her own expansionist attentions southwards, towards the Mediterranean, this would not bring her into conflict with Germany but would rather tend to bring her into friction with France and Britain.

It should be noted that Hitler's calculations regarding the desirability of alliance with Italy (and other states) was an expression of geopolitical realpolitik rather than the result of ideological promptings. Thus alliance with Italy made sense to Hitler irrespective of he fascist character of the regime, while the desirability of such an alliance meant that he was willing to sacrifice the principle of a Grossdeutschland regarding the South Tyrol – a German-speaking region of the former Habsburg empire which constituted one of Italy's territorial gains at the end of the First World War – despite the fact that the very first point of the 25-point party programme of 1920 had consisted of the demand that all Germans should be united into a Greater Germany.

Notwithstanding the claims of the Yamoto race to purity and Japanese 'proof' of racial supremacy in the Asiatic sphere by virtue of its fledgling empire over Koreans and Chinese, Hitler's avowed desire for a Germano-Japanese alliance once again illustrates the primacy of power politics over ideology in his thinking on foreign policy. He regarded such an alliance as desirable because it would threaten the Soviet Union with a war on two fronts and might oblige the United States to turn its attention towards the Pacific and the Asian mainland, rather than towards the Atlantic and European affairs.

To sum up, Hitler sought to isolate France and create a Grossdeutschland prior to securing Lebensraum to feed Germany's surplus population in the East. To put it another way, he sought to undo the 1919 Treaty of Versailles so that he could reimpose something akin to the 1918 Treaty of Brest–Litovsk, which had deprived Russia of her most fertile and industrialised lands.

Thus *Mein Kampf* shows that even if Hitler was not thinking in terms of global domination, he was certainly thinking globally, and was prepared to sacrifice ideological consistency in favour of geopolitical coherence. The fact that he did ultimately achieve alliance with Italy and Japan, pursued an understanding with Great Britain (which took concrete form in the Anglo-German Naval Agreement), and invaded the USSR, also provides at least *prima facie* evidence of Hitler's possessing long term goals which he pursued with great consistency.

1933–1937: from the Concordat to the Hossbach Memorandum

Hitler's pre-war foreign policy once in power naturally falls into two phases, namely, 1933–37 and 1938–39. When Hitler was appointed Chancellor on 30 January 1933, Germany was both militarily weak (given the disarmament clauses of the Treaty of Versailles) and economically weak (given the impact of the Wall Street Crash, which had resulted in withdrawal of short-term US loans and meant that Germany had over six million unemployed). Moreover, the extent to which the German people had a stomach for bloodshed after the losses of the First World War remained in dispute. Hence publicly Hitler posed as a man of peace while privately indicating to those who needed to know that his agenda was still that outlined in *Mein Kampf*. Thus General Liebmann's notes show Hitler telling a group of army officers after a dinner party on 3 February 1933 that he remained committed to 'the conquest of new living space in the east and its ruthless Germanization'.[1]

The 1933 Concordat with the Vatican, whereby Hitler promised not to interfere in church matters if the church did not interfere in politics, gave the new regime legitimacy and prestige, at least in the eyes of the Roman Catholic community, while withdrawal from the Geneva Disarmament Conference and the League of Nations was presented as entirely reasonable, for why should Germany alone be disarmed if countries like France failed to fulfil the ideals of the Fourteen Points and the Covenant of the League? Moreover, the League's recent failure to take strong action over the Japanese aggression in Manchuria in 1931 had exposed the flawed character of that organisation for all those who had not yet already arrived at that conclusion.

A ten-year Non-Aggression Pact with Poland in January 1934, although it had the practical effect of puncturing the system of French alliances in Eastern Europe, also provided reassurance for those who wished to believe that Nazi diplomacy would be more moderate than Hitler's speeches and writings prior to the seizure of power had suggested.

However, in July 1934 the Austrian Nazis attempted to seize power and the Austrian Chancellor, Engelbert Dollfuss, was killed in the course of the coup. Hitler felt obliged to disown his comrades after Mussolini sent Italian troops to the Brenner Pass. II Duce's distrust of Der Fuhrer was further indicated by his joining Britain and France in the Stresa Front the following year, which condemned German rearmament following the formal recreation of the Luftwaffe and the reintroduction of conscription, both of which actions were in breach of the Treaty of Versailles. However, the Stresa Front did not survive the year of its birth as Britain signed the Anglo-German Naval Agreement, which also violated Versailles, without consulting her partners, and Britain and France felt obliged to play a leading role in the League in condemning Italy's invasion of Abyssinia. Hitler, by contrast, supported Italy's action, not least because it provided a distraction (compounded by the exceptionally fractious French elections) which helped him to remilitarise the Rhineland, in breach of both the Versailles and Locarno treaties in March 1936. This move was enormously popular at home, not least because it meant that the military balance tipped decisively in Germany's favour in relation to France.

The process whereby Italy drew closer to Germany was further accelerated by the outbreak in 1936 of the Spanish Civil War, where both fascist powers assisted Franco's Nationalist forces, and opened up the prospect of France being confronted with a third fascist neighbour. Italy's willingness to countenance greatly increased German influence in Austria had already been conceded by Mussolini in January 1936, and was accomplished to a considerable extent by the Austro-German agreement of July 1936. The shift in Italy's alignment was symbolised by the signing of the Rome–Berlin Axis in October 1936, while Hitler's long-term goal of allying with Japan also moved a step closer in November 1936 with Tokyo's accession to the Anti-Comintern Pact (the secret clauses of which included an agreement of benevolent neutrality in the event of either party going to war with the Soviet Union).

However, it was 1937 which marks the real watershed in Germany's pre-war foreign policy when the pace quickened. There are several reasons for this change. The 'threat' posed by the 'Jewish-Bolshevik world conspiracy' appeared more immediate to Hitler than hitherto given increasing support by Moscow for the Republican forces in Spain; the advent of a 'Popular Front' administration in France; and ratification of the Franco-Soviet Pact. Moreover, he was painfully aware that the lead which Germany had secured in the rearmament race was fast being eroded and might disappear altogether if she did not act 'by 1943–45 at the latest'. That quotation comes from the Hossbach Memorandum – a key but highly contentious document – for charting the development of Nazi foreign policy at this critical time.[2]

Colonel Friedrich Hossbach was Hitler's military adjutant in November 1937, whose responsibilities included liaison between the NSDAP and the armed forces. The so-called Hossbach Memorandum consists of his notes of the meeting he observed held in the Reich Chancellery on 5 November 1937, which was attended by Hitler, von Neurath (Foreign Minister), Goering (Commander-in-Chief of the Air Force), Fritsch (Commander-in-Chief of the Army), Raeder (Commander-in-Chief of the Navy) and Blomberg (Reich War Minister). The meeting had been called by the last two named in the hope that they might persuade Hitler to adjudicate on disputed allocations of raw materials and labour, of which Goering had been managing to appropriate the lion's share in part by virtue of his position as Head of the Four Year Plan Office. However, as was his wont, Hitler took the opportunity to expound at considerable length upon his grand plans for the future, after having apparently told his select audience that 'his exposition be regarded, in the event of his death, as his last will and testament'.[3]

Ironically his words became a matter of life and death for some of those present because the Hossbach Memorandum was used by the prosecution at the Nuremberg War Crimes Tribunal as evidence of Nazi crimes against peace. At face value the document represents a timetable for aggression with Hitler expressing his 'unalterable determination to solve Germany's problem of space by 1943–45 at the latest'.[4] This urgency was predicated upon the considerations that equipment would become obsolete; the secretive nature of 'special weapons' might leak out; no further reserves could be recruited from older age groups; a food crisis might provoke a foreign exchange crisis which would undermine the regime; the NSDAP and its leaders were aging (the forty-eight-year-old Hitler appears to have had his own mortality in mind); and, most fundamentally, the clock was ticking with regard to rearmament, with the economy overheating and Germany's rivals stripping away her relative advantage. In short, time was working against Germany.

Hitler envisaged two contingencies in the event of which action might be taken before 1943–45, namely, if internal strife in France or war between France and a third party rendered its army incapable of action against Germany. The first objective 'in the event of our being embroiled in war,' according to Hitler 'must be to overthrow Czechoslovakia and Austria simultaneously in order to remove the threat to our flank in any possible operation against the West'.[5]

Hitler expressed the belief that 'almost certainly Britain, and probably France as well, had already tacitly written off the Czechs',[6] however, this did not prevent Hitler from characterising the British as a 'hate-inspired antagonist'[7], reflecting the fact that Hitler's hope of securing alliance with Britain had been stymied, despite the Anglo-German Naval Agreement of 1935, and that for the time being he would have to choose Italy in preference to Britain, as circumstances currently prevented him from embracing both, and the events of 1934 had shown that Italian acquiescence was a precondition of Anschluss with Austria. Hitler's willingness to go to war with Britain or at least threaten her with war, if she stood in the way of his ultimate aim of achieving Lebensraum in the east, is indicated by his authorising naval expansion, with particular reference to the construction of U-boats.

Blomberg, Fritsch and von Neurath counselled caution both at the Hossbach conference and shortly thereafter. Hitler's unwillingness to delay resulted in their replacement as part of a general process of removing the more timid members of the 'old guard' in what is sometimes referred to as 'the second purge' (to distinguish it from the more bloody Night of the Long Knives of 30 June 1934). Fourteen senior generals were retired and a further forty six were required to change their commands in a major shake up of the Army High Command. Sex scandals saw Fritsch replaced as Commander-in-Chief of the Army by Brauchitsch, while the post of War Minister was abolished after Blomberg was forced to resign, Hitler assuming the title of Commander-in-Chief of the Armed Forces, in addition to that of Supreme Commander which he had held since Hindenburg's death and the amalgamation of the roles of head of government and head of state in August 1934. Hjalmar Schacht, who was forced to resign as Minister of Economics in November 1937 (having already been marginalised by the creation of the Four Year Plan) was replaced by Funk, and the Anglophobe Ribbentrop replaced von Neurath as Foreign Minister in February 1938.

Those historians who deny the significance of the Hossbach conference tend to overlook the fact that just two days later General Jodl, the Chief of Operations Staff at OKW (the Armed Forces High Command), amended Germany's war plans so that 'Operation Green', the putative attack upon Czechoslovakia became offensive rather than defensive and took priority over 'Operation Red': the attack on France. In the event, however, it was Austria that took priority.

1938–39: from Anschluss with Austria to the invasion of Poland

As late as December 1937, Hitler had declared that he wanted an 'evolutionary' rather than a 'revolutionary' solution to the Austrian 'problem'.[8] That is to say, in the light of the failed 1934 coup he hoped that the Austrian Nazis might achieve power like the party in the fatherland: by a mixture of electoral success, the threat of force and backstairs intrigue.

Von Papen, who had been prevailed upon to exchange the post of Vice-Chancellor for that of ambassador to Vienna, had arranged a meeting between Hitler and Kurt von Schuschnigg, the Austrian Chancellor, at Berchtesgaden on 12 February 1938, at which Hitler had bullied his guest into accepting a role for the Austrian Nazis in government, including their control over the police. However, on 9 March the worm had turned and Schuschnigg called for a plebiscite on Anschluss for 12 March, where the manner in which the question was framed and the raising of the voting age to 24 offered a chance of the proposal being rejected. Hitler decided on possible military intervention to avoid any risk of humiliation but first needed reassurance regarding Italy's response, so as to avoid any repetition of the events of 1934. Thus on 10 March Hitler dispatched a letter to Mussolini via Prince Philip of Hesse in which he reassured Il Duce that the Brenner represented the 'definite boundary ... between ourselves'[9] in an effort to reassure him that he renounced all claims to the South Tyrol. This met with a favourable response which was communicated to Hitler by Hesse by phone at 10.25 pm on 11 March.

Given the general improvement in Italian-German relations since 1934, and the overextension of Italy's armed forces in Abyssinia and Spain, Hitler had been sufficiently confident of a favourable response from Mussolini to have already issued Directive No 1 for 'Operation Otto' (the invasion of Austria) at 2.00 am on 11 March (although this order only committed Germany to act militarily 'If other measures prove unsuccessful ...').[10] With German troops massing on the border, Schuschnigg resigned, President Miklas appointed the Austrian Nazi Seyss-Inquart in his place, and German troops made an unopposed crossing of the frontier on 12 March. Hitler announced the Anschluss in the course of a triumphant tour of his country of birth.

The absorption of Austria into the Third Reich acted as a catalyst for the 'Czech problem' as the Sudeten Germans stepped up their demands for Anschluss, and the Czech state became increasingly vulnerable to German attack. Thus on 28 March Hitler stated his intention of settling the Sudeten German problem in the 'not-too-distant future',[11] and Konrad Henlein, the leader of the Sudeten German party, acting on instructions from Berlin, made a series of demands which looked reasonable to outsiders but which could not be granted by the Prague government without fatally compromising its sovereignty.

Hitler's interim draft for 'Operation Green', issued on 20 May, stated 'It is not my intention to smash Czechoslovakia by military action in the immediate future without provocation …'[12] However, that provocation occurred almost immediately in the shape of the so-called 'May weekend crisis'.

Alarmed by German troop movements which it thought might presage an imminent attack, the Czech government mobilised on 20 May. It received diplomatic support in this action from the British and French governments. Hitler felt obliged to deny that he had intended invasion and was infuriated when the international press interpreted his action as a climb down. Thus Czech fears of German invasion plans proved self-fulfilling, as Hitler on 30 May issued a new order for 'Green' in which he stated it was his intention to 'smash Czechoslovakia by military action in the near future'.[13] Thus a perception of damage to his prestige pre-cipitated a radical change of pace, if not direction, in Hitler's foreign policy over a space of not more than ten days.

Hitler's increasingly bellicose statements regarding Czechoslovakia in turn persuaded Chamberlain to intervene to try to regain the initiative by discovering precisely what Hitler wanted and delivering his demands by means of international negotiation rather than unilateral military action. This policy of appeasement resulted in Britain, France, Italy and Germany deciding at the Munich Conference that Hitler should receive the Sudetenland. Neither the Czechs nor the Soviets were consulted (despite the latter being pledged by treaty to come to the assistance of the Czechs if France did).

Although hailed in Germany as a masterly triumph of diplo-macy, there is evidence to suggest that Hitler would have pre-ferred to conquer all of Czechoslovakia by military means rather than gain the Sudetenland bloodlessly at Munich.[14] His grudging willingness to come to the conference table rather than imple-ment Operation Green were attributable to Mussolini's ostenta-tious unpreparedness for war in September 1938 (which was manifested by an inflated 'shopping list' of all that would be required before Italy felt that she would be able to engage in further hostilities) and, more importantly, the German public's evident lack of enthusiasm for war (which was manifested by the cheering for Chamberlain and the disappointing turn out for a military parade through Berlin), notwithstanding propaganda designed to show the alleged indignities and atrocities inflicted upon the Sudeten Germans by the Prague government.

In his secret speech to 400 representatives of the (Nazi-controlled) German press in Munich on 10 November 1938, Hitler admitted that in part this lacklustre response was the inevitable consequence of the role which he had felt obliged to play since attaining office:

> For years circumstances have compelled me to talk about almost nothing but peace. Only by continually stressing Germany's desire for peace and her peaceful intentions could I achieve freedom for the German people bit by bit and provide the armaments which were always necessary before the next step could be taken. It is obvious that such peace propaganda also has its doubtful aspects, for it can only too easily give people the idea that the present regime really identifies itself with the determination to preserve peace at all costs.[15]

Hitler's claim to be a patriot merely seeking the just application of the Wilsonian principle of national self-determination which had been denied to Germany at the Paris peace conference could not be maintained after March 1939. The Sudetenland was overwhelmingly Germanic but the Czech rump, which Hitler had guaranteed at Munich was Slav, so when he carved it up six months later, albeit without bloodshed and with Polish and Hungarian connivance, there was no disguising the fact that he was acting aggressively. It was this action which provoked the British and French governments into offering guarantees to both Poland and Rumania although, as will be shown in the following chapter, this did not mark the end of appeasement.

The Nazi–Soviet Non-Aggression Pact of August 1939 provides the supreme example of Hitler's willingness to sacrifice ideological consistency on the altar of geopolitical expediency. By temporarily burying the hatchet with Russia in Poland, Hitler calculated he would deter Britain and France from honouring their commitment to Warsaw. He miscalculated and thus ended up, on 3 September 1939, with a war in the West which he did

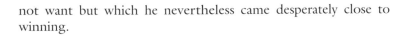

not want but which he nevertheless came desperately close to winning.

The Mason thesis

According to the late British Marxist historian T.W. Mason, economic factors were decisive in determining the timing of the war in Europe.[16] In essence, Mason argues that the Nazi economy was proving increasingly incapable after 1937 of meeting both the needs of the extensive public works programme and escalating rearmament and the desires for goods and services of the fully employed workforce. The strains inherent in this situation were manifested in a variety of ways including shortages of skilled labour and raw materials in key areas, rising inflation and an increasingly strained balance of payments situation. However, the Nazis did not dare dampen down consumer demand dramatically in favour of giving absolute priority to rearmament because, according to Mason, they feared that if they pressed the working class too hard in this manner they would risk provoking a revolt comparable to that of 1918–19. The only means of squaring the circle and providing a release valve for the overheated German economy was allegedly to plunge Germany into war. Short successful wars of plunder would unite, or at least distract, the nation and provide the means of delaying any economic reckoning. Nazi economic thinking and planning certainly sheds light on Nazi foreign and military policy, although not in the manner outlined by Mason.

Notwithstanding the rhetoric of the 'stab in the back' myth, Hitler and the German military appreciated the damage which the Royal Navy's blockade had caused to Germany's economy and morale in the First World War. To avoid any future enemy exerting a similar stranglehold over Germany's material resources and moral reserves, emphasis in the inter-war period was placed upon the creation of a *Wehrwirtschaft* or defence-based economy, capable of meeting internally all the needs of total war. Hence General Groener established an army economic office, headed by Colonel Georg Thomas, which in 1933 was absorbed into the Defence Ministry as the Economics and Armaments Office. However, Hitler typically encouraged the armed services to fight out with one another the acquisition of labour and other resources, with the consequence that already by 1936 this competition was threatening to impact adversely not only upon Germany's military capabilities but upon the economy as a whole.

In short, domestic factors may have added pressure for Germany to go to war but Hitler was set upon his path for Lebensraum by geopolitical and racist assumptions rather than economic considerations.

3　Appeasement

In the 1920s Britain appeased Germany in an effort both to counteract French antagonism towards Germany and to persuade
Germany to accept its diminished power within Europe. The
appeasement of Germany in the 1920s (which centred upon a willingness to see Germany's reparations burden reduced) differed from
that of the 1930s because the first was undertaken from a position
of relative military strength whereas the latter was undertaken
from a position of weakness, albeit not as great as was imagined
at the time. Chamberlainite appeasement also differed from that of
his predecessor Stanley Baldwin because Neville Chamberlain was
dynamic and proactive, whereas Baldwin, the truer conservative,
had been masterly in his inactivity. Thus appeasement changed from
passive acceptance of Germany's unilateral breaches of the Treaty of
Versailles into an active mission to discover her grievances and seek
to satisfy them through peaceful negotiation.

The policy of appeasement is indeed indelibly associated with
the foreign policy of Chamberlain after he became Prime Minister
in May 1937 and it had its finest hour in September 1938 with
the Munich Agreement. However, the trickle of criticism voiced
at that time subsequently swelled into a tidal wave whose roar at
one time threatened to drown out measured appreciations of the
policy. While appeasement seems unlikely ever to shed the pejora-
tive connotations which it acquired in the 1940s, Chamberlain's
reputation has undergone positive re-evaluation and while he is
still dismissed as a naïve dupe or reviled as worse by some, others
regard him as having done as much, or even more, than Churchill
to ensure Britain's survival and Nazi Germany's ultimate defeat.

What follows will consider British inter-war foreign policy
with particular reference to Chamberlain's premiership in order to
assess whether he deserves opprobrium or approbation. The analytical framework for this assessment will involve consideration or four
subsidiary questions, namely: Why did Britain oppose continental
commitments after 1918? How far and why did Britain's attitude to

Germany change between 1918 and 1938? Why did Chamberlain pursue the policy of appeasement, and was there an alternative? And finally, why did Chamberlain take Britain to war in 1939?

Why did Britain oppose continental commitments after 1918?

The Great War had supposedly been 'the war to end wars' and there was a widespread feeling of 'never again' compounded by the facts that it had been the bloodiest war in British history and the slaughter seemed futile to many. Conversely the League of Nations and collective security were widely thought to offer the possibility of a new, peaceful international order. It took time to appreciate that the League was fatally flawed (in its membership, decision-making apparatus and powers) and those who believed in collective security were often reluctant to contemplate rearmament, let alone armed action by the League.

As the world's greatest naval and imperial power Britain was traditionally isolationist, not concerning herself in the affairs of continental Europe unless some power threatened to dominate it (and especially the Channel coastline), such as Philip II's Spain in Elizabethan times, Louis XIV's France at the time of Winston Churchill's illustrious forbear, the 1st Duke of Marlborough, or the Kaiser's Germany.

However, the advent of modern air power undermined Britain's traditional foreign policy, making the Rhine rather than the Channel Britain's strategic frontier. Hence Britain's formal abandonment of isolationism by acting as co-guarantor with Italy of the Locarno Pact of 1925 (whereby Germany, France and Belgium accepted their frontiers with one another as laid down at the Paris Peace Conference). Hence, too, a shift in defence expenditure towards the Royal Air Force (RAF) (first Bomber Command, and later Fighter Command).

When the First World War ended, however, there had been no immediate threats to Britain's global position, with Japan an ally (since 1902), America isolationist, the Soviet Union weak after the Great War, revolution and civil war, and Germany disarmed under the terms of the Treaty of Versailles.

Britain could therefore afford to disarm. Hence the ten-year rule (the assumption that Great Britain faced no threat for the next decade) which Churchill as Chancellor institutionalised in 1928 (so that it was automatically extended each year) and which led to a progressive reduction in defence spending. It was only abandoned in 1932 as the impact of the Wall Street Crash stimulated aggressive nationalism, specifically the 1931 Manchurian Incident (which led to Japan's departure from the League in 1933). The Treasury, however, remained opposed to rapid rearmament as both unnecessary and economically damaging, while the seeming fulfilment of the Keynesian prophecy that heavy reparations would damage the German and global economy, strengthened the commonly held view that the Versailles had been too harsh and therefore required revision and many, including the trade union movement and the Labour party believed that money could be better spent on social reform and/or welfare rather than rearmament.

As a great imperial power Britain had to try to strike a balance between defence of the mother country (which might involve continental commitments) and imperial defence, such as the development of the naval base at Singapore. The problem became critical when British policymakers were contemporaneously confronted with the Japanese threat to the Far Eastern empire, the Italian threat to the Mediterranean empire (which provided communications with the Far Eastern Empire), and the German threat to the homeland itself. This was a major argument (pushed by the Service Chiefs) in favour of appeasing one or more of the hostile powers.

How far (and why) did Britain's attitude to Germany change between 1918 and 1938?

In helping to draw up the Versailles Treaty, Lloyd George, unlike Clemenceau's France did not want to see Germany crippled economically, militarily and territorially because he believed this would make Germany want revenge, damage British trade, and allow Soviet communism (or France) to dominate the continent. Lloyd George believed, moreover, that allowing the Wilsonian principle of national self-determination to determine the shape of central and eastern Europe, would render European peace more, rather than less, fragile, stating:

> I cannot imagine any greater cause of future war than that the German people, who have proved themselves to be one of the

most powerful and vigorous races in the world, should be surrounded by a number of small states, many of them consisting
of peoples who have never previously set up a stable government for themselves.[1]

However, Lloyd George had to pose as tough on Germany in
order to secure re-election in 1918 and felt obliged to make some
concessions to the tough French bargaining position.

John Maynard Keynes felt no such constraints and resigned
from the British delegation at Paris over the allegedly harsh treatment of Germany. He consistently argued thereafter that reparations were set too high (a view expressed in his book *The
Economic Consequences of the Peace*). This 'Versailles guilt' in governing circles in Britain helps to explain British dislike of the 1923
Franco-Belgian occupation of the Ruhr (in response to Germany
defaulting on her reparations payments) and British support for
the 1924 Dawes Plan, the 1925 Locarno Pact, the admission of
Germany to the League (with a permanent seat on the Council)
in 1926, the 1929 Young Plan and the 1932 cancellation of reparations payments (at Lausanne).

'Versailles guilt' persisted after the Nazi takeover in 1933. That is
to say, appeasement was based upon the assumption that Germany
had been treated too harshly and had legitimate grievances. As
shown in the previous chapter, Hitler cleverly exploited this sentiment, for example by arguing at the time of Germany's 1933
withdrawal from the League and the Geneva Disarmament
Conference that it was only fair for Germany to rearm if other
powers failed to disarm (in line with the universal disarmament
which was one of Wilson's Fourteen Points and a stated aim of
the League). Moreover, Hitler had claimed with apparent sincerity as early as *Mein Kampf* (1924) that he admired Britain, had no
quarrel with the British Empire and desired alliance between
Germany and Britain. In addition, those in Britain who disliked
and/or feared the USSR more than Germany and who actively
welcomed the prospect of Hitler seeking Lebensraum in the East
were obviously not upset by the prospect of Germany rearming
or expanding.

For all the above reasons there was relatively little resistance
within Britain to the reintroduction of conscription and formal
recreation of the Luftwaffe in 1935, the remilitarisation of the

Rhineland in March 1936, Anschluss (union) with Austria in March 1938, and the acquisition of the Sudetenland in September 1938. Indeed, when Lord Halifax visited Germany in November 1937, ostensibly to hunt, he had been authorised by Chamberlain to tell Hitler that Britain was not opposed to German revisionism regarding Austria and Czechoslovakia, so long as this was achieved peacefully. Shortly thereafter Chamberlain had signified his unwillingness to brook any questioning of his desire to appease Germany and Italy by two changes of personnel. Firstly, he sidelined the Germanophobe Robert Vansittart (making him chief diplomatic adviser to the government rather than permanent under-secretary at the Foreign Office) in favour of Sir Horace Wilson (who became his chief diplomatic envoy). Secondly, he replaced Eden with the more supportive Halifax as Foreign Secretary. Eden had resigned on 20 February 1938 because Chamberlain had not consulted him before rejecting Roosevelt's proposal to convene a conference to establish agreed principles of international conduct and because Eden disagreed with Chamberlain's willingness to consider ending the League's sanctions over Abyssinia as the price of improving Anglo-Italian relations.

Why did Chamberlain pursue the policy of appeasement, and was there an alternative?

Chamberlain's reasons for pursuing the policy of appeasing Germany can be deduced from his speeches and actions, but in the absence of his memoirs the best source for his real thinking consists of his letters to his sisters (Ida and Hilda). Nevertheless, there is ample scope for differences of interpretation. There are essentially three schools of historical thought on the subject.

Firstly, there are those like 'Cato' (the three Beaverbrook journalists – Michael Foot, Frank Owen and Peter Howard – who collectively used the pseudonym 'Cato' for their 1940 book entitled *Guilty Men*,)[2] and Churchill who followed the 'Guilty Man' thesis that Chamberlain was naive and outmanoeuvred in his dealings with Hitler.[3]

Secondly, there are revisionists like John Charmley[4] who defend Chamberlain's actions as farsighted or at least as sensible given the constraints under which he was operating (including the state of Britain's finances, defences, public opinion and friends and allies abroad).

Thirdly, there are post-revisionists or counter-revisionists like McDonough[5] who are more sympathetic towards Chamberlain than the first school but more critical towards him than the second.

Evaluating the policy of appeasement depends in part upon deciding whether or not there was a realistic or viable alternative, which principally means whether Hitler might have been deterred and war avoided by alliance with the USSR. R.A.C. Parker argued that this could have worked,[6] but conversely it can be argued that neither side liked or trusted the other; countries like Poland and Rumania deeply distrusted the USSR (with good reason) and would not allow the Red Army onto their soil; experts considered the Red Army to have been gravely weakened by Stalin's purges; and Hitler could always 'outbid' Chamberlain, for example, by offering Stalin land at Poland's expense.

The attitude of the Labour party and the influence of public opinion (as shown by the 1935 Peace Ballot) suggested strong opposition to rapid and extensive rearmament, let alone war – at least up to Hitler's March 1939 takeover of the 'Czech rump'.

Churchill was Chamberlain's arch-critic, condemning appeasement and urging rearmament and a 'Grand alliance' (which would include the Soviet Union) to resist German aggression but until March 1939 his was largely a voice in the wilderness because his judgment had long seemed suspect (for example, over the Dardanelles, the gold standard, India and the abdication); he was widely distrusted within the Conservative party as disloyal (having first defected to the Liberals and then returned to the Conservatives); and was widely considered to be motivated more by the desire to humiliate the Chamberlain cabinet and force his way back into office rather than disinterestedly serving the national interest.

Why did Chamberlain take Britain to war in 1939?

The German occupation of Bohemia–Moravia in March 1939 marked a turning point in international relations because Hitler's action manifestly broke the assurances he had given at Munich just six months earlier that he had no further territorial demands and the action (as shown above) was blatantly aggressive, as the land acquired was not German-speaking, like the Sudetenland, but Slav.

Hence Chamberlain offered the Polish Guarantee in order to warn Hitler that he risked war if he continued to act unilaterally, using force or the threat of force to gain territory. It should, however, be noted that the policy of appeasement while arguably dead was not yet buried to Chamberlain's mind. His action was partly designed to silence domestic critics (chiefly Churchill). Moreover, the guarantee related only to Poland's independent existence not to its existing frontiers. That is to say, it left the door open to a second Munich-style conference and territorial adjustments.

The idea of an Anglo-Russian alliance was pursued largely because Churchill pushed for this as a means of making the Polish Guarantee more meaningful militarily but Chamberlain did not pursue the idea seriously as shown by the low profile of the British delegation; the leisurely manner of their travel to the Soviet Union (by ship rather than by plane); and their lack of treaty-making powers.

The Nazi–Soviet Non-Aggression Pact of August 1939 sealed the fate of Poland, and Hitler thought that it would ensure that Britain and France would not go to war over Poland.

Germany invaded Poland on 1 September 1939 and Britain and France declared war two days later. The delay occurred because the French claimed that they needed more time to mobilise before they were subject to German bombing but to advocates of the 'Guilty Man' thesis it is evidence that Chamberlain was still hoping to cut a deal with Nazi Germany so as to avoid war.

In fact, Chamberlain had little or no room for manoeuvre as the Poles would not negotiate with the Nazis and Churchill would have had much more popular support than he had at the time of Munich for depicting any further deal with Hitler as dishonourable.

Revisionists would argue that the year gained at Munich was vital for national survival – producing the Spitfires, Hawker Hurricanes and radar that ensured success in the Battle of Britain. Chamberlain's critics – advocates of the 'Guilty Man' thesis – would argue that Britain would have been better off fighting in September 1938 than September 1939 because Germany would then theoretically have been faced not only with Britain, France and Czechoslovakia but also the Czechs' Soviet ally.

Post-revisionists, by contrast, sympathise with Chamberlain's predicament, credit him with making good use of the 12 months 'bought' at Munich to improve Britain's bargaining position, and would point out that there is no guarantee that the USSR would have stood by the Czechs if Britain and France had not appeased Germany and that Russia's military weight would, in any case, not have been sufficient at the time either to deter Hitler from aggression or, necessarily, to ensure his defeat, given Stalin's Red Army purges and the refusal of Rumania or Poland to cooperate.

Whether Chamberlain is ultimately perceived as weak, cowardly and indecisive or competent, strong-willed and clear-sighted depends not only upon one's reading of Chamberlain's reading of Hitler's foreign policy aims but also on Chamberlain's appreciation of all the relevant domestic and international factors.

Ironically, the greatest tribute paid to Chamberlain's policy of appeasement came from Hitler himself when he comment that 'That damned fellow has ruined my triumphant entry into Prague'.[7] Hitler had wanted a short, victorious war against Czechoslovakia which would have blooded his army, put heart into his nation and totally destroyed the democratic Slav 'aircraft-carrier' which appeared to threaten the heart of the Grossdeutschland. It is true that the Munich Conference allowed the Sudetenland to be incorporated into Nazi Germany by 10 October 1938, thereby rendering the Czech 'rump' economically and militarily highly vulnerable as it had lost the bulk of its manufacturing capacity (including 70 per cent of its electricity power plants and iron and steel factories, and nearly all of its chemical plants) together with all of its heavily fortified defences along the German border (and the Skoda armaments works). Moreover, the failure to consult the Soviet Union perhaps fatally increased Stalin's distrust of the western democracies and thus helped produce the Nazi–Soviet Non-Aggression Pact of August 1939, which helped to seal the fate of Poland and much else of eastern Europe besides.

In this sense the infamous 'piece of paper' pledging that Britain and Germany would never to go to war with one another again, which Chamberlain persuaded Hitler to sign on 30 September 1938 and which he brandished upon his return to Britain, was manifestly worthless. However, symbolically it was priceless, indicating that without a shadow of doubt any further demand on Czechoslovakia – as materialised in March 1939 – constituted a blatant act of aggression. Such a lesson was invaluable in educating international opinion – particularly in the Dominions and the United States – of Hitler's untrustworthiness and unreasonable insatiability. Historians disagree over whether Britain or Germany made better use of the 12-month postponement of war which Munich meant but what is irrefutable is that Britain's armed forces, and particularly its fighter squadrons, were in a much better shape in September 1939 than in September 1938 to resist Hitler (with British expenditure on rearmament increasing from 8.1 per cent of GNP to 21.4 per cent) and that opinion at home and in the Dominions was much more united in September 1939 than in September 1938 regarding the need to resist Hitler. The policy of appeasement manifestly failed to prevent war but at least provided the preconditions for a successful outcome.

Missed opportunities?

The story of appeasement does not end with the British declaration of war on Germany on 3 September 1939 or even with Churchill's replacement of Chamberlain as prime minister in May 1940. Lloyd George, who as early as 1919 had asked who was prepared to 'die for Danzig', on 24 September 1939 published an article in the *Sunday Express* criticising the Polish regime and on 3 October, following the Polish collapse, in a speech to the House of Commons he hinted at the possibility of coming to some understanding with Germany. The expression of such views did not prove an obstacle to Churchill later twice offering Lloyd George a post in government (in May and June 1940). Indeed, Lentin has even considered the possibility that Churchill wanted Lloyd George at his side precisely because of the possible need to negotiate with Hitler.[8] There were certainly several in the cabinet at the time and there have been several historians since who think British national interests would have been better served by continuing to appease Hitler rather than continuing to fight him.

The Polish guarantee (like those to Greece and Rumania) was a commitment that could not be honoured unless, and possibly even if, Britain had been allied with the USSR, as Britain was suffering from 'imperial overstretch', with large numbers of troops tied down in Palestine and India, and the BEF and the Army generally neglected relative to the RAF, while the Maginot Line symbolised the defensive mentality of the French. A significant part of the Conservative party, led by Lord Halifax, felt that the war was being fought out of moral indignation rather than the clear-sighted defence of British interests, and was being waged with little or no prospect of success, and wanted to sue for peace after the fall of France in 1940. Churchill, however, managed to outmanoeuvre and outvote Halifax in the War Cabinet, arguing that Britain should fight on until Germany was utterly defeated. Some critics question whether Churchill's motives in hindering the peace process were completely disinterested. Opposition to appeasement in the 1930s had given him office in 1940. If peace had been concluded with Germany in 1940 Churchill would either have felt obliged to resign or his removal would have been a German precondition for agreeing to peace.

According to Alan Clark national interests would have been better served by a compromise peace with Hitler, although he believes that negotiating peace in 1940 would have been unwise, as Britain would have been in the role of a supplicant and would have received harsh terms.[9] However, while Clark regards Churchill as having saved the country in 1940 he argues that in early 1941 Britain was in a much stronger bargaining position to come to terms with Germany as the Battle of Britain had confirmed RAF command of the skies and obliged Hitler to postpone his invasion plans; the British had defeated the armies of Hitler's Italian ally in North Africa; and Hitler wanted to concentrate his energies on invading the USSR: a fact known to the British thanks to their interception and decoding of German Enigma signals.

Thus Britain could have negotiated a peace between equals in 1941 that would have reduced British bloodshed; removed the need for Britain to become dependent upon American finance (after losing our gold and overseas assets); enabled forces to be moved to the Far East so that there would have been a better chance of deterring Japanese aggression; and rendered the fight between the Red Army and the Wehrmacht more evenly matched. an attritional war between these two being in the best interests of the British Empire and the world.

The advocates of appeasement argue that the best outcome for Britain would be if Germany and the USSR fought a long war of attrition in which they were both gravely weakened. They point out that ever since at least the time of *Mein Kampf* (1924) Hitler had, with apparent sincerity, protested his admiration for the British and his desire for an alliance which would give them a free hand as a great maritime and imperial power, so long as they left him with a free hand to conquer Lebensraum in the East. Once allied with the USSR there was always the danger, they argue, that Russia might ultimately make a separate peace with Germany at Britain's expense, as had happened at Brest–Litovsk in March 1918, while if Germany was defeated by the Red Army then Eastern and Central Europe would almost certainly lose their independence to the Russians, as had already happened to the Baltic States, Bessarabia, eastern Poland and parts of Finland in 1939–40. Thus peace with Germany in 1941 might have preserved the Empire and Britain's great power status as well as preventing hundreds of thousands of Britons from being killed or wounded without making a great, if any, difference to Central and Eastern Europe.

Those who believe in an ethical foreign policy will object that it would have been immoral not to have carried on fighting Germany in 1941 but the Wannsee Conference which is commonly characterised as having organised the Final Solution (see Chapter 8) did not take place until 20 January 1942, while Stalin's record on human rights (as symbolised by the Ukraine famine and the purges, to say nothing of Katyn Wood) was even more appalling than Hitler's when Britain allied with the USSR in June 1941.

However, any chance of a 1941 peace deal between Britain and Germany was destroyed by Churchill's sending British forces against the Germans in Greece. It could be argued that by 1939 Britain had already shot its bolt as a Great Power and the real choice for Britain's policymakers was whether to become a junior partner of the United States or a junior partner of Germany. If this was the stark choice facing Churchill in 1940 then few would doubt that he made the correct choice, given the nature of the Third Reich.

Historians such as Alan Clark and John Charmley nevertheless feel that Britain actually enjoyed more room for manoeuvre in 1941, and that had Britain negotiated peace with Germany, such a deal would certainly have resulted in Britain being stronger and richer than proved to be the case in 1945, while such an accommodation might even have perpetuated Britain's Great Power status for the foreseeable future. Instead Britain became dependent upon the United States, which effectively made its aid conditional upon the liquidation of British investments overseas (a precondition of Lend–Lease) and the British Empire (as symbolised by the 'bases for destroyers' deal). Moreover, Britain remained dependent upon the United States after the war as shown by the loan negotiated by Lord Keynes (1945), Marshall Aid (1948) and Suez (1956), when Eisenhower forced British withdrawal by refusing to take action to stop the run on sterling. According to this interpretation, Churchill successfully defended British territorial integrity from Germany at the cost of mortgaging British sovereignty to 'Uncle Sam'. To all but a few this, if true, appears to have been a price worth paying.

4 The fall of France

On 3 September 1939, two days after the German invasion of Poland, Great Britain and France declared war on Germany. They were, however, unable to do anything to save Poland, especially as the Red Army, in accordance with the secret clauses of the Nazi–Soviet Non-Aggression Pact, invaded Poland from the east on 17 September.

A period of deceptive quiet followed the defeat of Poland, which became known as the Phoney War. Then on 9 April 1940 Hitler launched his Blitzkrieg tactics against Denmark and Norway. A month later, just before dawn on 10 May, it was the turn of neutral Holland and Belgium. The war in the west now hinged upon the ability of France to halt the German juggernaut. However, within six weeks of the initial German assault and to the surprise of most pundits, French military resistance had crumbled. What follows is an attempt to explain this collapse.

The debate on the fall of France

The conventional interpretation of the fall of France is that the Third Republic was in a terminal state of decline, aggravated by geriatric generals and squabbling politicians. Their professional incompetence and incessant in-fighting, respectively, produced a spiritual malaise which made defeatism a self-fulfilling prophecy. Thus France's leaders lacked both the discipline to organise a war and the moral conviction to fight one. Internecine warfare militated against military success.

Alternative interpretations rebut the claims of a degenerate and decadent political culture by alleging that a remarkable recovery in national confidence and resolution occurred from late 1938 onwards (only to be sapped once again during the Phoney War), and/or point out that systemic weaknesses, such as a relatively low birth rate, that might have had a bearing in a protracted attritional conflict are irrelevant given that France succumbed in six weeks to the German blitzkrieg.

German war plans

Hitler issued Fuhrer Directive No. 6 for an offensive in the West on 9 October 1939. The plan of attack, codenamed Case Yellow, was to be worked out in detail by the OKH (Army High Command). General Halder, the Chief-of-Staff, proposed an extremely cautious campaign which would have effectively postponed a decisive offensive against France until 1942. Not surprisingly, Hitler was unimpressed and ordered that Case Yellow begin by 12 November (although the start date was later postponed). Hitler's boldness was backed by several professionals including Gerd von Rundstedt, the Commander-in-Chief of Army Group A; von Rundstedt's Chief-of-Staff, Erich von Manstein, and the prime theorist and ace practitioner of Blitzkrieg tactics, Heinz Guderian.

Two chance incidents played an important role in the unfolding of events. Firstly, Yellow was compromised when two Luftwaffe officers with detailed documentation regarding the operation crash-landed in Belgium on 10 January 1940. Hitler reacted by demanding a new plan. Secondly, a new plan which coincided with his own intuitions fell into his lap when Halder sought to sideline Manstein after the latter had written six memoranda for OKH critical of the former's plan. Halder arranged for Manstein's promotion to command a corps based in East Prussia but Hitler's Wehrmacht adjutant, Schmundt ensured that Manstein's formal courtesy call on the Commander-in-Chief on 17 February turned into a prolonged briefing session. Hitler adopted the Manstein plan as his own and under the codename Sichelschnitt ('sickle stroke') it formally replaced Yellow.

Whereas the Schlieffen plan had sought to cut off the Anglo-French forces by swinging south-east through Belgium, Sichelschnitt sought to outflank the allies as they pushed into Belgium by means of an armoured thrust which would cross the Meuse after passing through the Ardennes, thereby by-passing the fortifications of the Maginot Line on the Franco-German border.

The Third Republic's faultlines

It has recently been suggested that 'it was not decadence that led to 1940; it is 1940 that has led us to view the late third Republic as decadent'.[1] Nevertheless the sickle stroke that cut a swathe through

France in 1940 and defeated it within six weeks shocked contemporaries and continues to perplex historians because superficially France was strong. In fact it was militarily, politically, demographically and economically enfeebled.

Although France was one of the Big Three victorious powers at the Paris Peace Conference, from which she emerged with the world's second largest empire, she had actually shot her bolt as a Great Power and was even more the victim of 'imperial overstretch' than Great Britain. Had it not been for first Russian, then British and finally American assistance it is difficult to imagine her having not succumbed to German arms between 1914–18 and her apparent dominance of the continent thereafter was based upon the temporary weakness of the Soviet Union and Germany. Her attempts to cripple the latter territorially, militarily and financially merely postponed the day of reckoning, with France's severe and deepening demographic deficit relative to Germany providing the writing on the wall unless France could construct a countervailing system of alliances. However, the Soviet Union was a pariah state, the buffer states of central and eastern Europe between Germany and the Soviet Union were too weak to counterbalance the revival of either, let alone both, which left the French dependent upon the goodwill of a Britain that was not so much 'perfidious' as constitutionally disinclined to commit itself to continental Europe and deeply distrustful of French desires to dominate the continent. France between the wars was deeply divided. Cabinets came and went in a cascade. Some lasted just a few hours. Rarely did one last a whole year. On the very day Hitler came to power, France was without a government. It was again without one when he marched into Austria five years later.

The Left in France was more concerned with hounding rogues in high places at home than in curbing fascism elsewhere. The Right so hated the Left that it was prepared to countenance dictatorship. As early as 1934 Marshal Petain, the victor of Verdun was proposed as France's saviour from communism, although he was then nearly 80. These deep divisions were to fetter France when she faced the need to rearm. France was even close to civil war in 1936.

However, the fall of the Popular Front on 30 November 1936 and Daladier's move away from Popular Front socialism from 1937 helped re-enlist the centre and right into a pro-war national consensus while Bill Irvine also suggests that the militant left became increasingly willing to cooperate with a government that was more willing to resist Hitler militarily, although this consensus fell short of that of 1914, and the mood when war actually broke out while not yet defeatist was certainly downbeat and dour.[2]

The Maginot line

Frenchmen numbering 1.3 million or 10.5 per cent of the active male population lost their lives in the Great War. Now French military thinking became wholly defensive, forgetting Napoleon's favourite maxim: 'The side that stays within its fortifications is beaten'. The Maginot Line allowed its 400,000-strong garrison merely to offer a frontal defence against a frontal attack. That is to say, it offered no scope for the French to mount a counter-offensive. Since the French spurned any notion of taking the offensive, the Maginot Line ironically protected Germany better than it did France.

The Maginot forts, constructed in the 1930s, were truly twentieth-century wonders. Electric trains took the troops from barracks to gun turrets and from arsenal to canteen. There were cinemas underground, air-conditioning and even sun-ray rooms.

In May 1940 half a million French soldiers garrisoned the Maginot Line. The fortifications of this defensive line were the most elaborate and expensive the world had ever seen. Unfortunately, however, they were not as extensive as they needed to be: their guns would only halt the Germans if they attacked across their common border. It was only 87-miles long and it stopped 250 miles short of the Channel, partly because the money ran out and partly because the Belgians objected to being left on the 'wrong' side of the line. French strategists argued that in the event of war they would need to confront the enemy on Belgian, if not German, soil. The folly of this thinking was shown up in 1936 when, following Hitler's remilitarisation of the Rhineland in March, King Leopold of Belgium, without consulting the French, declared Belgium independent and neutral and to that end revoked the military treaty with France and closed the border, even to French military observers. Too late, the French began extending the Maginot Line to the sea but by May 1940 it was far from finished.

Thus when war broke out Anglo-French forces would have to advance into Belgian territory without having been able to co-ordinate plans with the Belgian General Staff or reconnoitre the ground (although in fact Leopold's chief military adviser, General Robert van Overstraeten did allow British and French officers wearing civilian clothes to reconnoitre the positions they intended to take up if Germany attacked and pass on intelligence, including details of the original Case Yellow plans captured at Mechelen on 9 January).

Blitzkrieg

Winston Churchill had thanked God for the French army when Hitler came to power in 1933, and a few days prior to the last peacetime Bastille Day (14 July 1939), the British War Minister, visiting Paris had said – and not apparently just out of politeness – that France had the greatest army in the world. These estimates were both absurdly optimistic. In the year that the Maginot Line had been completed, Guderian, had published his *Achtung Panzer* which expounded a new form of warfare, centring upon highly mobile armoured divisions closely supported by dive bombers, for which neither the British or French General Staffs were adequately prepared.

The common training shared by German air force and army officers ensured that the former could provide the latter with close support, and while Britain and France had over-diversified in aircraft production, Germany had concentrated on developing a relatively small number of aircraft specialising in certain roles – such as the Junkers 87 ('Stuka') dive-bomber – which could then be mass produced.

German tanks were often inferior, model for model, compared with their British and French counterparts. The Mark III Panzer, for example, was inferior in terms of armour to both the British Infantry Tank Mark I and the French Somua. However, whereas the allies tended to disperse their tanks in penny packets, the Germans concentrated theirs in ten Panzer divisions. The French actually had 3000 tanks to the Germans' 2400 but they frittered them away, with 1500 allocated to their slower-moving infantry divisions, 700 allotted to hybrid 'cavalry' and 'mechanised' divisions, and only 800 retained for five armoured divisions, of which in 1940 only three were active.

The Phoney War

While their Polish allies were being routed in the east, the French and British did little in the west. There was the so-called Saar offensive: the only French offensive of the war. A few French divisions advanced five miles but they did not even try to penetrate the Siegfried Line, at that time still unfinished. And while Poland fought on, there were no German tanks at all on the western front.

Had the French attacked in strength in September 1939 their superiority at that time on the Western Front would have overwhelmed the German forces there within one to two weeks. But even before the Poles had surrendered, the French commander had ordered withdrawal from German territory to back behind the Maginot Line. Even bombing of the Ruhr was forbidden for fear of Luftwaffe retaliation against French factories. As one Frenchman commented at the time, after the prologue of a phoney offensive, they were well prepared for a Phoney War.

The winter of 1939 was the coldest for half a century. Even the Channel froze at Boulogne. The French halted work on the Maginot extension. The Germans, however, forged ahead with their plans. As winter wore on, French morale sank. Discipline deteriorated and drunkenness became rife. Special rooms were set aside in railway stations where men could recover before rejoining their units.

The Maginot mentality

Command arrangements were superior on the German side but structural deficiencies on the Allied side were compounded by personal failings on the part of Gort, Georges and Gamelin.

Few French generals bothered to inspect, let alone meet, their troops but then their commander, General Maurice Gamelin, rarely set foot outside his own headquarters, at Vincennes near Paris. After March 1940, Gamelin paid no further personal visits to inspect preparations along the front. Already 68 at the beginning of 1940, his military record was so impeccable that no one dreamed of asking him to make way for a younger man. Gamelin was clever but lacked guts and regarded the French government rather than the Germans as the enemy.

Unbelievably Vincennes had no radio communications or teleprinter links with the outside world. Instead, motorcycle riders dispatched messages every hour. Gamelin rarely issued orders, preferring to suggest guidelines. His long-term strategy was to wait until the Allies could match the Germans in numbers and equipment before launching any major offensive, even though that would mean waiting until 1941. Meanwhile he was concerned to keep the war away from French soil. Hence his interest in plans such as an attack on the Baku oilfields from Syria, a landing in Salonika or an attack on Russia through Norway to aid Finland.

The latter plan had serious domestic repercussions. Daladier was keen to satisfy the centre right by being seen to stand up to communist aggression but could not persuade Chamberlain to join him in this adventure. His consequent resignation from the premiership in March 1940 left a leadership vacuum.

In May 1940 Gamelin had 100 divisions on the Western Front plus another 10 of the British Expeditionary Force. Forty manned the Maginot Line, while five guarded the Swiss frontier. Another 40 – the best – were to go into neutral Belgium once Germany attacked but when that happened the pivot of Gamelin's strength would lie in the supposedly impenetrable Ardennes. Gamelin chose to place 10 of his weakest, least-trained, worst-equipped divisions to guard this 100-mile portion of the front.

The French chose to ignore reports that nearly 50 Panzer divisions were on the move. They even learnt the date of the attack but still did nothing. As Gamelin put it, they preferred to await events.

Sickle stroke

Anglo-French forces were to be tempted as far eastwards as possible by Army Group B with three Panzer divisions, under General Fedor von Bock, attacking into Holland and northern Belgium. Meantime, in the south, Army Group C, under General Wilhelm Ritter von Leeb, engaged the Maginot Line. However, the main German thrust came from Army Group A with the remaining seven Panzer divisions (comprising 1800 tanks), under Rundstedt in the centre, which was to pass through the Ardennes, seize crossings over the Meuse between Sedan and Dinant and then drive north-west, along the line of the Somme, to Amiens, Abbeville and the Channel coastline.

The attack began at 5.30 am on 10 May 1940 with an airborne invasion of neutral Holland. The Germans' 118 infantry divisions,

10 Panzer divisions and 6 motorised divisions were ranged against 101 French divisions, the 13 infantry divisions of the British Expeditionary Force, the Dutch army's 10 divisions and the Belgian army's 22.

The French rushed into the trap set for them by the Germans, with Gamelin pushing 40 of his best divisions – almost half of his total force, including the whole of the BEF – northwards into Belgium and Holland, thereby depriving himself of a reserve force strong enough to mount an effective counter-attack in the event of a German breakthrough. Such a breakthrough was assisted by the fact that the Ardennes section was poorly defended by 2 Belgian divisions of forest riflemen, followed by Corap's Ninth Army and part of Huntziger's Second, who abandoned their position on the Meuse, allowing Allied defences to be breached as the Germans crossed the river during the afternoon of 13 May, assisted by a poorly defended bridge at a weir 40 miles north of Sedan which the French had left intact, alone among the bridges over the Meuse, for fear that its destruction would lower the water level to such an extent that the river could have been forded.

By 14 May not only were the Germans over the Meuse but they had secured command of the skies and the Dutch had surrendered. The following day de Gaulle, as commander of the 4th Armoured Division, was ordered to mount a counter-attack in order to win time for the allies to consolidate a new front north of Paris but this and subsequent counter-attacks on (19 May and 28–30 May) proved unavailing.

The Panzers now broke out from their bridgehead, assisted by the withdrawal of troops along the Meuse to defend Paris and by Gamelin's panic-stricken sacking of roughly 20 of his frontline commanders. Panic also characterised the political scene, although here it took the form on 16 May of Reynaud, the French premier, sending to the Madrid embassy for the 84-year-old Petain to join him as his deputy, and to Syria for the 73-year-old Weygand to replace the 68-year-old Gamelin.

On 17 May Brussels fell and the German High Command, at Hitler's behest imposed a temporary halt on the advance. Nevertheless by 20 May Guderian's divisions had reached Abbeville at the mouth of the Somme. German success, in advancing 200 miles in just 7 days, not only effectively divided the Allied armies into two but drove a figurative wedge between the British and

French, who hereafter agreed upon little other than that they had both been let down by the Belgians.

Rommel badly overestimated the strength of a British counter-attack at Arras on 21 May, believing the 2 British divisions, supported by 2 tank battalions to have comprised a force of 5 divisions. In a reversal of roles, Brauchitsch and Halder sought to press ahead but Hitler and Rundstedt now urged caution, believing that the Panzers should not continue their advance until infantry had moved up to protect their flanks. Thus the advance was not resumed until the afternoon of 26 May by which time Operation Dynamo – the evacuation of the BEF from Dunkirk – had been formulated and put into practice. Thus when Hitler's 'stop order' was revoked the BEF and a substantial portion of the French First Army had escaped into the relative sanctuary of the 'Canal Line', protected by the Aa and Colme Canals. By 4 June, when Dunkirk fell, 338,000 Allied soldiers (including 110,000 Frenchmen) had been safely evacuated by the Royal Navy assisted by an armada of small boats.

The following day the Panzers resumed their offensive and broke through the 'Weygand Line', which ran from the Channel coast to the rivers Somme and Aisne before joining the Maginot Line at Montmedy. Within three days Rommel broke through the Seine at Rouen and on 10 June Reynaud's government left the capital and Italy declared war. The Italian advance stalled, despite a massive numerical advantage but elsewhere the news was bleak. On 12 June, 52nd Lowland and the Canadian Division were landed at Cherbourg to help French troops returning after evacuation from Dunkirk to open a new front, but they had to be evacuated almost immediately in order to avoid being taken prisoners. On 14 June, the Germans entered Paris and three days later Petain broadcast to the French nation announcing that he had become head of government (following Reynaud's resignation) and applied to the Germans for an armistice.

The armistice was signed on 22 June in Marshal Foch's old railway carriage in the woods of Compiegne, where the Armistice of 1918 had been signed. It came into effect on 25 June. Under its terms a humiliated France retained a shred of dignity in the shape of Vichy France: a nominally sovereign entity under the control of Petain's government, which also retained control over the French fleet and colonies. However, Germany occupied the rest of France, including the Atlantic seaboard, apart from some scraps of south-eastern France thrown to the Italian jackal. Moreover, 'occupation costs' were to be met from the French budget while all French POWs (amounting to roughly 25 per cent of her active manhood) were to act as a surety of good behaviour by remaining in German hands for an unspecified duration.

The consequences

The fall of France rendered Britain increasingly vulnerable to U-boat and aerial attack and to invasion. In Churchill's words, 'What General Weygand called the Battle of France is over. The Battle of Britain is about to begin'.[3] The British appear to have genuinely welcomed the prospect of fighting on their own in Europe, unencumbered by allies. Thus Chamberlain remarked that '[W]e are at any rate free of the French who have been nothing but a liability to us' and Lord Hankey stated that '[I]n a way it is almost a relief to be thrown back on the resources of the Empire and of America'.[4] Nor was this sentiment restricted to the 'Great and the Good'. Nellie Carver was probably typical of the British nation in recording 'The dominant feeling' as one of 'relief' on news that France had asked for an armistice. 'I'm absolutely sure', she went on, 'we can do better if we have nobody with us. They've let us down time and time again. Now we can really get on with the job'.[5]

However, Churchill recognised the need for American 'tools' if Britain were to 'finish the job' and the fall of France inclined him, and other British policymakers, to place even greater emphasis than hitherto upon cultivating the so-called 'special relationship' with the United States.

The fall of France persuaded Washington to accelerate its own rearmament programmes and to send aid to Britain once she had shown her capacity to survive the Nazi onslaught by defeating the Luftwaffe over the skies of Britain and once she had shown her will to carry on the fight by opening fire and drowning over 1000 Vichy French sailors at Oran and Mers-el-Kebir in July 1940 after they refused an ultimatum to side with the Royal Navy, scuttle their ships or sail them to the West Indies.

As already mentioned, the imminent prostration of France meant that Italy decided to enter the war on 10 June. The fall of France also encouraged the Japanese to throw in their lot with

Nazi Germany and take aggressive action in south-east Asia because the Dutch, French and British colonies were vulnerable as a consequence of the humiliations suffered by their mother countries at German hands and the need to strip their defences in order to bolster those closer to home. The Italian threat to Britain's position in the Mediterranean had already obliged the British government to tell the governments of Australia and New Zealand on 28 June that it would not be able to send a fleet to Singapore in the foreseeable future.

In the longer term, wartime dependence upon British and even scarcer American goodwill, persuaded de Gaulle to favour a post-war rapprochement with Germany or Russia rather than seeking closer relations with the 'Atlanticist' Anglo-Saxon powers. Hence in large part his vetoing of Britain's applications to join the European Economic Community in 1963 and 1967. The fall of France also helps explain why French decolonisation in Indo-China and Algeria was so much more bloody than the British experience in, say, the Indian sub-continent. France felt a need to cling to its empire as a sign of its Great Power status to offset the German occupation, while Britain having escaped this particular humiliation found it easier to allow the 'liberation' of its own colonies.

All this is, however, looking far beyond the immediate consequences of the fall of France. Hitler's longstanding aim remained the conquest of Lebensraum in the East and the war with Britain represented an unwelcome distraction from that conflict. Nevertheless, the fall of France, ended the threat of a serious war on two fronts for the foreseeable future, provided Germany with much-needed resources (including 650,000 civilian French workers compulsorily drafted to work in German factories), and discouraged the German public and High Command from questioning the Fuhrer's judgment by providing sweet revenge for the humiliations of 1918–19. Stalin having hoped for a protracted war in the West comparable to the stalemate of 1914–18 now had to prepare for Hitler turning eastwards much sooner than anticipated. He was thus encouraged to accelerate rearmament and to protect the soil of Mother Russia by annexing the Baltic States on 15–16 June 1940 and seizing Bessarabia and Bukovina from Rumania on 26 June 1940. The latter action, by bringing the Red Army even closer to the Ploesti oilfields if anything merely encouraged Hitler to strike sooner rather than later.

5 Great Britain alone

The Battle of Britain

The Battle for France nearly lost the RAF the Battle of Britain. Air Chief Marshal Sir Hugh Dowding, the Commander-in-Chief of Fighter Command, had to fight Churchill tooth and nail on 15 May 1940 to prevent him from fatally dissipating Fighter Command's meagre resources by siphoning off further fighters for France. Fortunately the claims of military prudence eventually prevailed over political considerations (namely vainly attempting to stiffen French resistance).

With 477 fighters and 284 pilots lost between May and 19 June 1940, when the campaign in France ended, Fighter Command was left with just 768 fighters in operational squadrons, of which only 520 were fit for operations. If they failed to deny the Luftwaffe control of the skies, then 'Operation Sealion', the proposed invasion of Britain, could proceed. By the time the Germans launched their air offensive in August 1940 the strength of Fighter Command had increased to 1032 aircraft at operational bases, of which 715 were ready for immediate action, with a further 424 in storage, ready for use the next day. During the Battle these figures remained roughly constant as increased aircraft production made good high losses.

Fighter Command's key aircraft were the Hawker Hurricane and the Vickers Supermarine Spitfire, both of which stood comparison with the very best fighters of the day, while the latter had already shown its ability to inflict serious damage on the Luftwaffe when in three days of fighting over the beaches of Dunkirk in the last week of May, they had inflicted 132 aircraft losses on the enemy at the cost of 155 Spitfires, 65 of them arising through accidents as aircrew attempted to master the new equipment.

The fact that the Battle of Britain was fought over home ground was advantageous in two respects. Firstly, it was easier to 'recycle' pilots insofar as they could rejoin their squadrons within hours if they bailed out safely, whereas their German counterparts would be taken prisoner (as was the fate of 967 Luftwaffe personnel between 1 July and 31 October). Partly for this reason, the Luftwaffe considered it legitimate to fire upon British pilots in the course of their descent by parachute. Nevertheless, this factor did something to offset the shortage of trained fighter pilots for the RAF (although nothing of course to counteract the more severe shortages of non-combat personnel, such as fitters, armourers and instrument mechanics). Secondly, the fact that the RAF was 'playing at home' allowed its aircraft more time in the air compared with enemy aircraft such as the Messerschmitt Me109 single-engined fighter, which had a relatively short range, which was further curtailed by the rapid manoeuvring required in a combat situation. Although the Germans used their bombers as bait to lure British fighters into combat it was actually German fighters who suffered most through this tactic, as being tied to the bomber stream limited their freedom of action, notably to fight at the higher altitudes where the Messerschmitt Me109 could outperform its British counterparts.

However, the key factor which allowed RAF Fighter Command win the battle by economising and focusing its efforts was the radar and signals intelligence it possessed regarding the enemy's operations. On the outbreak of war there were 21 Chain Home radar stations circling the coastline, providing information on the height and range of approaching aircraft for up to 200 miles. However, the average range was only 80 miles and these stations could not detect aircraft flying at below 1000 feet. Thus a supplementary chain of radar stations was established just after the outbreak of war to detect low-flying aircraft (and coastal shipping), with a range of 30 miles. Enigma also helped identify the German order of battle while low-level radio interception from the RAF wireless interception station at Cheadle provided regular information on the range, destination and origin of enemy aircraft.

On 1 August 1940, Hitler issued a directive instructing Geoering's Luftwaffe 'to overpower the English air force ... in the shortest possible time' by attacks on the whole air force structure and its supporting industries. However, the German air force had been developed to provide close support for ground operations rather than independent air operations and unlike the RAF it lacked either any means of tracking where the enemy was, or controlling the whole fighter force from the ground once it was airborne. Thus when news of one of the postponements of *Adlertag* (the Day of Eagles), the codename for the operation to destroy the RAF, arrived too late to prevent hundreds of aircraft being launched prematurely in poor flying conditions, no means existed to secure their recall.

In June, RAF Coastal Command monitored and harassed the French coast, and the Germans responded by probing RAF defences throughout June and July before the rather scrappy opening of *Adlertag* already referred to in August. Between 12 August and 6 September there were 32 major raids against Fighter Command airfields and 6 against radar stations but from 7 September, when the first daylight raid was launched on London, German efforts were focused on bombing the capital by both day and night. This change of tactics was in line with Hitler's announcement in a speech on 4 September that henceforth the Luftwaffe would concentrate its efforts on attacking British cities in general and London in particular.

This change of strategy from targeting air bases to targeting industry and communications, or, increasingly targeting civilians, is conventionally attributed to a German desire for revenge for RAF raids on Berlin. It was apparently based upon a mistaken belief in the power of German bombing both past (assuming that Fighter Command was virtually eliminated) and prospective (assuming that British morale would be made to crack). There was certainly very limited success in targeting the aviation industry as throughout the battle, the British aircraft industry out-produced Germany's by a substantial margin, allowing Fighter Command to make good the higher loss rates it suffered.

The German change of strategy certainly proved decisive for between 7 and 15 September, the date of the last great daylight raid, the Luftwaffe lost 298 aircraft, including 99 fighters to Fighter Command's 120. On 17 September Hitler postponed Sealion indefinitely and accordingly from 19 September the Germans basically switched to night-time raids, although fighter bombers continued to launch 'nuisance' daylight raids until the end of the month, by which time the Luftwaffe had manifestly failed in its aim of driving the RAF from the skies and the air battle gradually diminished. Between 10 July and 31 October the RAF had lost 915 aircraft to the Luftwaffe's 1733 but the comparison in terms of single-engined fighters was much closer, the higher German losses being attributable to its more vulnerable bombers.

Churchill famously celebrated the event by proclaiming that 'Never in the field of human conflict has so much been owed by so many to so few', and the Battle of Britain certainly boosted British morale and played a key role in persuading America that the British war effort was worth supplying as it was no longer in danger of imminent collapse. However, Richard Overy's revisionist *The Battle* (Penguin Books, 2000) claims that the campaign is still shrouded in myth.

Firstly, Overy claims that the RAF did not face seemingly overwhelming odds for, 'If Fighter Command were the "few", German fighter pilots were fewer'.[1] It is true that, as Overy points out, Fighter Command had slightly fewer than the Luftwaffe's operational establishment of 1011 single-engined fighters assigned to the battle over Britain on 10 August 1940 but as Overy himself concedes, the German forces 'enjoyed a marginally better serviceability record'[2] and German fighter forces concentrated their attacks on southern England, while Fighter Command was dispersed so as to defend all of Britain within range of Germany's bombers. Overy's claim also discounts the German bombers and dive-bombers, on the grounds that they 'were not a major threat to fighter aircraft ...'[3] However, while this was true in terms of aerial combat, it ignores the damage which they could do to Fighter Command on the ground. Indeed, it is widely accepted that the Luftwaffe's best chance of winning the Battle of Britain had consisted of attacking Fighter Command directly, rather than switching the bomber force to targeting Britain's cities. In short, the rough parity in fighter numbers over the course of most of the battle does not detract from the fact that in broad terms RAF Fighter Command constituted a thin defence which was badly overstretched and which might well have been brushed aside had the Germans engaged in different tactics. Pointing to the Messerschmitt Me 109's capacity to outperform both the Hurricane and the Spitfire at higher altitudes thanks to its two-stage supercharger, Overy himself writes that 'If the Battle of Britain had been fought at 30,000 feet, the RAF would have lost it'.[4] (p. 57) Overy's own account, then, is that the Battle of Britain was only won by virtue of good fortune or German misjudgement.

Secondly, Overy states that it was certainly a myth to claim that Britain 'stood alone' in 1940, as she received crucial support from the Commonwealth and Empire. Fighter Command drew support from even further afield, possessing not only a Canadian squadron but also a Czech and two Polish squadrons. This is clearly true but the 'Britain alone' rhetoric of the time was shorthand for the inescapable fact that following the Fall of France Britain stood alone, for roughly 12 months, as the sole sovereign state within Europe fighting Nazi Germany, until Hitler launched his attack upon the Soviet Union on 22 June 1941.

Thirdly, Overy states that the popular image of a nation united under Churchill's leadership to fight to the bitter end to defeat fascism is also a myth insofar as there was defeatism along with defiance as the Foreign Secretary, Lord Halifax, asked the Cabinet to consider a negotiated peace at the end of May, while in June around 30 MPs joined in urging Lloyd George to campaign for peace. The question which needs to be considered, however, is how representative was Halifax and those who thought like him in the summer of 1940. Insofar as one can ever speak of a nation as being united it seems fairly safe to say that the nation, and not just parliament or the cabinet, was united behind Churchill in 1940.

Finally, Overy seeks to undermine the traditional significance invested in the Battle of Britain by suggesting that Hitler's aim was always Lebensraum in the East and thus Operation Sealion amounted to nothing more than an elaborate bluff to persuade the likes of Halifax to make peace. In short, 'The Royal Air Force did not repel invasion for the ... simple reason that the Germans were never coming'.[5] However, while Hitler's heart was clearly not in fighting Britain in 1940 so that 'not a lot was needed to deter Hitler from the idea of invading Britain' Overy himself concedes that 'Fighter Command tipped the scales' by ruling out the possibility of 'a cheap, quick end to the war in the west' and by thus keeping 'alive an armed anti-Axis presence in Europe'[6] the Battle of Britain not only ensured Britain's survival but helped lay the foundations for ultimate victory.

The Battle of the Atlantic

The first casualties of the Battle of the Atlantic were suffered within nine hours of the British declaration of war on Germany on 3 September, when the captain of *U-30* mistook the *Athenia*, an ocean liner bound for Canada, for a British merchant cruiser and accordingly fired his torpedoes without warning. One hundred and eighteen members of the 1418 passengers and crew on board, including 28 Americans, lost their lives, prompting Hitler to tighten restrictions on U-boat operations, beyond even what was required under international law, only to loosen them once again after the *U-47* daringly infiltrated the main naval base for the British Home Fleet at Scapa Flow on 14 October and sank *HMS Royal Oak*, with the loss of 883 of the ship's complement of 1200 officers and men.

The Battle of the Atlantic was to become the longest campaign of the entire war and it was at least as important as the Battle of Britain for national survival and ultimate victory. As Churchill himself said, it was 'the dominating factor all throughout the war ... Battles might be won or lost, enterprises might succeed or miscarry, territories might be gained or quitted, but dominating all our power to carry on the war, or even keep ourselves alive, lay our mastery of the ocean routes and the free approach and entry to our ports'.[7]

Britain had imported 55 million tons of supplies in 1939, although its needs were later reduced to 43 million tons through substitution and rationing. Germany's U-boat fleet, although numbering only 57 vessels of which only 27 were large enough to carry out Atlantic operations at the outbreak of war nevertheless constituted a formidable threat to Britain's essential supply lines, particularly after the fall of France in 1940 meant that Germany acquired the Atlantic ports of Brest, Saint-Nazaire, La Rochelle and Lorient.

Admiral Doenitz, himself a former First World War U-boat captain, had claimed prior to the war that with 300 U-boats he could starve Britain into submission (at any one time 100 of which would be on active service, 100 would be sailing to or from the combat zone, and the remaining 100 would be undergoing repairs and refitting). When this figure was finally achieved in July 1942 the Allied escort fleet in the central Atlantic had been weakened as a result of transferring British ships to help the Americans introduce a convoy system on their eastern coast and into the Gulf of Mexico so as to bring an end to the so-called 'Happy Time', when U-Boats had enjoyed easy pickings (sinking 1.25

million tons of shipping between January and March 1942). Moreover, U-boat range was being extended by refuelling at sea from submarine 'milch cows' and Doenitz was becoming more skilful at organising patrol lines and directing wolf packs against convoys because of the cryptographic advantage that the B-Dienst (Observer Service) currently enjoyed in reading convoy traffic over Bletchley Park's efforts to locate U-boats (a serious interruption of Ultra decrypts of U-boat radio traffic lasting for almost a year from February 1942 and the Enigma 'Shark' key used by the U-boat service not being broken until December 1942 and not being regularly deciphered until May 1943). All these factors enabled Germany to sink ships at a rate more than 5 times greater than the British rate of replacement launchings.

However, the tide in the Battle of the Atlantic – the struggle for supremacy between convoy escorts and U-boat packs – had actually turned in Britain's favour by this stage of the war as the result of a number of factors of which the most important had been the entry of the United States into the war in December 1941 as this allowed merchant ships to be launched at a rate which exceeded U-boat sinkings, increased the provision of naval escorts, and narrowed the 'air gap' in which U-boats could operate safely on the surface by allowing long-range aircraft, such as the Liberator (B-24), to operate from bases in the United States as well, Canada, Iceland and Britain.

U-boat losses gradually crept up to equal launchings (at a monthly rate of about 15) and by May 1943 U-boat losses exceeded replacement by more than twice. This trend was thanks largely to the increased availability of long-range patrol aircraft, improved Asdic (echo-sounding equipment), radar (which proved increasingly capable of providing early warning or accurate ranging) and new depth-charge launchers (Hedgeghog and Squid). Increased protection was provided by the creation of 'support groups' of escorts (of which there were five by April 1943) which sailed to the rescue of any convoy under attack, and the adaptation of merchant ships to fly their own aircraft.

With U-boat losses currently totalling 696 out of the 830 dispatched on active service (almost all in the Atlantic) and 25,870 out of 40,900 crewmen killed, and a further 5000 taken prisoner, Doenitz felt obliged to withdraw his U-boat fleet from the Atlantic on 24 May 1943.

The development of the schnorkel, a retractable air-breathing tube, which allowed a submarine to recharge its batteries while cruising submerged, safe from anti-submarine aircraft, was a technological innovation which offered the possibility of Germany regaining the upper hand in the Battle of the Atlantic. However, this invention came too late in the war to have a decisive impact upon its course as the trial cruise of a schnorkel-equipped U-boat occurred only in May 1944, the month before D-Day, and the Germans lost their main Atlantic ports to the American army in August.

John Keegan correctly takes the view that, 'Had Hitler achieved the creation of a 300-boat fleet before 1942, added significantly to its size thereafter, or managed to introduce his advanced schnorkel and revolutionary hydrogen-peroxide types before 1944' the Battle of the Atlantic might have been won by Germany, and Britain would have succumbed to 'total strangulation' of its supplies.[8]

6   The Eastern Front

Russo-German relations before 1917

In 1938, film director Sergei Eisenstein returned to favour with Stalin with the release of *Alexander Nevsky*, the climax of which was the recreation of the 1242 Battle on the ice of Lake Peipus when Nevsky's forces decisively defeated the Teutonic Knights. The film dramatised a significant period in the centuries-long conflict between the Germanic and Russian peoples.

Having failed in a frontal assault, Germanic influences entered Russia by the invitation of her rulers, notably Tsar Peter I – Peter the Great – who in his bid to modernise or westernise Russia, imported many foreigners. Russia even had a German government when, shortly before her death in 1740, Empress Anna appointed her favourite Ernst Johann Biron (Buehren) as regent. He was shortly overthrown by other members of the German ruling clique, headed by Burkhard Münnich and Andrey Osterman, before they in turn were ousted by Peter the Great's daughter Elizabeth. However, the number of Germans in high places in the Russian administration and military (to say nothing of the artisanal class) did not diminish in the second half of the eighteenth century and their continued presence fostered Russian nationalist sentiment.

Thus by 1812, sixty generals were of German origin and as late as the 1880s Russians of German origin occupied roughly 40 per cent of the posts in the higher command, while the figures for the ministries of War, Foreign Affairs and Posts and Communications were, respectively, 46, 57 and 62 per cent. And all this was at a time when Germans constituted less than 1 per cent of Russia's population.

Russo-German relations were further strained by virtue of the fact that several Tsars placed Germans in charge of implementing their most repressive and unpopular policies. Thus the names of Benckendorff and then Dubbelt were associated for several years with running the 'third department' (the political police and the censorship), consolidating the image of Russia as being ruled over by a brutal and reactionary set of Germanic foreigners.

Nicholas I's successors showed less preference for Germans and their share of the top posts gradually declined but any residual German influence was resented all the more bitterly as Panslav sentiment and the policy of 'Russification' prevailed within Russia, while the wars of German Unification (1864–71) saw Germany, under Prussian leadership, emerge as a Great Power with the potential to threaten Russian security.

More immediately, however, Russia felt itself threatened economically by Germany and its industrialists demanded protectionist policies in order to shield native industry against foreign competition; a demand echoed by the Prussian Junkers in relation to their government because they feared the competition from Russian wheat. The 1880s were therefore marked by a customs war that was only ended by a trade agreement in 1894, which was renegotiated and extended a decade later. However, this economic competition left a lasting scar upon Russo-German relations insofar as Russia never completely recovered its position as Germany's principal supplier of grain, while French and Belgian investment in Russia came to eclipse that of Germany.

However, the fundamental and lasting damage done to Russo-German relations occurred at the diplomatic level and centred upon the Balkans where Russia's desire to exploit the power vacuum created by Turkish decline brought her into conflict with Germany's Austrian ally. The circle might have been squared had Bismarck continued to control German foreign policy, but in 1890, in a bid to assert himself by distancing himself from Bismarck's policy, Kaiser Wilhelm II decided to allow the Reinsurance Treaty with Russia to lapse. The consequence was that four years later Russia had entered into military alliance with France, and Germany drew ever closer to Austria–Hungary because of the threat this posed of a war on two fronts.

Nicholas II of Russia and Kaiser Wilhelm II of Germany – Nicky and Willy – were not merely cousins with a shared view regarding their roles as emperors. They both believed in the need to keep down the Poles and the Jews, but these common interests were outweighed by the geopolitical considerations which resulted in their belonging to rival sets of alliances and which brought them into war with one another in August 1914.

The First World War gave fresh impetus to the strain of anti-Russian feeling in Germany, which had always looked down upon the Russian state as a primitive 'Asiatic' and artificial creation of inferior peoples which had only been held together hitherto by a combination of Tsarist despotism and Germanic administrative efficiency.

Soviet–German relations, 1917–33

The view that Russians had never achieved anything without German help was confirmed by the October Revolution insofar as Lenin's success in seizing power was predicated upon the assistance he received from the German High Command, symbolised by the sealed train which took him from Switzerland to the Finland station in Petrograd.

This investment paid Germany handsome dividends insofar as Lenin was prepared to pay any price to end the war so as to consolidate the Bolshevik hold on power. Hence the March 1918 Treaty of Brest–Litovsk whereby Soviet Russia lost the Ukraine, its Polish and Baltic territories and Finland. Although the Treaty was effectively annulled by the defeat of Germany in the west, the USSR was as much a losing power as the defeated Central Powers when the victorious allies assembled for the Paris Peace conference. Lloyd George was sufficiently fearful of these two pariah powers making common cause that he circulated a confidential memorandum at the peace talks in which he shrewdly stated that

> The greatest danger that I see in the present situation is that Germany may throw in her lot with Bolshevism and place her resources, her brains, her vast organizing power at the disposal of the revolutionary fanatics whose dream is to conquer the world for Bolshevism by arms. This danger is no mere chimera.[1]

The accuracy of Lloyd George's analysis was shortly borne out. Once the Bolsheviks had survived the worst of the Civil War and Wars of Intervention, they began to seek a means of placing relations with the rest of the world on a firmer footing, if only to facilitate the importation of badly needed technology. There was also interest on the German side in reviving Russo-German trade, if only as a way of generating the means whereby Germany could meet her reparations payments.

As early as May 1920 a German-Soviet trade agreement was signed and direct trade exchanges multiplied, as did German acquisition of a number of concessions for the exploitation of raw materials, in line with the foreign trade policy of Lenin's New Economic Programme (NEP). However, the real breakthrough came in the course of the Genoa Conference of 1922 when the Soviet and Weimar delegates slipped away to meet on their own and sign the Rapallo Treaty whereby the two countries resumed full diplomatic relations, with the former agreeing not to demand reparations while in return the latter renounced any claim to pre-war Russian debts or compensation for nationalised German property in Russia. This bilateral deal shocked the rest of the world, which would have been even more appalled had they been aware of the secret agreements, which flowed from Rapallo, between the Russian and German General Staffs.

Soviet–German military co-operation, which ran from July 1922 until September 1933, took three forms. Firstly, there was a constant exchange of staff officers. Secondly, training schools were established in Russia so as to allow German military personnel to use weaponry banned under the military provisions of the Treaty of Versailles. Thirdly, the German armaments industry established branches in the Soviet Union and engaged in research in such areas as chemical warfare. Both parties gained a great deal through these arrangements, Marshal Tukhachevsky going so far as to describe the Reichswehr as 'the teacher of the Red Army'.[2]

Even Goebbels, in the days when he was closer to Gregor Strasser than to Hitler, initially favoured an accommodation with the Soviet Union, writing in 1925 that 'Russia is our natural ally against the devilish temptations and corruptions of the West'.[3] However, what became the dominant Russophobic strain in National Socialism was enunciated even earlier by a group of German Balts, of whom the most important were two political refuges from Riga: Alfred Rosenberg and Max Erwin von Scheubner-Richter.

Historically the German Balts played a disproportionately important role, relative to their numbers, in shaping Russo-German relations. It was the Baltic Germans who among all foreigners tended to monopolise the higher posts in Russia from the time of the Petrine reforms and conversely they tended to be the chief targets of vilification from Russian nationalists and Panslavists. The Baltic had suffered more than most other provinces of the Russian empire during the 1905 Revolution and the subsequent repression, and the Balts were especially embittered by the Bolshevik takeover and were fearful of its avowed intention of spreading proletarian revolution. Rosenberg and Scheubner-Richter were among the Baltic Germans who migrated not only to Germany proper but to Munich: the centre of extreme right-wing politics in Germany.

Hitler was an anti-Semite who was contemptuous of the Slavs but it was Balts such as Rosenberg (the Nazi party's chief ideologist and editor of the *Völkischer Beobachter* when it was made a daily paper in February 1923) and Scheubner-Richter (secretary of the Kampfbund and liaison man between Ludendorff and Hitler), who taught him to make the fateful equation of Bolshevism with Jewry and claim that communism was part of the Jewish world conspiracy.

When events of great magnitude occur there is a natural tendency to assume that their causes are proportionately profound. Thus rather than explain a war, a revolution or the death of a public figure as caused by 'chance' factors, there will always be some keen to attribute these events to the workings of some sinister conspiracy. This tendency will be even more pronounced if those accused of conspiracy act as scapegoats: bearing a burden of guilt which more properly belongs with their accusers. Such was the case with the downfall of the Romanov dynasty. Rather than look to themselves, the imperial family and their supporters, and more particularly the proto-fascist 'Black Hundred' or *Soyuz Russkogo Naroda* (Union of the Russian People) had presented the events of 1917–18 as the consequence of a *Zhidomasonstvo* or Judeao–Masonic conspiracy. This idea of a conspiracy which embraced Jewish revolutionaries as well as Jewish capitalists, already successfully articulated in 'The Protocols of the Elders of Zion', was adopted by Rosenberg and through him by Hitler. The claim was that Bolshevism was not a genuine political movement but rather a tool of Jewish financial capital.

Thus by 1923 the Nazi view was that Bolshevism was not an ideology but a conspiracy whereby Jewish elements in Russia had deposed the Germanic or Aryan elements. The logical consequence of this belief was that there could be no reconciliation or compromise between the USSR and Germany as they were mortal enemies. As Hitler wrote in *Mein Kampf*: 'We are taking up where we left off six hundred years ago … putting an end to the perpetual German march towards the south and west of Europe and turning our eyes towards the east'.[4]

The equation of Jews with communists had just enough truth to facilitate Nazi propaganda and fuel anti-Semitic prejudice insofar as revolutionaries from Karl Marx down to Trotsky and Zinoviev were of Jewish origin. Moreover, five of the seven leaders of the short-lived Soviet Republic in the Bavarian capital in April 1919 were Jewish, allowing the Nazis to claim that the tentacles of the world conspiracy threatened the heart of Germany itself. Anti-communism certainly played well in terms of domestic German politics and anti-Bolshevism directed against 'the enemy within' as well as the enemy to the East assumed an increasingly central role in Nazi rhetoric.

Weimar, however, remained wedded to the amicable relations with the USSR symbolised by Rapallo, particularly during the 'Stresemann years'. Thus although Locarno in 1925 could be perceived as reducing German dependence upon Soviet goodwill by guaranteeing her western frontiers with Belgium and France, Stresemann still took care to negotiate the Berlin Treaty with the USSR in the following year, which guaranteed Russian neutrality in the event of an attack upon Germany and vice versa.

Nazi–Soviet relations, 1933–39

When Hitler came to power in Germany on 30 January 1933, relations with Russia opened a new phase, although the change was not as dramatic as one might suppose. As mentioned above, military co-operation did not cease overnight but continued until September. German exports to Russia declined dramatically but it is worth bearing in mind that while 47 per cent of Russia's total imports came from Germany by 1932 (a figure comparable to the situation in 1914), this figure represented just under 11 per cent of Germany's exports. In other words, trade between the two countries was badly imbalanced and even at its greatest, the volume of German exports to Russia was exceeded by that with the Netherlands.

Problems in achieving economic self-sufficiency in key areas, nevertheless, resulted in the Third Reich making a credit agreement with the Soviet Union in 1936 designed to improve German access to Russian markets and raw materials, especially metals and oil, while allowing the Soviets to gain access to machinery and other manufactured goods that it lacked.

This agreement was due to expire at the end of 1938 but both parties were so keen to keep this economic dialogue going that they opened negotiations to extend the agreement in March. It was not, however, until 19 December 1938 that the two sides agreed to extend the March 1938 trade agreement through to the end of 1939. In the meantime Anglo-French appeasement of Nazi Germany climaxed with the Munich Agreement in September. This laid the foundations for not just Nazi–Soviet economic co-operation but for political *rapprochement* insofar as the failure to consult the Soviets at Munich, despite their defensive alliance with Czechoslovakia, helped to confirm Stalin in his beliefs that not only were the Western powers unwilling to fight Germany but that they were willing to see her expand eastwards, where she would eventually be embroiled in war with the Soviet Union.

The Nazi–Soviet Non-Aggression Pact and the German–Soviet Boundary and Friendship Treaty

When the news of the Nazi–Soviet Non-Aggression Pact of 23 August 1939 was announced, its cynicism was breathtaking given the rhetoric with which both parties had previously regaled one another. Typical of Hitler's output was his speech to the Nuremberg rally just two years previously, in which he referred to the Soviet leaders as an uncivilised Jewish-Bolshevik international guild of criminals and characterised the Soviet Union itself as the greatest danger for the culture and civilisation of mankind which has ever threatened it since the collapse of the states of the ancient world. Equally stunning in the light of such pronouncements was the official optimism on both sides regarding the Pact's prospects insofar as it was slated to last for 25 years.

Hitler's motive in agreeing to the Pact was that it removed the threat of Soviet intervention when he attacked Poland. Moreover, he calculated that Britain and France would be more likely to appease Germany than stand by their guarantees to Poland in the event of Soviet neutrality. The Pact certainly put an abrupt end to the Anglo-French negotiations which had been dragging on since

April and which had entered a new but hardly more dynamic phase following the arrival of an Anglo-French military delegation in Moscow on 10 August.

Stalin's motive, equally clearly, was to gain territory and time. He was not so naïve as to believe that war with Germany could be postponed indefinitely but he wished to delay that conflict as long as possible – preferably by seeing Germany engaged in a protracted conflict with Britain and France – in the meantime gaining as much land as possible so that when the fighting came there would be a buffer zone before the Soviet Union proper was invaded (although he also coveted the territory which made up that buffer zone as land which had previously part of the Russian Empire).

Thus the secret clauses of the Nazi–Soviet Pact divided Poland and the Baltic States (Latvia, Lithuania and Estonia) and Finland into German and Soviet spheres of influence, with the northern boundary of Lithuania representing the furthest extent of the German sphere in the Baltic States while the Polish boundary would be broadly defined by the line of the rivers Narew, Vistula and San.

Nine days after Germany invaded Poland from the west, the Soviet government announced to the Germans that it would assume control over its half of Poland, and on 17 September, the Red Army invaded from the east, claiming that an independent Polish state had collapsed and that the USSR was merely reclaiming Ukrainian and Belorussian lands invaded by Poland during the Russo-Polish War of 1920–21. However, while it had taken the Germans under three weeks to establish control over their half of Poland it took the Red Army, despite acting in the role of jackal, almost a month to establish control over its share of Poland: a point not missed by Hitler and his generals.

The German–Soviet Boundary and Friendship Treaty was signed on 28 September 1939 after Ribbentrop had flown again to Moscow. This agreement adjusted the frontier between the two states in occupied Poland in Germany's favour (gaining the province of Lublin and parts of the province of Warsaw) and compensated the Soviets by transferring Lithuania to their sphere of influence. The pact ushered in a period of extensive economic co-operation between the two states.

The Soviets asserted their 'rights' under the secret terms of the new treaty by forcing Latvia, Lithuania and Estonia to sign mutual assistance treaties with the USSR and agree to the establishment of Soviet air and naval bases on their territories. However, when similar pressure was exerted upon Helsinki to allow access to Finnish resources and ports, the Finns resisted and in the resulting 'Winter War' (30 November 1939–12 March 1940) the Red Army was badly mauled, suffering almost 127,000 dead and 265,000 wounded, and only ultimately triumphing by flooding Finland with troops: according to some estimates in numbers exceeding that of the indigenous population (of 3.5 million). In March 1940 the Finns sued for peace on Russia's terms, fortunately forestalling plans for an Anglo-French expeditionary force to come to their aid (via Norway) as the British and French had more than enough on their hands dealing with Germany.

In July 1940, in response to the success of Hitler's Blitzkrieg in the West, Stalin tightened his grip over the Baltic States by occupying Latvia, Lithuania and Estonia and incorporating them into the USSR as soviet republics. Moreover, following a Soviet ultimatum to Rumania issued on 26 June 1940, Bessarabia and North Bukovina were ceded to Stalin. Although Stalin once again claimed to be merely reasserting rights to traditional Russian territories, Hitler regarded this move as very threatening to German interests, given that it brought the Red Army so close to the vital Ploesti oilfields. Thus Hitler guaranteed Rumania against any further Soviet encroachments, which prompted the Soviets to accuse the Nazis of violating the terms of the Nazi–Soviet Non-Aggression Pact insofar as this provided for consultation on matters of mutual interest.

Stalin made an effort to repair the damage done to Nazi–Soviet relations, or at least to discover Hitler's true intentions, by sending Molotov to Berlin in November 1940. Ribbentrop actually initiated the conference because he still hoped to get the Soviet Union to join Germany, Italy and Japan in a 'continental bloc' against the 'Anglo-Saxon' powers of Great Britain and the United States (with the Soviets encouraged to expand towards the Indian Ocean so as to bring them into conflict with Britain). Hitler had, however, already made up his mind to go to war with the Soviet Union and on 18 December 1940 he issued the order for Germany's armed forces '*to crush Soviet Russia in a quick campaign* ... even before the conclusion of the war against England'.[5]

Despite numerous warnings of the German military build up from a very wide range of sources, Stalin persisted in the belief that the Germans were not planning an attack but were merely engaged in exerting pressure so as to gain economic and political concessions from the Soviet Union. Stalin made every effort to avoid any action which might be construed as provocative by Germany, including putting his own forces on a war footing. Thus when Operation Barbarossa was launched on 22 June 1941 the Nazis were able to make sweeping gains which soon included all the territory, bar that in Finland, which the USSR had gained as a result of the Nazi–Soviet Non-Aggression Pact and German–Soviet Boundary and Friendship Treaty.

The Nazi–Soviet Economic Agreements of 1939 and 1940

Although the Soviet Union appears to have regarded improved trading relations with Nazi Germany as principally of significance because indicative of improved political goodwill, and insisted upon an economic treaty being signed before they would agree to the Non-Aggression Pact, the economic agreements of 1939 and 1940 were very important in their own right, not least because of the substantial assistance they provided for the German war economy. Indeed, several historians view these economic agreements as being more important than the political deal done by Molotov and Ribbentrop.[6]

On 19 August 1939, an economic treaty was signed in Berlin. On 23 December, an agreement allowing Germany to ship goods using the Soviet railway system (which was especially important for imports of wolfram, molybdenum, chrome and rubber) was added as a postscript, and the 1939 agreement was amended in 1940 in ways which were even more advantageous to the Nazis. Indeed, in the 22 months between August 1939 and the Nazi invasion of the Soviet Union, Russo-German trade increased ninefold compared to the period between 1936 and 1938 with the terms of trade showing a balance of 230 million Reichsmarks in Germany's favour, while the Third Reich not only gained access to vitally important supplies of Russian oil, iron, manganese, phosphates, platinum, cotton, lumber and food but was also assisted in breaking the British blockade (not only through the railway agreement referred to above but also by the Soviet Union agreeing to act as a third party buyer of metals and other goods for Germany). Stalin's economic appeasement of

Hitler was so great that there is a good case for arguing that he seriously damaged the Soviet economy in the process, and one may even wonder why Hitler felt any need to conquer Russian resources when he enjoyed such easy access to them without bloodshed.

The answer, of course, is that Hitler regarded war between the Soviet Union and Germany as inevitable and desirable, as geopolitical and racial considerations rendered them mortal enemies.

Planning Barbarossa

On 22 November 1939, Hitler addressed 200 senior members of the armed forces. His audience was plainly sceptical for notwithstanding the success of the Blitzkrieg in Poland, a campaign against Britain and France seemed a daunting prospect. Hitler tried to suggest that there was nothing to fear by suggesting that he had a master plan that had yielded nothing but success, even when the wisdom of his actions had been questioned beforehand by his generals and other expert advisers.

In one respect, however, Hitler had to admit that the master plan had gone somewhat awry. He had never wanted war with Britain and the need to protect his rear meant that the final reckoning with his real enemy – the Soviet Union – would now have to be postponed until victory over the western democracies.

When it came, Hitler's offensive in the West had exceeded expectations, with France falling in the space of six weeks. However, the British, now led by Churchill, refused to negotiate terms and the victory of the RAF in the Battle of Britain resulted in the indefinite postponement of Operation Sealion if, indeed, its implementation was ever seriously considered. However, Britain could do little to challenge Hitler's mastery of the continent, so he turned his attention once again to his original and over-riding objective of conquering Lebensraum in Russia.

Hitler's formal military directive for Operation Barbarossa, the invasion of Russia, was issued on 18 December 1940, although initial planning had been proceeding since August 1940. The immediate spur to action was provided by the failure of two sets of negotiations. Firstly, Molotov, failed to accept proposals for increased trade, although the Soviet Union continued to fulfil to the letter the arrangements agreed at the time of the Nazi–Soviet Pact. Secondly, Petain's Vichy France and Franco's fascist Spain had refused to be drawn into conflict with Britain, despite Hitler holding out the prospects of gains at Britain's expense in the Mediterranean.

There are essentially two schools of thought regarding Hitler's reasons for launching Operation Barbarossa. On the one hand, intentionalist historians regard it as fulfilling his longstanding aim, repeatedly expressed since at least the time of *Mein Kampf* that Russia represented the heartland of the 'Jewish-Bolshevik' racial-ideological foe, whose defeat would provide the abundant land which Germany's surplus population required and deserved. On the other hand, structuralist historians claim that Hitler's thoughts only seriously turned towards Russia once it became clear that Britain would not succumb to German arms or entreaties in 1940. According to this scenario Hitler's position resembled Napoleon's after 1805. Neither could invade Britain nor need fear Britain inflicting much damage on their rear were they to turn eastwards. Turning eastwards, it is argued, allowed both Napoleon and Hitler scope to use their finely honed army, which would otherwise languish unemployed, in consolidating control of the continent. Moreover, conquest of Russia would snuff out any last flicker of hope of national salvation on the part of the British and oblige them to see sense and enter into peace negotiations.

For those who wish to draw facile parallels between Napoleon and Hitler, one can of course add that the invasions of Russia in 1812 and 1941 both began on 22 June, that Moscow provided a point beyond which neither army advanced, that 'General Winter' compounded the sufferings of the invaders in their retreat from the Russian Motherland, and that defeat in Russia marked the decisive turning point in the fortunes of both dictators. The fact that Stalin drew parallels between 'the Great Patriotic War' of 1941–45 and the events of 1812 should not, however, lure the unwary into assuming that History is cyclical or that its parameters are set by geopolitical verities or that it is powered by human vanity.

There are, in fact, several reasons for the German invasion of Russia taking place on 22 June 1941. Firstly, and most fundamentally, there was the racial-ideological desire to destroy Jewish-Bolshevism and subjugate and enslave the inferior Slavs. Hitler despised all talk of egalitarianism and communism, as the most extreme, was in his eyes the most pernicious, preaching in favour not only a classless society but of an international brotherhood of man.

The identification of Jewry with Bolshevism was child's play to a mind such as Hitler's given that Karl Marx was of rabbinical stock and that many communists similarly happened to be of Jewish descent. The fact that Bernstein, Luxemburg, Bela Kun and the other revolutionaries of Jewish stock had abandoned their faith and attacked institutionalised religion was, of course, irrelevant to Hitler as Jewishness was for him defined by blood rather than religious affiliation.

The geopolitical desire for Lebensraum at Russia's expense obviously overlaps with Hitler's racial-ideological antipathy towards the Soviet Union. The latter consisted of abundant land whose native peoples had no right in nature to possess it, by virtue of the fact that they were *untermenschen*.

Strategic considerations underlay the decision to invade Russia for not only did it possess valuable resources, many of which were currently untapped or inefficiently exploited, but it also appeared to threaten Germany's economic lifelines, posing a threat not only to Rumania's Ploesti oilfields but also to iron ore supplies from neutral Sweden. Conquering Russia would thus enrich Germany and remove this threat to her security. Invasion could also be seen as desirable as a form of pre-emptive strike, as it was feared that Stalin might realise Soviet Union's latent potential and seek to dominate Germany and the continent. As has already been noted (in Chapter 2), in the Hossbach conference of 5 November 1937, Hitler had shown himself acutely conscious of the need to strike before Germany lost its lead over its rivals in terms of rearmament and he was aware that Germany was already losing the 'battle of births' insofar as the Slavs could boast a higher birth rate.

As a strictly secondary consideration, successful invasion of Russia might offer the only means of forcing Britain into submission by demonstrating Germany's power and removing for all time any prospect of an Anglo-Soviet alliance. This was certainly an argument which Hitler used with his generals. For example, on 31 July 1940, he told a collection of military commanders at the Berghof that, since Britain forlornly hoped that the USSR might one day come to its aid, its conquest in revealing the bankruptcy of this view would remove Britain's last reason to carry on the fight. This is not to say that Hitler's commanders necessarily needed a great deal of convincing. Chief of Staff Franz Halder, for example, was already trying to anticipate the Fuhrer's desires in this regard as his diary entry of 3 July 1940 reveals him already toying with the idea of an attack upon the Soviet Union to 'compel Russia to recognise Germany's dominant position in Europe'.[7]

The generals realised that their long-term future depended upon their correctly anticipating and implementing Hitler's wishes. Moreover, having raised objections to Hitler's strategy in the West which had proved groundless, they had ground to make up in terms of the relationship which could only be achieved by enthusiasm for his long-standing aim of conquest in the East. Nor were they any more immune than Hitler himself from the hubris attendant upon Blitzkrieg's successes in the West, notwithstanding the escape of a third of a million men from the beaches of Dunkirk and the RAF's success in retaining mastery of the skies over Britain: both of which could be conveniently – if privately – explained as resulting from Reichsmarshall Goering's overweening arrogance.

German over-confidence most fundamentally stemmed from the belief that the Slavs were an inferior race and that the Soviet state was a rotten edifice requiring little outside pressure to make it crumble. General Jodl claimed that 'The Russian colossus will be proved to be a pig's bladder', requiring merely to be pricked in order to see it burst.[8] Or as Hitler told his officers, 'We only have to kick in the front door and the whole rotten edifice will come tumbling down'.[9]

There was much circumstantial evidence to suggest that this might be more than mere wishful thinking, not least of which was the impact on the Red Army of Stalin's purges. There are still disputes among historians regarding the precise extent to which the officer corps was culled but there is no denying the fact that the purges were significant not just numerically but because of the damage they did to those who remained in place, or were promoted into positions for which they had not been properly trained. Moreover, Stalin's purges were calculated to stifle the taking of initiative, with potentially disastrous results. The German officer corps' low estimation of their Soviet counterparts appeared, as mentioned above, to be amply confirmed by the Red Army's poor showing in eastern Poland and in Finland. Thus the German General Staff might be forgiven for assuming that the quality of the Wehrmacht's troops would outweigh the numerical advantage enjoyed by the Red Army.

The Suvorov thesis

In the late 1980s, as glasnost resulted in an opening of the Soviet archives, the Russian Viktor Suvorov (a former intelligence officer whose real name is Vladimir Rezun) offered an account of Stalinist thinking in the late 1930s and early 1940s which represented a radical revision of the traditional understanding of this period.[10]

In essence Suvorov argued that the Nazi–Soviet Non-Aggression Pact was not agreed to by Stalin out of disgust and despair with Anglo-French appeasement of Hitler in the wake of Munich and in order to secure the defence of the Soviet Union by gaining territory and time. Rather, according to Suvorov, the deal was done in order to reclaim the territories to the West that the Tsars had formerly held and, most importantly, to be in a position for the Red Army to assist western revolutionaries when an attritional war between Germany and the western democracies produced conditions comparable to those which had prevailed in Russia in 1917. In short, Stalin's motive in signing the Non-Aggression Pact with Nazi Germany was offensive not defensive: buying time to prepare for an attack planned for the early summer of 1941, which would belatedly fulfill Lenin's dream of 1918 of a Russian-led international revolution.

Suvorov's claim that a comprehensive political plan existed for Soviet intervention in the West has received indirect support from Semidetko's suggestion[11] that the reason why the Wehrmacht so easily smashed through the Red Army on the central, White Russian, front in June 1941 was because the latter was already in an attack position. In other words, Hitler was right to speak of the need to attack the Soviet Union pre-emptively and Stalin's plan to attack west in was wrong-footed as a result of the Germans attacking first.

There are, however, good reasons for not allowing the above revisionist exercise to overturn the conventional explanation of events. Firstly, there is a difference between wishful thinking and concrete intention. There is good reason to suppose that Stalin and his henchmen speculated on the desirability of a scenario such as Suvorov depicts, namely, a situation arising in the west in the early 1940s approximating to that exploited by the Bolsheviks in Russia in 1917 which would enable the Red Army to export revolution. However, it is inherently unlikely that detailed military planning which stood a serious chance of being implemented would have ensued given that the fall of France in May 1940 invalidated the assumption of a protracted war and thus undermined the expectation that the strains of war would create the potential for revolutionary unrest on the part of the proletariat. Nor need one invoke Semidetko's elaborate arguments to explain the Soviet Union's defensive failure in June 1941: the Red Army was simply taken by surprise by the German Blitzkrieg and temporarily outclassed by their foes – as so many nations had been before them. Sometimes the simplest commonsensical explanations really are the best.

The Eastern Front: The road to Stalingrad

Three million men were in the attacking force, divided between three great army groups, namely, Army Group North which was targeted towards Leningrad (now St Petersburg), Army Group Centre, which had the objectives of taking Smolensk and Moscow, and Army Group South which headed for Russian grain and oil in the Ukraine via Kiev.

However, this disposition of forces meant that the guiding principle of Blitzkrieg – the concentration of maximum force against a single weak objective – had been neglected. Nevertheless, at first the Germans enjoyed great success, assisted by the facts that Stalin had refused to believe warnings from numerous quarters that attack was imminent, while his purges of the Red Army meant that many officers in the middle and higher grades occupied commands beyond their levels of competence. Thus the Germans destroyed roughly 1500 Soviet planes on the ground, took many prisoners (almost three-quarters of a million as encirclements around Smolensk were mopped up), and captured a great deal of territory. In early September, for example, the Germans reached the south-western shore of Lake Lagoda completing Leningrad's isolation and beginning a siege that would last for two and a half years and claim more than a million Soviet lives. Moreover, Stalin's rule had been so harsh that people in areas like the Ukraine rose to greet the invaders as liberators.

However, as the Army Groups advanced they moved further and further away from each other, rather than coming closer together. Furthermore, the sheer size of Russia, with its seemingly endless horizon, depressed many German soldiers as they moved ever further from their homeland.

Transport was difficult as Russia had mostly dirt roads which easily turned to mud, in which German men, horses and vehicles floundered, while Germany's increasingly long line of communications created supply problems. These were compounded by the Soviets adoption of a 'scorched earth' policy, destroying everything as they retreated which might be of use to the invader and by partisan groups or guerrilla fighters operating behind the German frontlines.

Indeed, short-sighted Nazi racism and atrocities turned potential collaborators and Russian soldiers reluctant to fight for Stalin into determined enemies, so that Soviet resistance, after the initial surprise, became increasingly tough. German intelligence had badly underestimated Soviet military strength. Thus despite the hammer blows it had sustained, the Red Army seemed able to field an unending supply of new divisions. Russian military manpower against the Germans increased dramatically after Pearl Harbor because troops once tied down in Siberia awaiting Japanese invasion could now be sent westwards.

By mid-October 1941, German forces occupied Soviet territory which produced 47 per cent of its grain crops, 60 per cent of its aluminium and over 66 per cent of its pig-iron, steel and rolled metals. This land also accounted for 45 per cent of the USSR's population and was where 64 per cent of its coal was extracted. However, Soviet industry, much of it hastily evacuated, was mostly beyond the range of the Germans' medium bombers, east of Moscow and in the Urals and Kuzbass basin regions, and capable of producing heavy and medium tanks, among other goods, which were superior to those of their German counterparts. Indeed, the Soviet T-34, with its sloping armour, wide tracks and advanced suspension, was arguably the finest tank of the entire war.

The winter of 1941 came early and was exceptionally severe. Few men had more than summer clothing and frostbite killed or incapacitated many. The Germans' machinery and guns had never been designed to function in such extremes of temperature, with the result that their lubricants froze, while the Soviets, by contrast, were accustomed to dealing with the fierce Russian winter.

Thus by December 1941, Blitzkrieg had failed and the German advance had ground to a halt within sight of Moscow.

In the spring of 1942, Stalin expected the new German offensive (Operation Blue) to target Moscow whereas it actually centred upon the Sixth Army under von Paulus encircling and destroying Soviet armies in the Don bend, driving east towards Stalingrad, and cutting off the Caucasus from the rest of the country while Hoth's Fourth Panzer Army would capture Rostov and strike south to the oilfields. The Sixth Army reached Stalingrad on 12 September, and on 8 November 1942 Hitler felt confident enough to claim that the city had been taken but for a few enemy positions still holding out.

However, the Germans lacked the strength to take the city, despite completely encircling it on 12 November, and on 19 November a Soviet counter-offensive (Operation Uranus) broke through the armies of Hitler's Rumanian allies and by 23 November the Soviet pincers met, completely encircling the attacking force. An attempted breakthrough by Manstein to relieve von Paulus began on 12 December but by Christmas Eve had ground to a halt, in part because of Soviet pressure on the Italians north of Stalingrad, in part because Hitler refused to order Paulus to break out and Paulus himself lacked the initiative to do so on his own account. Whereas Stalin had already learnt that 'stand fast' orders issued for their own sake merely played into the enemy's hands, Hitler refused von Paulus permission to attempt to break out, just as he had refused his earlier request to break off the fighting in Stalingrad and withdraw. Moreover, Goering's boast to apply to supply von Paulus by air proved as empty as all his other boasts (deliveries by the Luftwaffe exceeding the minimum requirement of 300 tons daily on only three days of the siege) so that by the end of January 1943 von Paulus surrendered, despite Hitler's having just made him Field Marshal, with the reminder that no German Field Marshal had ever been taken alive. The Soviets took 110,000 prisoners, of whom 20,000 were wounded.

The armies of Hitler's Rumanian, Italian and Hungarian allies had been destroyed and the heart had been ripped out of the German army on the Eastern Front. Goebbels seized on the opportunity to push for the full mobilisation of Germany's resources but Hitler's conversion to 'total war' came too late.

The Eastern Front: The road to Berlin

On 15 April 1943, Hitler signed the order committing the Army Groups Centre and South to pinch off the Kursk bulge (Operation Citadel), with Model's Ninth Army in the north and Hoth's Fourth Panzer Army in the south. However, when the offensive finally opened on 5 July the date of attack had been postponed no less than four times (namely, 3 May, and 6, 18 and 25 June) and during that time the Soviets, having correctly anticipated the aim of the German offensive, had taken the opportunity to reinforce the Kursk salient and to strengthen it for defence in depth, with eight defensive lines, covering 100 miles.

Facing crushing Soviet counter-attacks and desperately needing to divert resources to Italy, Hitler ordered an end to Operation Citadel on 13 July. By fatally eroding Hitler's central armoured reserve, which could not be rebuilt out of current production, Kursk may be said to mark a decisive shift in the balance of forces on the Eastern Front as henceforth the Red Army rather than the *Ostheer* possessed the initiative.

Thus by mid-December 1943, the Soviet forces had recovered over half the territory the Germans had occupied since June 1941, and the siege of Leningrad was formally declared to be over on 26 January 1944. In the following month, Hitler reluctantly agreed to the withdrawal of German forces to the 'Panther line': the only section of the defensive East Wall actually to have been completed. Hitler's reluctance arose partly from the fear that this would encourage the Finns to attempt to negotiate a separate peace with the Soviets: a fear that came to fruition by August. In the meantime, the Soviets spring offensive in the south had met with great success, clearing the Germans from the Crimea and pushing them back 165 miles, which included successful crossings of the rivers Bug, Dniester and Prut. In the process Army Groups A, South and Centre had suffered irreparable damage.

Moreover, while Stalin was grudgingly prepared to give a freer hand to his professionals, symbolised as early as 1942 by the relegation of political commissars from an equal to an advisory status beside his generals, Hitler's inclinations were all in the other direction and his increasing interference in detailed operational matters unnecessarily strained both his and his generals' nerves.

On 22 June 1944 – the third anniversary of the opening of Operation Barbarossa, and just 16 days after the D-Day landings in Normandy – the Soviets launched 166 divisions comprising 2.4 million troops, 5200 tanks, and 5300 aircraft in Operation Bagration, which decimated the 37 divisions of Army Group Centre. Germany's allies began to drop out of the conflict (Rumania on 23 August, Finland on 2 September, and Bulgaria four days later).

By 10 July, the Red Army had 'liberated' Vilna, the capital of Lithuania, and by the end of the month was on the banks of the rivers San and Bug, within striking distance of Warsaw (promoting the ill-starred uprising by the Polish Home Army).

The heaviest single offensive of World War Two was launched by the Red Army on 12 January 1945, although the Berlin garrison only finally surrendered on 2 May: two days after Hitler had committed suicide.

With never less than 55 per cent of Germany's divisions committed there, the Eastern Front dominated the Second World War. At their most successful, the Germans and their Finnish, Hungarian, Italian, and Romanian allies had advanced 1240 miles (2000 km) into Soviet territory, taking over 50 per cent of the European Soviet Union, 63 per cent of Soviet coal, 71 per cent of its iron, and potentially over 80 per cent of its oil. However, Soviet materiel, supplemented by that of her British and American allies, and manpower ultimately told. The ultimate price was perhaps 5.5 million Germans dead compared with Soviet civilian and military losses of between 20 and 27 million.

7 The strategic bombing offensive against Germany

Introduction

In the long period, when the Red Army was bearing the brunt of the fight against the Axis and Stalin's western allies repeatedly delayed the opening of the Second Front, Churchill pointed to the strategic bombing offensive against Germany as making a material contribution to the Allied war effort at substantial cost. The effectiveness of that effort in strategic terms and its cost – to those in the air and, more particularly, to those on the ground – remain highly controversial questions.

Detlef Siebert has argued that 'The bombing of Dresden cannot be equalled with the horrors of Auschwitz'.[1] Yet this is precisely what some have sought to do, arguing that the area bombing that characterised the strategic bombing offensive against Germany, and which enjoyed its greatest successes in the raids which inflicted firestorms on Hamburg (27–28 July 1943) and Dresden (13–14 February 1945) constitutes a war crime comparable to the Holocaust as 'In both cases it was a question of the well-organised mass murder of innocent people, sanctioned at the highest level but contrary to international law'.[2]

Just as the Sonderkommando had to disentangle human pyramids in the gas chambers as those exposed to Zyklon B gas struggled to escape the fumes so the rescue teams making their way into Hamburg's bomb shelters found 'intertwined piles of people, killed by fumes and pressed against the vents and the barricaded doors'.[3]

Lindqvist and Englund, nevertheless, admit three crucial differences between the German and British holocausts. Firstly, the order of magnitude: the Nazis murdering an estimated six million Jews and five million others, while the Allied bombing offensive killed about 500,000 civilians. Secondly, the Germans' victims were almost completely defenceless, whereas roughly 140,000 American and British airmen were killed in the course of the Allied strategic bombing offensive (approximately 85,000 American and 55,000 'British' of whom the major contributors in round figures were nearly 40,000 British, heading towards 10,000 Canadians and over 5,500 Australians and New Zealanders). Third, and most crucially, the British and their allies aimed at forcing Germany's surrender rather than at genocide. Nevertheless, to those like Lindqvist, targeting of German civilians constitutes a war crime and those who advocated, approved or implemented that strategy are war criminals who only escaped justice because it is the winners who write war crime indictments, if not History itself.

The controversy surrounding the bombing offensive shows little sign of abating with the passage of time. Demonstrations attended the unveiling by the Queen Mother in 1982 of a bronze statue to Sir Arthur 'Bomber' Harris outside the RAF chapel in London (St. Clement Danes church) near Trafalgar Square, and in 2002 Jörg Friedrich's book *The Fire: Germany Under Bombardment 1940–45*[4] excited strong feelings by arguing, among other things that Churchill's policy of area bombing Germany means that he should be regarded as a war criminal.

While what follows may shed light on the legal and moral status of the strategic bombing offensive, its focus will be a consideration of the psychological, military and diplomatic imperatives which drove the campaign together with an assessment of its military effectiveness.

A brief history of bombing before the Second World War

The Great War of 1914–18 is often portrayed as the first total war. The term certainly first became current in France during the First World War and was popularised by Field Marshal Erich Ludendorff in his 1935 publication *Der Totale Krieg*. However, the American Civil War of 1861–65 in this regard, as in so many others, has the dubious distinction of having acted as a harbinger of the First World War. Thus despite General Order No. 100, published on 24 April 1863 which stated that 'The unarmed citizen is to be spared in person, property, and honour as much as the exigencies of war will admit', Sherman's 'march through Georgia', epitomising his determination to ensure that the ordinary people of the south felt 'the hard hand of war', represented a landmark in that erosion of the distinction between soldiers and civilians or combatants and non-combatants which is one of the defining characteristics of total war.[5]

During the First World War both sides bombed enemy civilians. In 1917, for example, 150 were killed and Liverpool Street Station was badly damaged in the first major raid by German bombers on London. In theory enemy industries and communications were the target, but in practise bombing was privately regarded by both sides as a legitimate means of killing or terrorising the enemy populace. In 1918, for example, the British Air Ministry wrote to Hugh Trenchard, commander of the RAF urging him 'not be too exacting as regards accuracy in bombing railway stations in the middle of towns' as 'The German is susceptible to bloodiness ...'. Trenchard was able to reassure his superiors that 'accuracy is not great at present ...'.[6]

Thus when there were calls after the war for the German pilots who had bombed London to be put on trial as war criminals, the British Air Ministry privately resisted such pressure on the grounds that their own airmen would be open to the same charge and it would tie their hands in future. Thus in 1921, the Air Staff considered it better 'to preserve appearances ... by still nominally confining bombardment to targets which are strictly military in character ... to avoid emphasizing the truth that air warfare has made such restrictions obsolete and impossible'.[7]

Britain also ensured that the commission on international law which met in the Hague during 1922–23 to formulate laws for air warfare did not adopt the American formulation that bombing should be limited to 'the combat area', defined as the area where land troops were engaged.

The nature of Germany's defeat in 1918 seemed to demonstrate that the key to victory now lay not in defeating the enemy's armed forces so much as in defeating the enemy nation on the home front. In 1914–18, the Royal Navy's blockade had been the instrument by which this could be accomplished. Henceforth, the long-range bomber appeared to offer the prospect of accomplishing the same result more quickly and economically (both in terms of finance and bloodshed). 'Air power was ... projected ... as a strategic stiletto, aimed at the heart of the enemy, much more economical than the heavy club provided by land forces or the slow strangulation provided by sea power'.[8]

Churchill, as ... was persuaded by Trenchard not to inflict cuts upon the RAF comparable to those imposed upon the other branches of the armed forces precisely by demonstrating that it was the most cost-effective means of disciplining unruly colonials. The test case was provided by 'the Mad Mullah' (Mohammed Abdille Hassan) of Somaliland, who was forced to submit within a week by a force of 12 planes and 250 men (costing £77,000), whereas the army would have needed to engage two divisions for at least a year to achieve the same effect. The RAF was duly engaged to take over the policing of Iraq for £6 million (the army having already consumed £18 million to this end).

Another key player in the future strategic bombing offensive against Germany – Arthur 'Bert' Harris – at this stage in his career a Squadron leader, was also impressed by the RAF's imperial successes, attributing the winning of the Third Afghan war in 1919 to a single strike with a ten-kilo bomb on the Afghani king's palace.[9] Although Overy states that Harris regarded demoralisation of the enemy as a by-product of the process of destroying Germany's industry through area bombing,[10] one should certainly not forget that Harris first saw bombing achieve results not through its impact upon infrastructures but at the much more elemental level of fear. The bombing of Afghans and Iraqis worked fundamentally because of the psychological effect of air power, the essence of which was the sense of powerlessness which it evoked in its victims, as much as through the physical destruction of their property or persons.

Inter-war strategic bombing doctrine found its foremost theorist in the Italian Giulio Douhet (1869–1930) whose 1921 text '*Il Dominio dell' Aria*' (*The Command of the Air*) asserted that the next war would be won by the side which achieved air superiority and used it to bomb the other side into submission by targeting its centres of civilian population with high explosives, incendiaries and poison gas. As Douhet put it, 'Aircraft enable us to jump over the army which shields the enemy government, industry and people, and strike directly and immediately at the seat of the opposing will and policy. Now, it is actually populations and nations, rather than their agents, which come to blows and seize each other's throats'.[11] Ethical scruples or the observance of international legal niceties inhibiting a side from attacking first would merely consign its own civilians to devastating defeat. The moral highground was the path to perdition for 'necessity will force every nation to use the most effective weapons available, immediately and with the greatest possible ruthlessness'.[12] Thus Stanley Baldwin warned in 1932 that 'The only defence is in offence, which means that you will have to kill more women and children more quickly than the enemy if you want to save yourselves'.[13]

If the British government did not accept Douhet's principles in their entirety, they reasonably enough took the view that other powers might do so and that accordingly a large bomber force was required in the hope that the prospect of massive retaliation might serve as a deterrent.

Popular belief in the war-winning potency of the bomber escalated in Britain, especially given London's proximity to the continent, as aerial technology appeared to improve exponentially and as newsreels and newspapers recorded the bombing of Shanghai in 1932 at the hands of the Japanese, the Italians' use of poison gas against the Abyssinians in 1935, and, most ominously, the destruction of the Basque capital of Guernica at the hands of the German Condor Legion in 1937 during the Spanish Civil War. Baldwin's famous warning that 'The Bomber will always get through'[14] was all the more chilling given his normally emollient and reassuring persona.

1939–42

During the Phoney War Chamberlain rebuked those desirous of bombing German cities stating that 'Whatever be the lengths to which others may go, His Majesty's Government will never resort to the deliberate attack on women and children, and other civilians for purposes of mere terrorism'.[15] Bomber crews rather risked their lives delivering free toilet paper to the Third Reich in the form of uninspired propaganda pamphlets.

Chamberlain was fearful of provoking retaliatory raids by the Luftwaffe but the harsh truth is that when war broke out Bomber Command was woefully prepared for launching either an offensive or counter-offensive, as it possessed just 488 light-bombers, whose range was generally too poor to reach the Ruhr from Britain, and was equipped with few bases capable of handling heavy bombers, few bombs larger than 250 pounds and even few maps of the likely target areas.

When Churchill replaced Chamberlain as Prime Minister (10 May 1940), he was determined to prosecute the war as energetically as possible and Bomber Command was the only branch of the armed forces, following the fall of France (June 1940), capable of taking the attack to the enemy. Thus among Churchill's earliest acts as Prime Minister and Minister of Defence were orders to adapt industry to the production of heavy bombers and the order (11 May) to bomb 'military targets' in Germany (including communication and transportation links such as railway stations). On 20 June 1940, the definition of 'military targets' was expanded to include industrial targets, including the homes of the workforce.

Hitting back at the enemy by any and all means possible was vital not only in terms of domestic morale but also as to show the enemy and neutral, especially American, opinion that Britain was determined, unlike France, to carry on fighting.

As mentioned above (in chapter 5) Bomber Command played a key role in the Battle of Britain, in provoking the Luftwaffe following five raids on Berlin between 25 August and 4 September 1940 to switch its tactics from targeting Fighter Command to bombing London and other urban centres: the Blitz. Mounting British civilian casualties undoubtedly increased the demand for similar suffering to be inflicted upon the enemy.[16] In Churchill's words: 'We ask no favours of the enemy. We seek from them no compunction [sic]. On the contrary, if tonight the people of London were asked to cast their votes as to whether a convention should be entered into to stop the bombing of all cities, an overwhelming majority would cry, "No: we will mete out to the Germans the measure, and more than the measure, that they have meted out"'.[17]

1942–45

Churchill's sentiments were echoed by Sir Arthur Harris when he stated that 'The Nazis entered this war under the rather childish delusion that they were going to bomb everybody else and nobody was going to bomb them. At Rotterdam, London, Warsaw and half a hundred other places they put their rather naive theory into operation. They sowed the wind. And now, they are going to reap the whirlwind'.[18]

Harris, who took over as Commander-in-Chief of Bomber Command on 23 February 1942, was to be Churchill's willing instrument in ensuring that 'the civilian population around the target areas must be made to feel the weight of war'.[19] The 'fiction that the bombers were attacking "military objectives" in towns was officially abandoned'[20] and area bombing (levelling the entire area in which a military target is located) was adopted before Harris' appointment but he had the will and the resources to make the strategy much more effective than hitherto. It should also be noted that, much to Harris's annoyance, the fiction that bombers were attacking military objectives was maintained *in public* throughout the war, or at least until the fallout from the destruction of Dresden.

The Secretary of State for Air, Archibald Sinclair, later referred to Harris' 'brilliant qualities as a Commander' namely, his 'energy, will-power, drive, originality, fertility in ideas and technical resource'. His alleged shortcomings were his 'egotism' and associated 'inability to see the war except through the blinkers of Bomber Command'.[21]

Harris later claimed that

The main task laid upon the Command by the Air Ministry directif letter numbered S.46368/D.C.A.S., of 14th February 1942 was "to focus attacks on the morale of the enemy civil population, and, in particular, of the industrial workers." This was to be achieved by destroying, mainly by incendiary attacks, first, four large cities in the Ruhr area and, then as opportunity offered, fourteen other industrial cities in Northern, Central and Southern Germany. The aim of attacks on town areas had already been defined in the Air Staff paper (dated 23rd September, 1941) as follows:-

"The ultimate aim of an attack on a town area is to break the morale of the population which occupies it. To ensure this we must achieve two things: first, we must make the town physically uninhabitable and, secondly, we must make the people conscious of constant personal danger. The immediate aim, is therefore, twofold, namely, to produce (i) destruction, and (ii) fear of death".[22]

However, after the war the Air Staff claimed that its intention, even when issuing the directive of February 1942 'was always to return to the bombing of precise targets as quickly as the tactical capabilities of the bomber force, and the improvement of night bombing technique, would permit'.

Moreover, it was claimed that believing 'a rapid development of tactical ability ... to be immediately practicable' the directive of 14 February 1942 had included various specific targets, in order of priority, in the Directive.[23]

In fact, the Directive stated that attacks should focus '"on morale of enemy civil population, in particular industrial workers," and "[the] aiming points [were] to be built-up areas, not, for instance, the dockyards or aircraft factories ... This must be made quite clear if it is not already understood"'.[24]

If, as later claimed, Air Staff 'hoped ... to be able to revert to the attack of precise targets' but knew 'from correspondence between the Air Ministry and the C-in-C. that he had little faith in the value of attacking precise targets', and resisted 'the large scale use of flares and the formation of a target-finding force' it is difficult to understand why Harris was appointed at all, let alone retained as Commander-in-Chief after 'the bomber force had become large enough to achieve the requisite degree of concentration, and when night bombing technique had been sufficiently improved' to allow area bombing to give way to precision bombing.[25]

Heavy losses had meant that early on Bomber Command had had to discontinue daylight raids in favour of night time flying but aircrews trained to attack in broad daylight had understandably found adjustment difficult. As Garro Jones pointed out in the House of Commons in February 1942, 'We know that these heavy bombers cannot operate except from extreme altitudes or by night. In the former case they cannot hit their targets; in the latter case they cannot find their targets and have not found them ...'.[26] The Butt Report of the summer of 1941 bore out Garro's stark assessment, concluding that only one plane in three got within five miles of its target, while on average a mere 20 per cent of aircraft managed to make an attack within the 75 square miles surrounding a target.

Harris' initial response to this state of affairs was to target the North German Baltic ports of Lubeck (on 28 March 1942) and Rostock (on 18 April 1942) for the simple reason that it was easier to find targets, even at night, if they were on the coastline. These raids were both successful in gutting large parts of the city. 30 May 1942 saw the first 1,000–bomber raid took place on 30 May 1942 on Cologne and rendered 45,000 homeless.

On 5 October 1942, Portal minuted his plans to increase Bomber Command's operations over the following two years, so as to kill almost one million civilians, seriously injure another million and leave 25 million homeless. The Air Ministry warned against such candour, stating, 'It is unnecessary and undesirable in any document about our bombing policy to emphasize this aspect, which is contrary to the principles of international law, such as they are, and also contrary to the statement made some time ago by the PM, that we should not direct our bombing to terrorize the civilian population, even in retaliation'.[27]

From August 1942, Bomber Command's night time bombing of Germany was supplemented by the US Eighth Air Force bombing by day. However, the American bombing campaign competed with rather than complemented Harris' strategy insofar as the Americans remained wedded to the notion of precision bombing. The American raid on Schweinfurt on 14 October 1943 revealed the potential gains and definite shortcomings of this policy insofar as a force of almost 300 planes managed to reduce Germany's ball-bearing capacity by 67 per cent but the cost – involving the loss of 60 bombers and damage to a further 138 – was such that the Eighth Air Force had to suspend attacks into Germany for the foreseeable future. It was not until the introduction of the P-51 Mustang, providing long-range fighter escort, that the American strategy really began to pay dividends.

In January 1943, Churchill and Roosevelt had met in Casablanca and decided to give priority to the bombing campaign. Thus on 21 January 1943, the Combined Chiefs-of-Staff issued a directive to the air forces in which their primary objective was stated as bringing about 'the progressive destruction and dislocation of the German military, industrial and economic system, and the undermining of the morale of the German people to a point where their capacity for armed resistance is fatally weakened'.

This demand was largely the consequence of the other major strategic decision taken at Casablanca – to postpone the opening of the Second Front in northern Europe. Bombing provided a means (together with the demand for the unconditional surrender of the Axis powers) of appeasing Stalin. Nor was it entirely rhetorical to present the strategic bombing offensive as a form of Second Front. Germany responded to the Combined Bombing Offensive by putting greater resources into counter-measures so that by the spring of 1943, for example, 70 per cent of German fighters were in the western theatre of operations, leaving a much smaller force facing the Red Army. As Albert Speer put it:

'There were thousands of anti-aircraft, heavy anti-aircraft guns, millions of ammunition for it and hundred thousands of soldier [sic] which were torn away from our fight in the Russian Front. So I should say, with air attacks on Germany you had, in an early stage, from '43 on, really a so-called Second Front'.[28]

In 1943, several factors contributed to Bomber Command's success in dropping more bombs on target, including the advent of new heavy bombers, including the Lancaster increasingly replacing the Stirling and Halifax, and new navigational aids which allowed bombers to be concentrated over the target. 'Gee' had first used against Cologne the previous year. It was supplemented by Oboe and H2S, although their full potential was not realised until 1944. Operational improvements included specially trained bomb-aimers and 'Pathfinders', who dropped flares on the target area for the other planes to follow.

The night of 24–25 July 1943 also witnessed the first use of 'Window' during a raid on Hamburg. This consisted of large quantities of small strips of aluminium foil, which were dropped en route to the target, jamming German radar and their gun-aiming apparatus. Several days of high temperatures and low humidity created ideal conditions for 1200 tons of incendiary bombs to create a firestorm of apocalyptic proportions. The British night attacks and American day raids lasted nearly a week. Apartment buildings numbering 16,000, roughly three-quarters of the city, were burned down and between 30,000 and 50,000 were killed: the latter figure approaching the number of fatalities (approximately 59,000) which the Luftwaffe inflicted upon all British cities put together. Indeed, at the time, no less an authority than Hitler's Armaments Minister, Albert Speer, expressed the opinion that six more raids of similar magnitude would finish the war,[29] yet historians such as Lindqvist still question the effectiveness of the bombing campaign comparing Harris with a First World War general repeatedly using the same impoverished attritional tactics in the hope that ultimately they might succeed and retrospectively legitimate the previous bloodletting or, in Lindqvist's words, 'Harris was forced to commit crime after crime in pursuit of the one success that would justify every crime that had gone before'.[30]

Buoyed by the example of Hamburg, Harris believed in late 1943 that with American support he could destroy Berlin and win the war within six months. However, two factors conspired against his being able to put this theory to the test. Firstly, the Eighth Air Force had been so badly mauled over Schweinfurt that they were unable to assist until escorted by Mustangs in March 1944. In the meantime, 1000 aircraft – the Command's first line strength – had been lost. Secondly, Harris was under increasing pressure from his own Air Ministry to engage in precision bombing of targets such as oil plants in preparation for the impending cross-Channel attack. Harris reluctantly complied, regarding such requests as 'diversions from the main offensive'.[31] In March 1944, both bomber forces were placed under Eisenhower's overall command to prepare for D-Day.

By the time of D-Day (6 June 1944), the Luftwaffe had lost control of their airspace even in daylight and had only 300 planes with which to face over 12,000 American and British aircraft.

With Allied command of the air, the bombing offensive could proceed largely unhindered. Thus of the 1.42 million tons of bombs dropped in the entire war by the British and Americans, 1.18 million tons were dropped in the last 12 months of the war. The culmination of Harris' air war, at least in symbolic terms, was the attack upon Dresden.

In October 1944, a report on Dresden had concluded that 'Compared to other towns of its size, Dresden is … an unattractive blitz target'. Yet on the night of 13/14 February 1945, a double attack by 805 British bombers, dropped 2690 tonnes of bombs creating a firestorm of 100 mph winds and temperatures of up to 1000 degrees Celsius (or 1800 degrees Fahrenheit), which covered 11 square miles of the city. On the two succeeding days the USAAF followed up with two smaller daylight raids, helping to level 1600 acres, destroying or seriously damaging 19 permanent and almost all of Dresden's temporary hospitals. Estimates of the dead vary enormously with Frederick Taylor at the more conservative end of the spectrum (25,000 to 35,000 dead), and David Irving at the outer limits of estimates (100,000 to 250,000 dead).[32] The actual figure can never be known because of the refugees crowding the city and the fact that many bodies were completely incinerated by the firestorm.

The decision was taken for two reasons. Firstly, because Dresden, in Harris' words 'had become of great importance as a communications centre and control point in the defence of Germany's eastern front'[33] and destroying this capacity would directly assist the advance of the Red Army into eastern Germany. Secondly, bombing Dresden was thought by Harris as likely to cause serious damage to German morale, not least because it had hardly been touched by air-raids hitherto and was poorly defended.

However, shortly after the event, Dresden became an embarrassment to Churchill and on 28 March he expressed himself thus

> It seems to me that the moment has come when the question of bombing German cities simply for the sake of increasing the terror, though under other pretexts, should be reviewed. Otherwise we shall come into control of an utterly ruined land. We shall not, for instance, be able to get housing materials out of Germany for our own needs because some temporary provision would have to be made for the Germans themselves. The destruction of Dresden remains a serious query against the conduct of Allied bombing. I am of the opinion that military objectives must henceforward be more strictly studied in our own interests rather than that of the enemy.
>
> The Foreign Secretary has spoken to me on this subject, and I feel the need for more precise concentration upon military objectives, such as oil and communications behind the immediate battle-zone, rather than on mere acts of terror and wanton destruction, however impressive.[34]

Churchill was prevailed upon to withdraw these reflections but still told his chiefs of staff that

> It seems to me that the moment [has come] when the question of the so-called "area-bombing" of German cities should be reviewed from the point of view of our own interests. If we come into control of an entirely ruined land, there will be a great shortage of accommodation for ourselves and our allies.[35]

Conclusion

The shameful shoddy treatment of Harris and Bomber Command continued after the war, as symbolised by the failure to create a campaign medal for the airmen who had carried the burden of the war for four years and who had suffered a higher casualty rate than any other branch of the British armed forces. Churchill's famed magnanimity in victory appears, on this occasion at least, to have extended to the defeated but not to his own comrades in arms and loyal servants. In an effort to win the hearts and minds of the Germans, Churchill implicitly gave credence to those who depicted area bombing as an act of terrorism rather than an act of war.

Area bombing had emerged in 1940 not in accordance with Douhet's dicta and from proven operational success but rather its reverse: the RAF could not hit precisely what they chose and thus opted to hit what they could, namely, large industrial centres. Precision daylight bombing proved not to be a viable option until early 1944.

Churchill chose to sanction the strategy of area bombing in 1940 for political reasons, namely, the desire to hit back, and to be seen to be hitting back, at the enemy. Political considerations buttressed pursuit of that strategy insofar as bombing represented one of the few means of reassuring Stalin that the enemy was being engaged and his capacity to wage war was being degraded by the western allies, when the Red Army was doing the bulk of the fighting and dying prior to the Second Front being formally opened by means of the cross-Channel attack of June 1944.

Critics of the strategic bombing offensive argue that the Blitz did not seriously damage British war production and so far from shattering British morale may actually have steeled it. In so doing, they often overlook the fact that the Luftwaffe was simply not equipped to perform those functions, whereas by 1943, Bomber Command, under Harris' inspired leadership, had developed the capacity to inflict such severe blows upon German industry and morale that Speer himself questioned the Reich's ability to survive another half a dozen Hamburgs.

8 The Holocaust

The journey to Auschwitz: crooked or straight path?

Persecution of the Jews is an historical commonplace. The genocidal anti-Semitism of the Third Reich requires deeper explanation. When and why was mass murder acknowledged as the 'final solution' of the 'Jewish question'?

Broadly speaking there are two schools of historians on this issue: the intentionalists and the structuralists. The former take the Fuhrerprinzip at face value and argue that to understand Hitler's will is to understand the policy of the Third Reich. Such historians tend to believe that Hitler, from at least the time of *Mein Kampf*, hankered after the liquidation of the Jews and that the 'road to Auschwitz' was essentially a straight one, once Hitler acquired the means to put his plan into practice.

Conversely, structuralists present the Third Reich as a polycratic structure, with overlapping and competing agencies exercising real power in the evolution and implementation of policy, partly as a result of Hitler's indolence, partly as a consequence of his Social Darwinist determination to encourage subordinates to decide issues by fighting it out among themselves, and partly in accordance with the traditional notion of 'divide and rule'.

These two views are not, of course, incapable of being synthesised. It can, for example, be plausibly argued that in anti-Semitic as in other areas of policy, Hitler established the framework and objectives but left others to furnish the details and influence the timing. More precisely, 'working towards the Fuhrer' involved initiating policies thought likely or known to conform to his wishes.

Part of the problem of divining Hitler's precise wishes is that he was careful to express himself publicly in ambiguous language. No one could be in any doubt from reading *Mein Kampf* or from hearing Hitler's speeches of his utter contempt for the Jews, but a staple of his vocabulary such as 'removal' may have referred 'simply' to expelling the Jews from Germany or from Nazi-occupied territory and only acquires genocidal connotations in the light of what we know ultimately happened.

One passage from *Mein Kampf* illustrates the problem:

> If we had at the beginning of, and during the war, subjected 12 or 15,000 of these Hebrew corrupters of the people to poison gas, as hundreds of thousands of our best German workers from all strata and occupations had to endure, then millions of victims of the Front would not have been in vain.[1]

Hitler can be read here as saying merely that the war need not have been lost if 12 or 15,000 of Germany's Jews had fought at the Front and been subjected to poison gas as troops such as he himself had been. However, it can also be argued from what he says that gassing Germany's Jews provides the means of preventing a second 'stab in the back' in the event of a future war.

Not least among the ironies of this passage are the facts that many more German Jews served and died at the front than Hitler imagined (see below) and that Fritz Haber, the inventor of poison gas, was a German Jew who wished to prove his patriotic credentials by presenting the Prussian officer corps with what he believed to be a war-winning weapon.

From the 1933 Boycott to the 1936 Berlin Olympics

Germany's Jews were small in number and relatively highly concentrated. According to the Reich Statistical Office's own figures 503,000 Jews lived in Germany in 1933. This represented just 0.76 per cent of the population. Over 70 per cent or 355,000 of Germany's Jews lived in cities of over 100,000 inhabitants (notably Frankfurt, Berlin and Breslau). Almost half (48.9 per cent) of this community made its living in commerce and trade but Jews were also disproportionately successful in the professions, comprising nearly 17 per cent of lawyers and public notaries and almost 11 per cent of doctors.

Moreover, Germany's Jews were very well assimilated as shown by their distinguished war record (100,000 had served in the armed forces during the Great War, 78,000 at the front. A total of 30,000 were decorated for their bravery, and 12,000 died in the service of their country) and by their hostility towards Jewish refugees from the East.[2]

Such sentiments did not, of course, preserve them from assaults in the street from members of SA and SS who, since the seizure of power, often appeared in the guise of police 'auxiliaries'. However, such seemingly random violence and locally organised boycotts of Jewish businesses attracted adverse criticism of the regime both abroad and in respectable circles at home.

In these early days of the regime, Hitler did not want to risk alienating the conservative elites by allowing lawlessness to flourish, or to damage the still fragile economy, or attract unfavourable international attention. Moreover, he had long advocated the need to replace traditional 'irrational' displays of anti-Semitism with more ordered, rational responses. As Heydrich was to remark in 1934: 'The methods of "rowdy anti-Semitism" are to be rejected. One does not fight rats with a revolver, but rather with poison and gas'.[3]

The announcement of a boycott of Jewish businesses and professionals, to begin on 1 April 1933, thus represented a means whereby the Party leadership could both provide a safe channel for the energies of party activists (a committee of hardliners, chaired by Julius Streicher being charged with organising the event) and test the precise strength of philosemitic sentiment both at home and abroad.

The fact that the boycott was abandoned after a single day, partly reflects behind the scenes pressure from both President Hindenburg and Foreign Minister Von Neurath, and partly reflects the mixed response which the experiment drew on the streets, with some members of the public ostentatiously ignoring the would-be intimidating presence of SA and SS pickets in order to demonstrate their loyalty to Jewish shopkeepers. However, the lessons to be drawn from the day were obscured by the typical Nazi failure to define their terms. For example, it was unclear whether a shop owned by but not run by Jews qualified as a 'Jewish shop'.

However, legal steps to purge Jews from Germany's professions and cultural life began within a week of the boycott's being called off with the Law for the Restoration of the Professional Civil Service (with those possessing a single Jewish grandparent being dismissed, unless – in deference to Hindenburg – they had either served at the front in the last war or were relatives of the fallen).

A total of 40,000 Jews left Germany in the first year of the Third Reich, including many of the most talented (Albert Einstein being one of twenty Nobel laureates), however, the situation quietened down until grassroots anti-Semitic agitation flared up once again in 1935.

The 25-Point Programme of 1920 had stated that a citizen could only be a person of 'German blood', but despite many years in the wilderness, the Nazis had entered office with no detailed plans for tackling this aspect of the Jewish 'problem', and by 1935 party activists thought the regime needed to address this state of affairs. The so-called Nuremberg Laws (passed by a special session of the Reichstag in Nuremberg on 15 September 1935) managed to satisfy both the desire of party activists for proof of the regime's continuing radical commitment (which had appeared problematical in the light of the Night of the Long Knives) and the desire for at least the appearance of legality and stability felt by the still influential conservative elites (who had been dismayed by the recrudescence of street violence as unseemly in itself and for what it meant in terms of Germany's image and sales abroad).

The Reich Citizenship Law, which in point of conception was actually the second of the two Nuremburg Laws, formally reduced Jews to the status of second-class citizens by redefining them as 'subjects'. Not only was it unclear what this precise status entailed, but it was also left unclear precisely who was affected by the law once Hitler had personally vetoed the suggestion that it only applied to full Jews. Hence the Supplementary Decree of the Reich Citizenship Law of 14 November was the first of thirteen such decrees which sought to clarify the situation. In essence those with three or four Jewish grandparents were defined as full Jews; those with two 'Aryan' and two Jewish grandparents were defined as 'half-Jews', and were considered Jewish only if they practised the Jewish faith, married a Jew or were the legitimate or illegitimate offspring of a 'mixed' marriage. The latter were designated *Geltungsjuden*, while those who did not meet these criteria were termed *Mischlinge*. The fact that the Nazis ultimately had to resort to religious faith in defining 'Jewishness' speaks volumes for the vacuity of their rhetoric regarding blood as the primary determinant of race. As Victor Klemperer remarked in his diary: 'race, in the sense of purity of blood, is a zoological notion ... which long ago ceased to correspond with any reality'.[4]

The other Nuremburg Law, namely, the Law for the Protection of German Blood and Honour, sought to preserve the purity of German blood from Jewish 'contamination' by banning marriage between Jews and Aryans and by outlawing sexual relations outside marriage between Jews and Aryans,[5] while German 'honour' was protected by limiting the employment of Aryan housemaids in Jewish homes and by forbidding Jews from raising the Reich or national flag. Those couples already partners in 'mixed marriages' were subjected to various pressures designed to encourage the instigation of divorce proceedings.

Many in Germany, including ironically many in the Jewish community itself, welcomed the Nuremburg Laws because they felt that the imposition of such a legal framework would at least stabilise the situation. They were, of course, to be proved wrong, although official anti-Semitism slackened somewhat until the autumn of 1937, in large part because the regime's energies were focused in the interim upon the remilitarisation of the Rhineland (March 1936) and the staging of the Berlin Olympics (between 1 and 16 August 1936).

The radicalisation of Nazi anti-Semitic policy culminating in Kristallnacht

The Anschluss with Austria of March 1938 radicalised Nazi anti-Semitic policy because Austrian Nazism was especially rabid on this question and because the Third Reich's acquisition of 195,000 more Jews – a figure greater than that forced to emigrate hitherto – put the regime back to square one, at least in numerical terms, in dealing with the 'Jewish Question'.

Efforts to encourage Jewish emigration were redoubled under the auspices of Department II–112 of the SS Sicherheitsdienst (SD) in general and Adolf Eichmann in particular. It was he who created the 'Central Office for the Emigration of Austrian Jewry' in Vienna for the express purpose of simplifying and thus speeding up emigration procedures. However, when 32 nations met at Evian on Roosevelt's initiative in July 1938, in order to co-ordinate the international response to the growing Jewish refugee problem, the conference tended rather to suggest to Berlin that the outside world was mostly prepared to abandon the Jews to their fate rather than offer them a safe haven. Leaving aside any suspicion of anti-Semitic prejudice, few countries were willing to welcome impoverished immigrants (and the Nazis made sure that they were shorn of most of their wealth before departure), not least in a time of global depression and mass unemployment.

Partly in response to the influx of Jewish refugees entering the country in the wake of Anschluss, the Warsaw government took steps, in March 1938, to deprive Polish Jews living abroad of their Polish citizenship. This move threatened to strand the 50,000 Polish Jews living in Germany. Rather than accept the responsibility for them by default, the SS, in October 1938, rounded up roughly 1700 of these people and unceremoniously and brutally dumped them across the border, or rather into the no-man's-land and legal limbo between the two countries as the Polish frontier officials refused to accept them.

The victims of this inhumane act included the parents and two sisters of Herschel Grynszpan, a young Jew living in Paris. He was so incensed at the maltreatment of his family and co-religionists that he bought a revolver with a view to shooting the German ambassador. On 7 November, Grynszpan was denied access to the ambassador but managed to shoot vom Rath, the Third Secretary. News of the latter's death arrived in Munich on the afternoon of 9 November, while Hitler was engaged in the emotionally charged annual commemoration of the martyrs of the 1923 Munich Putsch. Now there was a new martyr to add to the Nazi roll of honour.

Goebbels, who was with Hitler in Munich, knew that one of the surest ways to the Fuhrer's heart was to suggest ways in which the Jews might be made to suffer. Moreover, Goebbels had an especial reason for currying favour as his affair with the Czech actress Lida Barova had strained Hitler's patience. This was not just because Barova was a Slav but because the romance was sufficiently serious at one point as to threaten Goebbels's marriage, which would have been a public relations disaster as Magda and the six Goebbels children represented a sort of substitute first family, given Hitler's reluctance to compromise his appeal for many German women by marrying.

Goebbels seems to have suggested that vom Rath's death might be made the occasion for unleashing the party's paramilitaries upon Germany's Jewish community. However, the stormtroopers and members of the SS would operate out of uniform in order to lend greater credibility to the claim that the action on the streets represented a 'spontaneous' expression of the anger of the ordinary Germans, incensed by the crime against vom Rath. This tactic would also deflect any international condemnation, although recent experiences regarding the Anschluss, Evian and the September 1938 Munich Conference all strongly suggested that Germany had relatively little to fear from that quarter.

Hitler appears to have given his verbal approval of this pogrom to Goebbels, who issued his instructions across Germany by means of a series of telephone calls. The night of 9–10 November 1938 became known as Kristallnacht because of the large amount of broken glass, notably from Jewish department store plate glass windows, which soon littered the gutters. An estimated 7500 business premises were damaged or destroyed, and many synagogues were fired. It was not, however, only Jewish property that was attacked. Over 90 Jews were killed and 30,000 were imprisoned in concentration camps.

If Hitler's March 1939 takeover of the Czech rump would come to represent a watershed for the international community, leaving no room for doubt regarding Hitler's aggressive intentions, Kristallnacht represented a comparable turning point in terms of domestic opinion. Although Hitler never publicly commented on the events of 9–10 November, those events made it no longer possible to ignore the fact that the regime was brutal and immoral, whatever its apparent economic and foreign policy successes.

To their credit, evidence from both Nazi and non-Nazi sources suggests that 'significant swathes of German opinion, especially, according to SD Reports, in the Roman Catholic south and west, regarded the pogrom with disgust',[6] although sometimes the revulsion was prompted more by the manifest disrespect for property rights than sympathy for the plight of the Jews themselves. Nevertheless, this backlash against the regime (albeit muted in form, given the limited scope for expressing critical sentiments) and the economic problems arising from Kristallnacht, provided the impetus for a high-level review of the whole affair and future policymaking with regard to the Jews.

The enemies of Goebbels, of whom there were many within the Nazi ranks, obviously saw a means of undermining him by pointing out that his initiative had been so costly as to risk destabilising Germany's fragile economic recovery. With half of Belgium's annual production of plate glass required to replace what had been smashed, at an estimated cost in foreign currency of 3000 million Reichsmarks, Kristallnacht placed enormous strains upon Germany's balance of trade, while equally unsettling were insurance claims estimated at 225 million Reichsmarks.

Hitler, however, stood by his Propaganda Minister, refusing to allow him to be made a scapegoat for the unforeseen consequences of scapegoating the Jews. Instead, he took the practical step of instructing Goering, as Head of the Four Year Plan Office, to chair a meeting on 12 November 1938 to address these economic problems. The result was the Decree for the Restitution of the Street Scene, making the victims liable for the damage they had suffered, with a 1000 million Reichsmarks fine on the Jewish community. The policy of Aryanisation was also accelerated by means of the Decree on the Exclusion of Jews from German Economic Life, which banned Jews from all independent business activity, and the Law on the Use of Jewish Assets, which meant that securities went into closed accounts and that Jews could no longer buy or sell jewels, precious metals or works of art freely. More ominous still was the closer involvement of the SS in initiating and implementing anti-Semitic policy with Heydrich pointing to Eichmann's 'Central Office for the Emigration of Austrian Jewry' in Vienna and successfully suggesting the creation of a similar agency to facilitate Jewish emigration in the old Reich.

Indeed, Kristallnacht represented the last gasp of the 'emotional' and 'spontaneous' anti-Semitism, as it gave way to the rational, cold-blooded and systematic persecution preferred by Hitler and implemented by Himmler's SS.

The war years

On 30 January 1939, Hitler made a speech to the Reichstag which is worth quoting at some length because intentionalists regard it as revealing Hitler's genocidal intent, by seeking to 'legitimate' it:

> In my life I have often been a prophet, and I have mostly been laughed at. At the time of my struggle for power, it was mostly the Jewish people who laughed at the prophecy that one day I would attain in Germany the leadership of the state and therewith of the entire nation, and that among other problems I would also solve the Jewish one. I think that the uproarious laughter of that time has in the meantime remained stuck in

> German Jewry's throat. Today I want to be a prophet again: If
> international finance Jewry inside and outside Europe again
> succeeds in precipitating the nations into a world war, the result
> will not be the Bolshevisation of the earth, and with it the vic-
> tory of Jewry, but the annihilation of the Jewish race in Europe.[7]

With the benefit of hindsight this 'prophecy' obviously acquired
great significance, not least for Hitler himself who twice referred
to it in 1942 and three times in 1943 as clearly pointing out what
would happen.[8] However, the 20–20 vision which hindsight
seems to offer can actually be misleading and once set in context
Hitler's pronouncement is susceptible to alternative readings,
namely as a threat to the United States not to interfere in European,
and specifically German, affairs and/or an attempt to exert pressure upon western governments to facilitate the emigration of
German Jews, not least by providing funding. In other words,
Hitler's words as uttered are threatening in the manner of a black-
mailer or extortionist rather than in the manner of a terrorist
promising bloodshed.

Just as the Anschluss with Austria resulted in a radicalisation of
anti-Semitic policy so did the war. This as so for four major reasons.
Firstly, warfare resulted in a closing of borders and therefore an
effective end to the option of migration, although the Madagascar
plan (shipping the Jews to the Vichy French colony) was seemingly seriously aired by sections of the SS after the fall of France).
Secondly, the Jewish 'problem' was magnified as more Jews fell into
the Nazis' hands. Thirdly, the problem became increasingly critical as the tide of war increasingly turned against the Nazis as this
meant that the 'biological balance' tilted in favour of the Jews and
against the Aryans, and made the latter increasingly vulnerable to
a second 'stab in the back'. Last but not least, war provided the
perfect setting for mass murder as information was even more
tightly controlled than in peacetime; any rumours of 'atrocities'
could be dismissed as enemy propaganda; and scruples regarding
the taking of 'civilian' life were eroded by experience of partisan
warfare and indiscriminate bombing.

On 31 July 1941, just over a month after the launch of Operation Barbarossa, Goering ordered Heydrich to carry out the 'final
solution' of the so-called Jewish question. In so doing he may
have been bowing to the inevitable: the SS had already succeeded
in asserting its authority in Jewish affairs and this was a role which

was likely to become more prominent still as more territory and hence more Jews fell into Nazi hands. Some might say that Goering's language allows the possibility that the 'solution' envisaged at this stage may still have represented forcible resettlement of the Jews rather than their extermination.

Any such lingering doubts should not survive an examination of the minutes of the Wannsee Conference of 20 January 1942, which was called by Heydrich to co-ordinate arrangements for the 'final solution'. The meeting, chaired by Heydrich and involving representatives of key ministries, including those of Foreign Affairs, the Eastern Territories and the Four-Year Plan, was the means whereby the SS asserted its authority over these other bodies and decided practical steps to implement the murder of Europe's estimated 11 million Jews. Evacuation of the Jews to the east was clearly nothing but a prelude to extermination as otherwise it was believed 'the Jewish race could regenerate itself'.[9]

If Dachau had been the model concentration camp under Theodor Eicke then Auschwitz–Birkenau became the model death camp under Rudolf Hoess. It became the scene of an estimated 1,080,000 murders (960,000 of the victims being Jewish), not least because Hoess improved upon the methods of mass murder he had observed at Treblinka: replacing carbon monoxide with Zyklon B cyanide; building gas chambers which could hold ten times as many people; and successfully disguising these units as showers.

The Goldhagen thesis

Daniel Goldhagen's bestselling 1997 book *Hitler's Willing Executioners* is subtitled 'Ordinary Germans and the Holocaust' and its controversial thesis is in essence that the Holocaust was not the work of Hitler, Himmler, Heydrich, the SS or even the Nazi party as a whole but was made possible by the German public as a whole subscribing to 'eliminatory anti-Semitism'.[10]

A moment's reflection should allow one to appreciate that the concept of 'ordinary Germans' is highly nebulous, as factors such as religion, region, class, age, gender and education are likely to produce a bewildering diversity of values which will issue in a variety of responses to any given situation. When Himmler reflected on the generality of Germans in his speech to a group of SS leaders at

Posen on 6 October 1943, he recognised that most Germans distinguished between their dislike of Jews in the abstract, and individual Jews whom they liked.[11] This is a perception borne out by sources such as Melita Maschmann's 'Memoirs' where she explains that she was personally able to engage in a form of 'double-think': finding it possible simultaneously to possess Nazi anti-Semitic opinions without this interfering in her personal relations with individual Jews.[12] If her experiences are at all representative then they may help to explain how the German people tolerated the Nazi persecution of the Jews: by accepting the Nazi propaganda image of the Jew as an abstract bogey-man who was behind both Bolshevism and the worst excesses of capitalism, they were able to avoid detailed consideration of the suffering which Nazism actually imposed upon individuals, especially as those individuals were marginalised, isolated and then removed from German society: out of sight, out of mind.

A minority of Germans were actively anti-Semitic and did harm the Jews with varying degrees of relish. Another minority put themselves at great risk by going out of their way to prevent harm befalling their Jewish neighbours. The overwhelming majority of 'ordinary' Germans by the winter of 1941–42 were passively anti-Semitic. That is to say, they had become indifferent to the fate of the Jews. Even this was due less, in all probability, to the success of Nazi propaganda than because of Allied bombing, and the increasing rigours of war focused their thoughts more narrowly upon their own survival and comforts, and that of their immediate circle of family and friends.

The International Military Tribunal which met at Nuremberg for the trial of 20 leading Nazis declared the whole of the SS to be a criminal organisation. This was an understandable but unjustified generalisation as many 'ordinary' Germans such as police reservists had been swept up into the SS and co-opted into the implementation of the final solution.

In addition to Nuremberg, there were approximately 1500 trials of concentration camp staff, Gestapo officials and Waffen SS by the Allies. The standard defence in such trials was that the accused had only been 'obeying orders' which could not have been disobeyed without the individual concerned being executed. It is true that there is no recorded example of death being administered to those who refused to participate in the killings. It is alleged that this was so because such individuals could not have been put before SS or police courts for disobeying what were manifestly criminal orders. However, before we condemn such men, we should bear in mind that if they were routinely witnessing their superiors engaging in manifestly criminal acts they were unlikely to imagine, indeed they could hardly be expected to conceive, that their disobedience would be dignified with a court proceeding. The majority probably expected, with some justification, that dissent would be met with summary execution rather than due process of law. So heinous were the acts that they were being ordered to perform that we can condemn them for failing to heed their conscience, but we should have the courage to admit that in any society it is only extraordinary men who are prepared to risk their lives for the sake of their scruples.

9 The Pacific war

Japanese-American relations to Pearl Harbor

World War Two only became a truly global war on 7 December 1941 when carrier-based Japanese aircraft launched a surprise attack upon the US Pacific fleet anchored at its base at Pearl Harbor, Hawaii, and both Germany and Italy, Japan's Axis allies, declared war on the United States shortly afterwards.

On the face of it, the Japanese action at Pearl Harbor was as suicidal as the kamikaze attacks which characterised their later efforts to humble American naval power. In order to explain the reasons why the Japanese attacked and why they thought they could win, it is necessary to examine Japan's relations with the United States, and the West generally, from the time of the Paris Peace Conference, as Japan was profoundly dissatisfied despite receiving Germany's former Pacific colonies north of the equator as mandated territories.

Although they were allies in the First World War, the United States and Japan were natural rivals in the Pacific, and relations between the two powers deteriorated sharply thereafter. In particular, the Japanese resented the blocking of any commitment to racial equality in the Covenant of the League in 1919 by Woodrow Wilson (with strong backing from the Australian delegation). The treatment of the Japanese by the Anglo-Saxon nations as inferiors was symbolised by the 1922 Washington Naval Disarmament Treaty where the 5:5:3 ratio agreed for the battleships of America, Britain and Japan, respectively, appeared to treat Japan as a second-rate naval power. It could be argued that Japan could not afford a major naval arms race with the Anglo-American powers, and it certainly was argued that the British and American had global naval commitments while Japan was merely a Pacific power. Nevertheless, in Japanese eyes the Anglo-Saxon powers were 'ganging up' against them: a feeling which was strengthened by the fact that the Americans also persuaded Britain in 1922 to drop its alliance with Japan, which dated from 1902. America's ban on Japanese immigration into the United States from 1924 and blatant discrimination against those Japanese who had already settled there were further sources of insult.

Long before Pearl Harbor, those of Japanese ancestry, and Asiatics in general, had been the focus of fears in the United States and the West generally, which went under the umbrella term of 'the Yellow Peril'. There was a 'widely held perception that as a group (and regardless of the level of assimilation or even citizenship), the Japanese were "sly" and "treacherous" ...'.[1]

Between 1861 and 1940, roughly 275,000 Japanese migrated to the United States, most between 1898 and 1924 when quotas first appeared. Although Japanese comprised less than 2 per cent of all immigrants, US newspapers characterised their advent as an 'invasion', 'The Sacramento Bee' warning that 'the Japs ... will increase like rats' and even San Francisco's Mayor declared that 'the Japanese are not the stuff of which American citizens can be made'.[2]

Such fears explain, although they cannot excuse, a series of Alien Exclusion Acts under which 'people of Japanese ancestry ... were not permitted to intermarry with US citizens, ... to own land or to take legal title to land and could not become citizens'.[3] Despite this discrimination, the Issei ('first-generation' Japanese in the United States) and the Nisei (second-generation Japanese, who were US citizens by birthright) assimilated and prospered. Thus, although 'Japanese Americans controlled less than 4 per cent of California's farmland in 1940 ... they produced more than 10 percent of the total value of the state's farm resources'.[4] However, in some quarters such economic success merely fuelled racism: the hardworking Japanese being perceived by 'the state Federations of Labor ... as unfair competitors on the job market'.[5] This resentment festered during America's slow recovery from the Depression when mass unemployment was a major problem. Moreover, tension increased as America's relations with Japan worsened.

This is not to say that America was unique in being racist. The Japanese themselves were at least as racist but despite, or because of, the fact that they held themselves superior to the Koreans and Chinese, they found it hard to accept that the Americans treated them in a similarly condescending manner.

The decisive factor in pushing Japan down the road to war was the crippling of her economy as a result of the 1929 Wall Street Crash which was compounded by US tariffs (such as the notorious Smoot–Hawley tariff of 1930).

The Japanese home islands, with more than half the land under forest rather than cultivation, and lacking natural resources, offered little but rice and fish. With little coal and barely 10 per cent of her needs for oil met internally, Japan depended upon the export of silk to pay for imported raw materials but the global economy was not conducive to the purchase of luxury items even if one ignores the impact of protectionist legislation.

Japan's need for raw materials, markets and living space resulted in her becoming increasingly aggressive. The Manchurian Incident of 1931 when the Kwantung Army staged an act of sabotage on the Japanese-controlled Manchurian railway in order to justify the complete takeover of this northern Chinese province was not just a strike against an enfeebled China, where Japan had traditionally claimed a privileged position, but also against those cosmopolitan democratic elements within the Japanese ruling elite, who had hitherto somewhat restrained militaristic and nationalistic sentiment. Lord Lytton's report of February 1933 condemning Japanese aggression merely precipitated Japanese withdrawal from the League. Tokyo hoped that this action, together with her repudiation of the Washington and 1930 London Naval Disarmament treaties in 1934, and 1936 withdrawal from the London Naval Disarmament Conference, would hasten the anticipated collapse of the Western-dominated international order in Asia.

The Marco Polo Bridge incident of 7 July 1937 (when Chinese and Japanese troops exchanged gunfire near the Marco Polo Bridge outside of Beijing), precipitated a full-scale Sino-Japanese war and destroyed any possibility of Japan being reintegrated into the international community.

From June 1938, the United States began helping China with loans (commencing with a credit of $25 million to Chiang Kai-shek) and arms as modest economic recovery encouraged Roosevelt to turn his attention from domestic to foreign affairs; Japanese atrocities against Chinese civilians, such as the 'Rape of Nanking' (now Nanjing), excited the moral indignation of the American media and public; and Japanese aggression increasingly came to be viewed as part of a global phenomenon in which the 'peace-loving' nations of the world were under assault from the aggressor nations. This last sentiment was strengthened by Japan's increasing friendliness towards Germany, which was first signalled by her signing of the Anti-Comintern Pact in 1936; by the sinking of the *USS Panay* in Chinese waters (notwithstanding Japan's apology for her 'mistake'); and by her November 1938 declaration of a 'New Order' in eastern Asia. The latter was condemned as a violation of the Open Door principle, and when America's 1911 commercial treaty with Japan, which accounted for 40 per cent of Japan's trade, expired in January 1940 it was only renewed on a day-to-day basis.

Japan's extending the hand of friendship towards Germany was partly motivated by admiration for the success of the revisionist fascist powers and the opportunity that success provided for it to exploit the weakness of the British, Dutch and French to defend their Far Eastern colonies. Equally important, however, was the hope that it might deter American 'meddling' in the Pacific (if she viewed the German threat in the Atlantic as her first priority) and the need to deter Soviet aggression by threatening the USSR with a war on two fronts, particularly after Japanese-Soviet clashes on the borders of Outer Mongolia borders in 1935 and the so-called Changkufeng incident of July 1938 which escalated into a full-scale conflict between Japan and the USSR on the heights of Nomonhan in August 1939, and resulted in 90,000 Japanese casualties (80,000 military and 10,000 civilian) before an armistice was signed on 15 September 1939 (allowing the Soviets to invade eastern Poland two days later, in line with the secret provisions of the Nazi–Soviet Non-Aggression Pact).

The fall of France in June 1940 radically improved Japan's prospects insofar as Germany was henceforth able to exert pressure upon Vichy France to allow Japan to station her troops in key towns in northern Indo-China; build airfields for use against the Chinese nationalists; and close the Haiphong–Kunning railway. Moreover, on 18 July 1940, Churchill agreed to close the Burma Road for three months and help Japan in negotiations with Chiang Kai-shek, after the Chiefs-of-Staff told him that the overriding consideration was to avoid war with Japan. The Burmese and Indo-Chinese borders with China through which outside aid had flowed into southwestern China, the stronghold of resistance to Japan, were now both sealed and the more optimistic elements within the Japanese military thus calculated that victory in China was now within sight.

On the very same day that the closure of the Burma Road was announced – 18 July 1940 – the triumph of the military over the civilians in Japanese politics was symbolised by the creation of the second Konoe cabinet, with General Hideki Tojo (former Chief-of-Staff of the Kwantung army) as war minister, Zengo Yoshida as navy minister and Yosuke Matsuoka (who had taken Japan out of the League in 1933) as foreign minister.

Among its first acts was the announcement, on 26 July, of the aim of creating the 'Greater East Asia Co-Prosperity Sphere', while the militarily dominated Liaison Committee decided on the following day that differences with the Soviet Union should be settled; steps should be taken to move closer to Germany and Italy; bases should be obtained in French Indo-China with a view to cutting Chiang Kai-shek's supply lines; pressure should be applied to obtain more oil, rubber and tin from the Dutch East Indies, and preparations should be made for war with the Anglo-Saxon powers.

With the European imperial powers clearly in no position to break the tightening and seemingly terminal Japanese stranglehold upon China with which America claimed its own long-standing special commercial relationship, the US State Department warned Tokyo against any further move into Indo-China, and on 25 July 1940 Roosevelt signed the order, which came into effect the following day, embargoing high-grade, high-octane aviation fuel. This was a gesture that caused Tokyo a little inconvenience – forcing her to switch to the purchase of middle-octane fuel – rather than obliging her to re-think her foreign policy. Instead she pushed ahead with the objectives outlined by the Liaison Committee, and on 22 September 1940, in return for recognition of French sovereignty over Indo-China, Vichy France agreed to allow Japan use three airfields in Tonkin province; to station her troops there; and to have free passage for her troops through Tonkin province to attack the Chinese in Yunnan.

Roosevelt responded by announcing increased loans to China and by extending sanctions on Japan through the export licensing system. Goods affected included machine tools, certain chemicals and metal products, with the result that 'by the spring of 1941 her industry was suffering from shortages of supplies, stockpiles were exhausted and the production of key items were being impeded'.[6] Roosevelt said that in his policy of sanctions he aimed to 'slip a noose around Japan's neck and give it a jerk now and then'.[7]

However, this action merely confirmed the Japanese in their intention of cementing their relations with Hitler's Germany and Mussolini's Italy, and on 27 September 1940 Japan signed the Tripartite Pact or Rome–Berlin–Tokyo Axis which promised mutual support, with all political, economic and military means to any member who was attacked *either openly or in a concealed form* by a power not involved in the European or Sino-Japanese wars.

Thus fortified diplomatically, Japanese troops landed in Indo-China following the aforementioned 'invitation' from Vichy France. By the summer of 1941 these forces were sufficiently well established so as to venture southwards, their rear being protected by a non-aggression pact with Moscow signed earlier that month (the Soviet–Japanese Neutrality Pact of 13 April 1941).

This effective takeover of Indo-China in violation of Washington's warnings regarding such a course of action and posing a direct threat to the security of the Dutch East Indies and the Philippines (now within striking range of Japan's strategic bomber force) provoked the final breakdown in Japanese-American relations. On 17 June 1941, Anglo-American pressure was instrumental in bringing about the breakdown of Japanese attempts to increase her supplies from the Dutch East Indies, and three days later the United States prohibited the export of oil from Atlantic and Gulf Coast ports to countries other than Britain and the Latin American states. On 26 July 1941, all Japanese assets in the United States were frozen and a de facto oil embargo took effect, bringing about virtually a complete cessation of trade between the two countries.

This represented an extremely serious threat to Japan at a time when 78 per cent of its steel and 80 per cent of its oil came from America or American-controlled sources. The fact that Britain and its Dominions and the Dutch East Indies had followed the United States lead meant that Japan, using oil at the rate of 12,000 tons daily, had reserves of crude and refined oil products roughly equivalent to the demand for 18 months. Strenuous efforts since 1937 to produce synthetic oil did not materially affect this situation. Thus a time bomb had been placed under Japanese policymakers and they knew that the longer they delayed the less capable Japan would be of fighting and winning a war to conquer the resources which she had been denied.

On 26 November 1941, US Secretary of State Cordell Hull called upon Japan to withdraw all military, naval, air and police forces from China and Indo-China if it wished to see these sanctions lifted, with Japanese assets in America "defrozen" and the two countries entering into a new commercial treaty on the basis of the principle of most-favoured-nation treatment.

In Tokyo the reference to 'China' in Hull's ultimatum was thought to include Manchukuo (as Manchuria had been renamed). That is to say, the Japanese were apparently being asked to give up all the hard-won gains they had made since 1931 or even earlier. In the Cairo Declaration of 1943, the United States, Britain and China dated Japanese aggression towards China not from 1931 but from 1894 and accordingly demanded the restoration to China of Taiwan and the Pescadores, and in the San Francisco Peace Treaty of 1951, Japan had to forfeit to China and Russia all territories seized since 1895. This broad interpretation of Japanese aggression was anticipated by Japan's civilian ministers when they agreed with their military counterparts on 1 December 1941, at a meeting at the Imperial Palace in Tokyo, that there was no honourable alternative to war with the United States for, 'If we give in, we surrender at one stroke what we won in the Sino-Japanese and the Russo-Japanese wars as well as the Manchurian Incident. We cannot do this'.[8]

Thus rather than suffer this dishonour and the emasculation of Japan's empire, with all of the adverse consequences this would have had for her future prosperity and security, the Japanese decided to cripple the American Pacific Fleet at Pearl Harbor and take the oil which they desperately needed (notwithstanding stockpiling and the production of synthetic oil) from the Dutch East Indies.

Reasoning that war was inevitable, the Japanese calculated that the sooner it began the better and that they should strike a decisive first blow at the very heart of American military power in the Pacific. 'In this sense, the surprise attack on Pearl Harbor was not surprising'.[9]

Some of the Japanese, at least, recognised that this as a gigantic gamble, given the relative size and potential of the economies of the two countries, with Japan at this time having a per-capita income that was one-tenth that of America's. Admiral Isoruku Yamamoto, as a graduate of Harvard and former naval attaché in Washington certainly had first hand experience of American industrial power, stating that 'Anyone who has seen the auto factories of Detroit and the oil fields in Texas knows that Japan lacks the national power for a naval race with America'.[10]

However, Hitler's launching of Operation Barbarossa on 22 June 1941 had removed any threat to Japan from the Soviet Union for the foreseeable future, the British had virtually stripped their Far Eastern defences to the bone in order to bolster their forces in the Mediterranean, and the Americans had boxed the Japanese into a corner in which the only honourable course was to come out fighting. Moreover, it was calculated that if the bulk of the US Pacific fleet was destroyed, then the Japanese would have a virtual free hand for six months to extend and entrench themselves to such an extent that the Americans might well balk at the blood that would have to be shed in order to dislodge them. In short, Japan's leaders believed that a nation's strength lay primarily in its spirit, and that the purity of the Yamato (Japanese) race gave them a moral or spiritual superiority to offset the undoubted materiel superiority of the United States.

Hence the Japanese attack upon Pearl Harbor in Hawaii on 7 December 1941.

How World War Two became truly global

It is still necessary to explain why Germany and Italy declared war on the United States on 11 December 1941, thereby uniting both the Pacific and European wars.

There is no difficulty in explaining Italy's action. Having been bailed out by Germany in North Africa and Greece, Mussolini had no real choice by this stage of the war but to do what Hitler wanted.

Hitler's decision to declare war on the United States is more difficult to understand. It is true that Germany, Italy and Japan were allies under the terms of the Tripartite Pact of 1940 but this was a defensive alliance committing each power to come to the aid of their allies if they were attacked. At Pearl Harbor Japan was the aggressor, and thus Germany was not obliged to enter the war against the United States – not that Hitler was in any case noted for honouring his treaty obligations.

Why then did Hitler declare war on the United States?

It may be that he was aiming for global domination and realised that in order to achieve this there would have to be a day of reckoning with the United States, sooner or later. He certainly viewed the United States with contempt as a multi-racial democracy with a strong Jewish and Negroid component.

However, the more immediate reason for Hitler's declaring war on the United States was resentment at the way in which the United States had bent over backwards to assist Britain's continued resistance to Nazi Germany after the Battle of Britain had ensured Britain's survival. Once Russia had survived the first onslaught of Operation Barbarossa, Roosevelt had similarly provided assistance to the USSR. Indeed, Hitler probably felt that he was already effectively at war with the United States and that his declaration of war merely formalised this state of affairs.

The long list of specific American actions which annoyed Germany included the freezing of Danish and Norwegian funds in the United States following Nazi occupation; the 'bases for destroyers' deal'; the Lend–Lease Act (which Stimson stated was 'a declaration of economic war'[11] and Carr describes as 'an act … which transformed the status of the United States from that of a non-belligerent to that of a quasi-belligerent'[12]); extending the Neutrality Zone eastwards to include the whole of Greenland and the Azores; taking Greenland under US protection; requisitioning Axis and Danish merchant vessels in American ports and pressing them into service in the Atlantic; removing the Red Sea from the list of combat areas forbidden to US shipping so as to allow American merchantmen to supply British forces in the Middle East; ordering American vessels to escort convoys in the Neutrality Zone in June 1941; occupying Iceland in July 1941 and ordering US navy vessels escorting American and Icelandic shipping to Iceland to destroy threatening vessels; unfreezing Russian assets and then allowing Russia to purchase war materials in August 1941; agreeing to escort British merchantmen as far as Iceland in September 1941; revising the Neutrality Act to allow American merchantmen to enter combat zones and carry war materials directly to friendly ports; and extending Lend–Lease to Russia in early November 1941.

When Japan struck against America at Pearl Harbor on 7 December 1941, Hitler may have believed that it had delivered a knock-out blow against the United States. At the very least he probably calculated that America was likely to be tied down in the Pacific and that an all-out U-boat offensive in the Atlantic might starve Britain into submission.

Thus on 11 December 1941 Germany and Italy declared war on the United States and the European war was transformed into a truly global one.

Japan's tragedy was that she learnt the lessons of the West only too well. She created a formidable fleet, using the Royal Navy as her template, and an efficient modern army, modelled on that of Germany, but when she sought to use these instruments to conquer colonies comparable to those carved out by the Western powers in the Pacific, in order to protect her economy, she discovered the true Anglo-Saxon gift for hypocrisy. Thus one has the irony of the archetypal racist Hitler being willing to encourage Japanese expansion for geopolitical reasons while the supposedly enlightened and principled Western forces who opposed Nazism provoked Japan into war, in part, because their treatment of her was based upon racist assumptions.

From Pearl Harbor to Midway

The attack on Pearl Harbor inflicted serious damage on the US Pacific fleet, sinking or seriously damaging six battleships and eight other ships and destroying almost 200 planes. Pearl Harbor did not, however, destroy the US Pacific fleet because its aircraft-carriers were fortuitously at sea. Nevertheless, the blow struck there and the speed and surprise that characterised simultaneous attacks elsewhere in the Pacific saw the Japanese enjoy a series of runaway successes. Thus by the end of 1941, Japanese Imperial forces had taken Guam (8 December), Wake Island (23 December) and Hong Kong (25 December). Moreover, in the Philippines, Douglas MacArthur had been forced to fall back on the Bataan peninsula on the north side of Manila Bay, and the battleship *HMS Prince of Wales* and the battle cruiser *Repulse* had been destroyed from the air (10 December 1941). Even greater humiliation for the British was to come in the new year when Japanese troops moved down the Malayan peninsula and forced the surrender at

Singapore of a recently reinforced British Empire and Commonwealth garrison of 130,000: twice the size of the invading force
(15 February).

Allied naval forces defending Java were destroyed in the Battle
of the Java Sea on 24 February, and the Dutch East Indies surrendered on 8 March. By 6 May 1942, the Philippines had fallen
(after island fortress of Corregidor in Manila Bay finally succumbed) and the British had undertaken the longest retreat in
their military history of 600 miles in Burma, so that the Japanese
were knocking on the door of British India.

The Japanese had thus secured their outer defensive perimeter,
which would be consolidated in the expectation that the Allies
would lack the stomach to submit to the casualties required to
dislodge them. In naval terms, the Japanese certainly appeared to
hold the advantage for although the Allies retained control of
Midway and Hawaii, their naval losses had been substantial while
the Japanese navy was intact.

The Battles of the Coral Sea (7–8 May) and, even more obviously, Midway (4–6 June) decisively altered this balance in favour of
America and its allies. The latter came about because the Doolittle
Raid launched on Tokyo from carrier-based planes at extreme long
range, which was more a gesture of defiance than of any military
significance, originated from the Midway area and this affront to
the Emperor allowed Yamamoto and the Combined Fleet, who
wished to provoke a decisive engagement with America's carrier
fleet by mounting an invasion of Midway, to overcome the Naval
General Staff, who would have preferred to capture more territory
in New Guinea, the Solomons and New Caledonia, from which to
threaten Australia. All four Japanese aircraft carriers – *Akagi*, *Hiryu*,
Kaga, and *Sorya* – were destroyed at Midway while the United
States just lost the *Yorktown*. Moreover, the United States could
make good its losses much more readily than Japan. Thus between
1942 and 1944 the Americans launched 14 fleet carriers to Japan's
six. Thus Midway manifestly forced Japan onto the defensive.

From Midway to Hiroshima

The American grand strategic offensive in the Pacific represented
an uneasy compromise between the rival claims of the army, represented by MacArthur, and the navy, represented by Chester

Nimitz. In the summer of 1942, it was decided that as the first step in the strategy of 'island hopping' (bypassing strong Japanese garrisons, but taking key islands as stepping stones across the Pacific towards the Japanese home islands) the latter should take Guadalcanal in the Solomons group of islands, east of New Guinea, while the former would clear New Guinea. By 9 February Guadalcanal was firmly in American hands but at the cost of 22,000 Japanese killed or missing to a little over 1000 Marines killed: an early indication of the very heavy losses which Japanese defenders were prepared to suffer.

The spring of 1942 saw two further blows inflicted upon the Japanese: at the Battle of the Bismarck Sea, US bombers sank all the transports of the 51st Division and four of the eight destroyer escorts, and utilising signals intelligence Yamamoto was ambushed and killed in mid-air. This was the most dramatic result of American superiority in signals intelligence which was an important factor throughout the Pacific war.

MacArthur's victory in Papua removed the immediate Japanese threat to Australia and cleared the way for advance through the Solomon and Bismarck archipelagos towards the Philippines. In April 1943, inter-service rivalries were addressed once again and it was decided to make Nimitz theatre commander for the whole Pacific, with Admiral William Halsey operating in the South Pacific (enveloping Rabaul from the north, via the Solomons and Bougainville) while MacArthur ranged over the South–West Pacific (enveloping Rabaul from the south, via New Guinea and the southern Bismarcks).

The fall of Tarawa in the Gilberts opened the way to the Marshalls, which in turn opened the way to the Marianas, including Saipan, Tinian and Guam. In the 'Great Marianas Turkey Shoot' of 19 June 1944, the Japanese lost 243 of their 373 Japanese aircraft, for the loss of just 29 American planes, while the Battle of the Philippine Sea halved the operational strength of the Japanese carrier force. Moreover, these islands brought the Japanese home islands within range of B-29 Superfortress bombers. They proceeded to launch a series of raids upon Japan using firebombs with devastating results. On the night of 9–10 March 1945 alone almost 85,000 were killed in one raid on Tokyo.

Okinawa represented the final stepping-stone before Japan itself. The cost of taking the island (7613 Americans killed or missing in action and 31,800 wounded, and Japanese casualties estimated at over 142,000) made many blanche at the prospect of similar operations against the Japanese home islands. That prospect was removed by the use of the atom bombs at Hiroshima and Nagasaki – and by Soviet entry into the Pacific war.

The nuclear option

Nuclear weapons were originally developed because it was feared that Hitler might procure them. If he did he would obviously have no qualms about using them and the only deterrent might be the fear of Allied retaliation (just as he seems to have vetoed the use of poison gas out of a calculation that the Allies might be able to hit back with even greater effect). In the event, however, Germany was defeated before the Manhattan Project successfully developed the Bomb and it was deployed instead against Japan.

The key question regarding Truman's decision to use the Bomb is whether he was motivated purely by military considerations – ending the war as quickly as possible with minimal loss of American lives – or whether he was also motivated by political considerations, specifically the desire to influence the Soviets so as to render them more co-operative, particularly in Europe where to some they appeared to be riding roughshod over what had been agreed between the Big Three at Yalta.

There is always friction between allies, and the strains in the wartime Grand Alliance were increasingly perceptible and serious as the coalition had only come into being and been sustained by Hitler. Once Germany's defeat appeared certain the Big Three powers reverted to policies which brought them into conflict with one another. In order to appreciate whether Truman used the Bomb as a form of leverage over the Soviet Union, it is worth examining all the sources of Soviet leverage over its Western allies and vice versa.

Soviet leverage over the Western allies was sixfold. First and foremost there was the sheer size and strength of the Red Army. Whereas the armies of the democracies would tend to 'melt away' as their governments came under increasing pressure to demobilise and 'send the boys home', the Red Army could be maintained for the foreseeable future in possession of 'liberated' territories in Central and Eastern Europe. Moreover, the sacrifices of the

Red Army and of the Russian people in general – sacrifices which dwarfed those of their Western allies – provided the Soviet Union with an enormous stock of goodwill and moral capital, at least among the peoples of the states with which they had been allies. The Red Army was also valued as a force which might enter and help end the Pacific War. Indeed, Stalin had largely been able to 'purchase' Allied recognition of effective post-war Soviet domination of Eastern Europe through prospective military help against Japan, which was first discussed at Teheran in 1943 and was then firmly pledged at Yalta and Potsdam so as to come into effect three months after Germany's defeat. Another Soviet source of leverage with the West arising out of its position in Asia was its ability to grant or withhold recognition of Chiang Kai-shek's regime in China. Thus Soviet concessions at Yalta included the negotiation of a 'pact of friendship and alliance' between Moscow and the Chinese nationalist government. Similarly the Soviets could facilitate or delay the access of its allies to Soviet-occupied territory to evacuate their POWs, and could choose whether or not to accede to American wishes for its participation in the United Nations Organization (UNO).

Anglo-American leverage over the USSR, by contrast, prior to the Bomb centred upon the ability to deliver or delay a Second Front and to provide aid, in the form of Lease–Lend or a post-war loan.

Even before D-Day on 6 June 1944, the first source of leverage was effectively renounced in November 1943 when Churchill and Roosevelt made a firm commitment to Stalin to open a Second Front in May–June 1944 in order to help gain the Soviet commitment to enter the war against Japan.

On 12 May 1945 (four days after VE Day) the Truman administration cut back lend–lease to all nations, including the USSR. However, the action in relation to the USSR accidentally appeared especially harsh as ships carrying lend–lease materials on board already en route to Russia were recalled.[13] However, dollar diplomacy had its limits as the conditions which America wished to attach to any financial aid entailed a political cost which the Soviet Union simply refused to pay.

This left the West with two remaining sources of leverage, namely, recognition of the new regimes of Soviet-liberated Eastern Europe and the possibility of Allied military penetration into

Central Europe. Churchill was keen for Eisenhower to push as far east as quickly as possible. Ideally he would have preferred to see Anglo-American forces rather than the Red Army take Berlin, Vienna and Prague, and would have extracted whatever advantage could be gained from trading land which had formally already been ceded to the Soviets. However, Eisenhower refused to act on Churchill's advice, claiming that a more cautious advance which consolidated control of the Ruhr would expose the Allied flanks to less threat of German counter-attacks, would generally result in the loss of fewer lives of American soldiers, and would avoid the risk of arousing Soviet distrust or even provoking hostilities.

The Soviet desire for recognition of their client states in Eastern Europe represented more than just a paradoxical desire for respect from the capitalist states which had shunned them for so long. By getting the West to accept the redrawn boundaries and questionable regimes of their puppet regimes, Moscow would confer legitimacy upon them in such a way as to undermine any indigenous resistance movements which might otherwise cling to the hope of Western support. However, this leverage could only be exercised up to a point and was lost in relation to Poland – the most symbolically sensitive of cases – when the British and US governments recognised the Warsaw government on 5 July 1945.

In general, then, the leverage of the Western allies over the Soviet Union was relatively slight, and was greatest in the early stages of the war on the Eastern Front. However, the Americans were reluctant to use what little leverage they had because they felt the need to win or recapture Soviet trust, especially given the delay in opening the Second Front and the gross disparity between the blood sacrifices made by the Soviet Union on the one hand, and its allies on the other. They also feared the possibility of the Soviets making a separate peace with Germany, in the light of the Treaty of Brest–Litovsk of March 1918 and the Nazi–Soviet Non-Aggression Pact of August 1939, and felt they needed Soviet help to finish off Japan.

It is in this context that the development of atomic weapons appeared to be a godsend for Truman, seemingly cancelling out the Soviet superiority in conventional military terms and providing the Americans with unrivalled power to get their own way by providing them with an unbeatable trump card.

Gar Alperovitz, the doyen of revisionist historians regarding the claim that Truman engaged in 'atomic diplomacy', claims that well before the Bomb was used it had a very significant impact on American diplomacy towards the Soviet Union.[14] More specifically it is argued that any showdown over Poland was deliberately delayed by Truman in the hope that the Bomb could be used as a master card. Conversely, the Bomb was used against the Japanese at Hiroshima not, as Truman claimed, 'to shorten the agony of war' and 'to save the lives of thousands and thousands of young Americans',[15] but rather in an effort to end the Pacific War before the Soviet Union entered it and to force Soviet concessions elsewhere (principally over Poland as the major issue then in contention between the superpowers).

There is certainly evidence to show that informed military and political opinion at the highest levels within the American establishment regarded use of the Bomb as unnecessary if the intention was merely to bring about the swift defeat of Japan. There was a range of alternative military and diplomatic means available in the pursuit of that policy. By the summer of 1945, Japan had lost control of the seas, as symbolised by the sinking in April of the *Yamoto* – Japan's last battleship – with its full complement of 3600 men. It had also lost command of the air, and American airfields on Guam and Tinian had brought all of Japan within bombing range. Thus Japan's cities were being systematically destroyed by conventional means, not least because the United States Army Air Force practised indiscriminate area bombing against the Japanese rather than the precision bombing which it had employed against their European allies.

One option was thus to continue the rain of destruction from the air and maintain the blockade of Japan until its people were bombed or starved into submission. Such a policy would risk the lives of fewer American servicemen than the projected D-Day style invasion of the Japanese home islands but would be so time consuming that it would inevitably result in Soviet entry into the Pacific War and thus do nothing to forestall subsequent Soviet gains. There are disputes as to just how costly a landing on the Japanese islands would have been but there was every reason to suppose that the cost in Allied – and Japanese – lives would have been very high indeed, as Japanese resistance seemed to increase in fanaticism the closer the Allies approached to the Japanese homeland. When the battle for Okinawa ended on 21 June 1945, for example, the Americans had suffered 72,000 casualties, compared to 131,303 Japanese military and 150,000 civilian casualties.

However, in the light of setbacks such as the fall of Saipan and Iwo Jima, certain elements within Japan's governing circles appreciated that defeat was inevitable and set out to explore the means by which they might secure most honourable peace which they could manage. To this end, Emperor Hirohito in early June had approved the suggestion of his Lord Privy Seal, Marquis Kido, to open peace negotiations via the Soviet Union – then still a neutral power in the Pacific. In return for their good offices in mediating an end to the war the Soviets would receive concessions in Manchuria and trade concessions. Kido and Prime Minister Suzuki, who had entered that post shortly before Truman became President, agreed on the need to end the war but saw this as prevented by the military, who claimed to be acting on behalf of the Emperor.

On 12 July 1945 Kido asked the Emperor's cousin, Prince Konoye, to go to Moscow on a State visit as the Emperor's personal envoy, conveying the message that Japan was willing to consider anything short of unconditional surrender, as long as the Emperor stays in place. Soundings were also made via Switzerland and Sweden (and were also known to the Americans). In part these avenues were explored because Konoye was sceptical of relying upon the Soviets. He was right to do so, as Stalin studiously avoided receiving him for as long as possible.

The Japanese were, of course, unaware of Stalin's promise to enter the war against Japan three months after the defeat of Germany, and there is some reason to suppose that the shock of Soviet entry into the war, destroying any vestigial hope of securing a negotiated peace, might itself have been sufficient to secure Japanese surrender. In short, even before the Red Army swept through Manchuria and Korea, the mere declaration of war by Stalin might have administered a psychological blow strong enough to give the initiative to the peace party within Japanese imperial counsels.

The existence of that peace party and their fumbling efforts to secure diplomatic assistance from the Soviets was apparent to the Americans through the success of their signals intelligence service in intercepting and decoding Japanese messages. Acting Secretary of State Joseph Grew, a former ambassador to Tokyo, was also able to enlighten Truman on the greatest stumbling obstacle to unconditional surrender by the Japanese, namely, their fear that their Emperor or Mikado, whom they regarded as a divine personage, would be displaced and the dynasty or even the institution itself destroyed. If the demand for unconditional surrender could be modified in such a way as to reassure them that this would not be the case then it might speed the end of the war, saving American lives and avoiding the risk of Soviet influence expanding in the region. If peace could have been obtained by these means, then the use of the Bomb, it is argued must have been designed to meet political objectives regarding the Soviets as much as, or even more than, military objectives regarding the Japanese.

Harry S. Truman had been Vice-President for less than three months during which time he had not attended Cabinet meetings nor been present during meetings with other heads of state. He was really unprepared for the job of stepping into Roosevelt's shoes on 12 April 1945 having not been at Yalta and knowing nothing about the development of the Bomb. Moreover, Truman was among those who revered Roosevelt as a giant of the domestic and world political stage. Not unnaturally in the circumstances, therefore, Truman suffered considerable doubt as to whether he was up to the task of leading America. The atom bomb would appear to have been the answer to his prayers.

Truman was informed of the Manhattan Project by Secretary of War Henry Stimson on 25 April, within a fortnight of entering the White House, and was told then that the weapon might be operational within four months. With American and Soviet troops having met at the River Elbe, the European war was as good as over and if the Bomb were to be used in combat it would therefore be used against the Japanese.

Truman was told that America would initially have just three atomic bombs. One was a uranium bomb and would be triggered by conventional means but the others were plutonium bombs and would require a new form of triggering through implosion. Hence the need to use one of these bombs to test the device. The earliest such a test could take place was July.

If it worked it might not only deliver a shattering blow to the Japanese comparable to or even greater than Soviet entry into the

Pacific War, enabling them to feel that they could surrender without losing face, but might also facilitate negotiations with the Soviets as they might be awed by American military power and accordingly be prepared to make concessions, perhaps in return for being allowed to share in nuclear secrets or seeing some international atomic agency created so that America's nuclear monopoly was ended. Stimson successfully suggested to Truman the creation of what became the Interim Committee to offer advice to the President after considering the use of the weapon.

The first meeting of the Interim Committee took place in Washington, DC on 9 May. Stimson summarised the conflicting and predictable preferences of the US military for dealing with Japan, with the army in favour of an invasion of the home islands, the navy opting for blockade, and the air force supporting conventional bombing. Byrnes intervened to state his belief that the Committee had not been set up to decide between these options but rather to report on the best possible use of the Bomb. He accordingly listed the options as follows:

(1) dropping the Bomb on a military target as part of an invasion
(2) a demonstration of the Bomb to Japanese observers
(3) a demonstration of the Bomb on a military target (such as Japanese naval vessels at anchor)
(4) hitting a 'mixed target' – which is to say a city with military installations – with prior warning
(5) hitting a 'mixed target', with no prior warning.

The latter choice might well, it was argued, scare Japan into surrender and would therefore mean that the United States owed the Russians nothing (if this could be accomplished before they entered the Pacific War). The fatal problem with either form of demonstration was that the Bomb might not work or even if it did, the Japanese might not be sufficiently impressed.

At the penultimate meeting of the Interim Committee on 31 May 1945, the scientists Oppenheimer, Fermi and Lawrence argued in favour of a demonstration of the Bomb, with the Soviets invited to the test. Byrnes and Groves opposed, arguing that not only might such a test backfire but that it would certainly remove any element of shock or surprise (on the Soviets as well as the Japanese). Moreover, if a warning was given, Japanese inhabitants could be evacuated from likely targets and American POWs brought in. In the event the Committee unanimously recommended that the Bomb be used as soon as possible against Japan, without warning, against war plant surrounded by workers' houses or other buildings susceptible to damage in order to maximise the impression caused by the blast (with the Soviets doubtless being impressed as well as the Japanese).

According to Alperovitz,[16] Truman appreciated that the atom bomb represented a potential master card in his dealings with the Soviets and thus delayed a showdown with Stalin in the hope that his hand in any future negotiations would be immeasurably strengthened if the Bomb could be shown to work and, better still, if America had demonstrated its willingness to use it militarily. The implication is that Truman did not want to see the Pacific War ended other than by dropping the Bomb, for example, by modifying the demand for unconditional surrender, as this would not allow the United States to impress upon Stalin the desirability of his making concessions to his ally.

It is true that Churchill, who was unaware of the detailed progress of the Manhattan Project, was trying to persuade Truman, from at least 11 May, to agree to a summit with Stalin and himself as soon as possible, as he considered the current deadlock over Poland critical and only likely to be resolved by a meeting of the three heads of government, preferably in some symbolically suitable shattered German city.

Churchill was concerned to expedite such a meeting as the redeployment of forces from the European to the Pacific theatres seemed to be weakening the American military presence in Europe far more than that of the Soviets, so that Stalin might have a vested interest in playing for time, postponing a tripartite meeting so as to accentuate that process and leave him effectively master of the continent. Churchill thus advocated a meeting of the Big Three for 15 June but Truman suggested 15 July on the grounds that domestic considerations required his presence in Washington until the end of the fiscal year in June.

This sounds dubious but it is worth bearing in mind three considerations which suggest that perhaps Truman should be given the benefit of the doubt. Firstly, Roosevelt had made similar noises in relation to Yalta for reasons which clearly cannot be linked with the development of the Bomb. Thus while Churchill urged a Big

Three summit for late November 1944 Roosevelt cabled him that, 'a meeting of the three of us just now may be a little less valuable than it would be after I am inaugurated'[17] and he wrote to Stalin to express his 'great hesitation in leaving here while my old Congress is in its final days'.[18] Secondly, it seems likely that Truman, having unexpectedly become President on 12 April 1945 needed all the time at his disposal to get up to speed on the home front as well as being briefed on international affairs before meeting Stalin face to face, especially if he felt that 'Uncle Joe' had managed to outmanoeuvre Roosevelt at Yalta despite FDR's delaying the summit until February 1945. Thirdly, one should not forget that the Bomb had still not been tested before the Potsdam conference opened. News of the successful Trinity Test at Alamagordo in the New Mexico desert, which actually exceeded expectations, was received by Truman on 16 July in the course of the negotiations. In other words, if he did delay the meeting to be sure of his trump card, he had still been obliged to gamble, opening the bidding with a hand that might have turned out to be a busted flush rather than promise a grand slam.

In the scenario presented by Alperovitz, the evil genius of atomic diplomacy is, however, not so much the new boy Truman as his Special Adviser turned Secretary of State (and effective Vice-President), James Byrnes, who had been present at Yalta and who dominated the Interim Committee set up to advise the President on the use of the Bomb. Byrnes believed, it is alleged, that the Bomb would enable America to dictate its own terms to the Russians by redressing the balance of power in Eastern Europe. For this reason Byrnes supposedly convinced the President not to give Japan reassurances about the Emperor because he wanted to ensure that Japan did not surrender 'prematurely' before the Bomb could be used to give America crucial leverage over the Soviet Union.

The machiavellian picture of Byrnes draws particularly on his 28 May meeting (when Secretary of State designate) with scientists Leo Szilard, Harold Urey and Walter Bartky at Spartanburg, North Carolina, just four days before the penultimate meeting of the Interim Committee. Szilard expressed the view that America had been wrong to start a nuclear arms race with Nazi Germany as it was now known that they had not even been close to getting the Bomb, and warned that if the Bomb was used against Japan it would provoke an atomic arms race with the USSR which might ultimately lead to the annihilation of the entire human race. Whereas General Groves (the military head of the Manhattan Project) had told Byrnes that the USSR would not have the Bomb for 20 years, Szilard estimated (much more correctly as it turned out) that the American nuclear monopoly might last just five years, as the real secret is that it can be done and that as soon as the USSR knew it to be feasible they would make available the necessary resources in order to engage in production. Byrnes sought to counter these arguments by pointing out that the United States had already expended $2 billion on the project and by arguing that if America impressed upon Russia the fact that they had the Bomb and were willing to use it, then it might prevent Russia from gobbling up countries like Szilard's homeland, Hungary (which the Red Army had entered as 'liberators' in 1944). Szilard remained unconvinced and was at the forefront of the protest by nuclear physicists against the Bomb. There is no record, however, of Byrnes having drawn Truman's attention to the reservations of Szilard and those like him.

Already on 12 June 1945 potential Japanese targets had been canvassed in the Map Room of the White House. They were all supposedly military targets and none had previously been damaged by conventional bombing. Stimson fiercely objected to the inclusion of Kyoto on the list because of the city's cultural and religious significance to the Japanese. For Groves, however, this was precisely why it should be the primary target: the shock to the Japanese would be all the greater.

When Churchill heard of the Bomb from Truman he expressed the view that the Bomb should be dropped on a Japanese city to end the war. Admiral Leahy shrewdly wondered whether Churchill was less concerned with the Bomb ending the war than in removing the need to move more US troops out of Europe to the Pacific and thereby weakening the position of the 'West' in relation to the Red Army.

When Stalin was obliquely informed of the Bomb by Truman at the end of an afternoon session at Potsdam, his reaction was so matter of fact that Truman wondered if he had misunderstood. In fact, Stalin already knew of the Bomb from spies like Klaus Fuchs and had known about the Manhattan Project long before Truman.

Stimson privately informed Truman and Byrnes that the Japanese peace party had communicated to their representatives in Moscow, their heartfelt desire for the swift termination of the war, so long as they are allowed to keep their Emperor. Byrnes, however, opposed acting on this information, preferring to drop the Bomb without warning, ostensibly in order to convince the more recalcitrant Japanese policymakers of the need to surrender unconditionally. Truman was placed under pressure to come to make up his mind over the use of the Bomb by a telegram from Groves informing him that delivery of the bombs was possible from 1 August and calling upon him to make a final decision.

Truman accordingly approved use of the weapon against Japan when it was ready but no sooner than 2 August. On 16 July the components for the 'Little Boy' uranium atomic bomb were loaded aboard the *USS Indianapolis*, in San Francisco, which sailed for Tinian: the home of the 509th B29 bomber group. Ten days later 'Little Boy' was unloaded. Its plutonium counterpart, 'Fat Man', arrived by plane.

Stimson was somewhat pacified by being told that Kyoto had been firmly declared off limits, in deference to his advice, and by being informed that the Japanese were to be offered a final chance to surrender and thereby avert nuclear attack in the form of the Potsdam Declaration, the text of which was both broadcast and dropped over Japan in leaflet form. However, Russia was not a signatory to the Declaration nor did it make explicit reference to America's possession of the Bomb. Hardliners within the Japanese military could, therefore, still dream of inflicting massive casualties on any invasion party in order to improve Japan's negotiating position through Russian intermediaries.

On 28 July the Japanese cabinet met to discuss the Potsdam Declaration. Anami and the military favoured its outright rejection. General Umezu, the Chief-of-Staff, spoke of the threat to morale and the threat of revolution if the Declaration was not rejected. Togo, nevertheless, advised a positive response.

Suzuki wished to sound firm for the sake of the military while still allowing room for diplomatic manoeuvre. Accordingly at a press conference later that day he referred to the Potsdam Declaration as a rehash of the Cairo Declaration and said 'we *mokusatsu* it'. Truman was informed later that day by a German expert in the Japanese language that this phrase literally meant 'to kill with silence' but could also signify, to those of a certain age and class, a willingness to negotiate while wishing to be seen to be treating the declaration with silent contempt. Such subtleties were either beyond Truman or he chose to ignore them, and merely voiced to his intimates his desire to be away from Potsdam (and Stalin) when the Bomb went off. News on 2 August 1945 of the sinking of the Indianoplis after it had unloaded the Bomb on Tinian and was heading towards Guam, merely confirmed Truman in his decision to use the Bomb to expedite the end of the war and the loss of American lives.

It is true that even Anami was facing up to eventual Japanese surrender but it is difficult to imagine how Truman could have been expected to renounce the demand for unconditional surrender and swallow the Army's conditions that the Emperor be retained; the military to be allowed to disarm itself; that Japan should not suffer an Allied occupation; and that war criminals would be prosecuted by the Japanese themselves and nobody else.

At 3.30 am on 6 August the *Enola Gay* took off, with 'Little Boy' in its modified bomb hold and Hiroshima as its primary target. At 8.15 am Japanese time the bomb was dropped and the plane banked sharply in order to escape, as far as possible, the shockwaves. Truman received the news of the successful mission in the course of his return voyage across the Atlantic, on board the *USS Augusta*. On broadcasting the news to the world he warned that if Japan's leaders 'do not now accept our terms they may expect a rain of ruin from the air the like of which has never been seen on this earth'.[19]

The Bomb did not come soon enough to forestall Soviet entry into the Pacific War as the Red Army poured into Manchuria and Korea on 9 August. Byrnes urged Truman to authorise the dropping of a second bomb in order to persuade the Japanese that they had further bombs which they were prepared to use, and to get the war over before the Soviet advance won them further concessions. Any vestigial Japanese doubts regarding America's possession of a stockpile of A bombs or their willingness to use them given the pressure of world opinion were extinguished on 9 August when a B29 dropped 'Fat Man' on Nagasaki (as poor weather had forced abandonment of the primary target of Kokura).

The Emperor now made a decisive intervention, coming down in favour of peace at an Imperial conference. In the early hours of

15 August junior officers attempted to stage a coup, trying in vain to prevent Hirohito's broadcast to the Japanese recommending capitulation.

It should never be forgotten that it took the dropping of two atomic bombs and the Soviet entry into the Pacific War before Japan surrendered. Undoubtedly Japan could have been defeated by non-atomic means but the process might well have been even more bloody and would certainly have been more prolonged. It would also thereby have strengthened the position of the Soviet Union, and it is thus difficult not to conclude that Truman and his advisers saw the Bomb as a weapon not just in the Pacific War against Japan but also in the emerging Cold War confrontation with Stalin.

10 The Second World War and the Cold War

The fundamental reason for distrust between the USA and the USSR

The Cold War is commonly defined as the state of tension and mistrust that characterised US–Soviet relations from the end of the Second World War until 1990. In fact, the Cold War had its origins long before 1939.

There are some who would argue that such mutual antagonism (and its corollary of near paranoia regarding national security) is inherent in any international relations scenario where two powers – or superpowers – confront one another. If this analysis is correct then the advent of bipolarity was a sufficient condition of Cold War and one needs to explain its appearance in terms of the decline of powers such as Great Britain. However, this is to ignore the ideological element. As a communist state dedicated to the overthrow of capitalism throughout the world, the USSR was bound to regard the United States as its arch-enemy and vice versa, given American belief in its 'manifest destiny' or civilising mission to extend the area of freedom by extending American influence. In short, the core values of the two states conflicted so completely that peaceful co-existence could only amount to an armed truce.

US–Soviet relations, 1917–41

Although allies in the fight against fascism, this was a marriage of convenience. The fact that US–Soviet relations 1941–45 should be seen as an aberration becomes clearer if one examines their history from the time of the Russian revolution.

The February 1917 revolution which saw Tsar Nicholas II and the Romanov dynasty deposed in favour of the Provisional Government was initially welcomed in the West as the new regime appeared more democratic than the old and was not only equally committed to continuation of the war against the Central Powers but initially seemed capable of prosecuting the war more effectively. However, the Bolshevik revolution of October 1917 brought to power men like Lenin who promised not only Land and Bread but Peace, and who for precisely that reason had received assistance (in the form of funds and the famous sealed train) from the German High Command.

Sure enough, in March 1918 by the Treaty of Brest–Litovsk, the USSR made a separate peace with the Central Powers, thereby placing Russia's allies in a very difficult situation insofar as the resources which the peace theoretically placed in the hands of the Central Powers would allow them to escape the ravages of the Allied blockade, while the bulk of troops engaged on the Eastern Front could now be transferred to the Western Front, providing Germany with the opportunity to launch a war-winning offensive there before the arrival of American troops across the Atlantic in large numbers tipped the balance of war irrevocably in the Allies' favour.

Furthermore, by revealing the details of secret diplomatic negotiations which were embarrassing to the West (such as the 1915 Treaty of London) the communists were able to claim the moral high ground in their effort to set the agenda for the new international order by showing that the Allies were fighting for land rather than ideals and that they had made promises that they could not keep (such as Britain's conflicting promises to the Arabs, the Jews and the French in the Middle East).

The seizure of western assets without compensation and the murder of the Russian imperial family (Nicholas and Alexandra and their children) confirmed the view of the Bolsheviks in Western diplomatic circles as barbarians, while the Soviet encouragement of revolution in the West (with the Third Communist International or Comintern, established in 1919, providing advice and funds) showed that the communist threat reached beyond the frontiers of the old Russian Empire to pose a threat of truly global proportions.

Not surprisingly, therefore, the United States and Great Britain were among those Allied powers which sent troops to Russia to intervene on the side of the anti-communist Whites in the Civil War of 1918–21. This attempt to strangle Bolshevism at birth, in which Churchill played a leading role, succeeded, however, merely in adding to the legacy of bitterness and mistrust on both sides.

Although the Soviet Union was officially recognised by the United States in 1933, this move represented a desire to stimulate trade rather than a genuine reconciliation, while the West's appeasement of Nazi Germany was interpreted in Moscow, with some justification, as signifying the desire of some in the democracies to see Hitler embroiled in war in the East at Russia's expense. Even before Hitler was appointed Chancellor, the fact that the Locarno Pact of 1925 appeared to give Germany the green light to revise its eastern frontiers was seen as evidence in the Kremlin that the West regarded a revived Germany as a bulwark against the spread of Soviet influence westwards. Such suspicions were compounded by the Anglo-French failure to ensure that the Soviets were consulted over the fate of the Sudetenland at the time of the Munich Agreement of September 1938, despite the fact that the Soviet Union had a defensive alliance with Czechoslovakia (which became operable if France stood by the Czechs).

The western democracies apparently having nothing to offer Stalin, other than the less than enticing prospect of manipulating the Soviets into a war with Germany, Stalin understandably decided to allow his Foreign Minister, Molotov, to negotiate the Nazi–Soviet Non-Aggression Pact between Germany and the USSR in August 1939. To the West, Stalin had rejected an alliance with them in favour of a cynical alliance with the Third Reich. To Stalin, secretly agreeing to carve up much of Europe with Hitler represented a means of gaining territory so that any German attack need not be fought, at least in the short term, on Russian soil.

The Soviet takeovers of eastern Poland, the Baltic States (Latvia, Lithuania and Estonia) and Bessarabia and Bukovina from Rumania were regarded in the West as aggression comparable to Hitler's attack upon western Poland. Moreover, the gallant defence of the Finns against the Soviets in the Winter War of 1939–40 aroused such strong feelings in the West that some in Britain and France seriously advocated sending military assistance even if this meant war with the Soviet Union (although this question was complicated by the desire to cut off Germany's iron ore supplies from Sweden and a desire, which was particularly strong in France, to take some military action during the Phoney War so long as it was far removed from French soil).

The launching of Operation Barbarrossa on 22 June 1941 transformed relations between the Soviet Union and the West. In Britain, and by extension America, Russia was now seen as worth backing in the fight against Hitler's Germany. When Hitler declared war on the United States four days after Pearl Harbor, the situation became even more simplified as Britain, the Soviet Union and the United States were all at war with Germany, although the Pacific and European Wars were not fully absorbed in one global conflict insofar as the Soviet Union and Japan were not yet at war with one another (and would not be so until the Soviets entered the Pacific War between the Hiroshima and Nagasaki bombs).

Wartime tensions (1): The Second Front

Stalin made a number of conciliatory gestures towards his new-found Western allies including expressing approval of the 1941 Atlantic Charter and 1945 Declaration on Liberated Europe, while in 1943 the dismantling of the Comintern in 1943, symbolised a suspension of the ideological war with the capitalist powers for the duration.

The Big Three of World War Two – Winston Churchill, Franklin D. Roosevelt and Joseph Stalin – first met at Teheran in November 1943. The conference lasted from 27 November until 1 December 1943, although much preparatory work had been done by the British, American and Soviet ministers – Eden, Hull and Molotov, respectively – and Churchill and Roosevelt had convened in Cairo en route for Teheran. The demand for the unconditional surrender of the Axis powers, which Roosevelt foisted upon Churchill, was designed to reassure Stalin that there would be no negotiated peace with Germany, as the USSR had done in March 1918 at Brest–Litovsk.

The Teheran conference of November–December 1943 marked a decisive turning point within the 'Grand Alliance'. The balance of military power within the Anglo-American alliance had shifted decisively in America's favour by this time. With British Imperial and Commonwealth forces only outnumbering American in the Italian theatre (which had opened with the invasion of Sicily in July), Roosevelt was increasingly in a position to call the shots as senior partner in the western military enterprise.

Roosevelt had over-ruled those advisers who had wished to see the defeat of Japan made a priority over that of Germany but he now backed those who wished to alter the focus of the European effort away from the Mediterranean, as favoured by the British, and towards the Western European focus favoured by the Soviets. This reflected a general move by the United States away from Britain and towards accommodating the Soviet Union because Roosevelt had no desire to be seen to be propping up the British Empire (particularly with 1944 being a presidential election year) and because he both feared that Stalin might seek a separate peace with Germany (notwithstanding the Casablanca demand for unconditional surrender) and wished to enlist Soviet support for the final assault upon Japan.

Agreement was reached at Teheran on grand strategy for 1944, with commitment to the long-anticipated and delayed opening of a Western Front in Northern France (Operation Overlord), and Stalin reciprocated by indicating that Russia would enter the war against Japan as soon as the war against Hitler had been won: a promise that was converted at Yalta in February 1945 into a firm pledge to enter the Pacific War three months after the conclusion of hostilities in Europe. Superficially this represents the most substantial concession yet made by Stalin to the Western allies but of course his assistance would come at a price. Participation in the Pacific War would enable him to regain the lands lost during the Russo-Japanese War and might even enable the Soviets to share ultimately in the military occupation of the Japanese home islands.

Teheran thus went a long way towards ending a major source of friction between the Big Three, namely, Stalin's requests for the opening of a 'second front' in Western Europe as soon as possible. Stalin had feared that this had been deliberately delayed in order to oblige the Red Army to bear the brunt of the fighting. Thus in July 1942, following Churchill's visit to Moscow, Stalin allegedly said, 'all is clear. A campaign in Africa, Italy. They simply want to be the first in reaching the Balkans. They want us to bleed white in order to dictate to us their terms later on ...'[1] Even after the opening of the Second Front, however, the Red Army engaged the bulk of Germany's armed forces and suffered accordingly.

The Mediterranean strategy

As early as December 1945 with the serialisation of Harry Butcher's *My Three Years with Eisenhower* (an edited diary of the period July 1942 to July 1945 by one of Eisenhower's aides),

Anglo-American arguments about the invasions of northern and southern France entered the public domain.[2] By April 1946, the claim that Churchill consistently pursued a Mediterranean strategy, focused on Italy and the Balkans, while the Americans tenaciously – and correctly – insisted that a cross-Channel attack provided the most direct and effective means of defeating Nazi Germany was popularised by the former Allied staff officer Ralph Ingersoll in his book *Top Secret*.[3] The charges became even weightier with the publication of Elliott Roosevelt's *As He Saw It* in 1946, when one of the sons of the former president claimed that Churchill's Mediterranean strategy was motivated by serving British imperial interests.[4] This image is now widely discredited. As Richard M. Leighton wrote in 1963, 'We now know ... that responsible British leaders never advocated an Allied invasion of the Balkan peninsula and that the "Balkans versus Western Europe" controversy referred to by many post-war writers is a myth. ... The familiar stereotype that pictures the British as persistently manoeuvring at the conference table and behind the scenes to weaken and postpone the cross-Channel invasion, while striving to build up the Mediterranean Theatre at its expense ... is not consistent with the findings of post-war research'.[5]

What follows will chart the evolution of Britain's Mediterranean strategy in some detail in order to show why it became so contentious in the historiography of the Second World War and the Cold War.

In line with historical precedent, Britain's strategy prior to the fall of France was not to force a decision on the Western Front but rather to rely upon its superior naval power and financial and imperial resources in a war of attrition. Germany's strength would be sapped by means of blockade, bombing and – after the Nazis overran most of Europe – by subversion.

Italy's jackal-like entry into the war in 1940 as France was about to fall had opened up the additional possibility of attacking Germany's ally in the Middle East. This made logistic sense, as Egypt could serve as a convenient staging post for most imperial forces. It made sense psychologically, as it provided a means of engaging directly on land with the enemy, and it made sense strategically as the Mediterranean was of vital interest to Britain, not least because of its role as route to Britain's Persian Gulf oil supplies and Far Eastern empire. Furthermore, Churchill as amateur strategist was always disposed to fighting on the flanks: a predisposition enhanced by memories of the carnage suffered on the Western Front in the First World War. Thus even before Italy invaded Greece on 28 October 1940, Britain had sought to create a Balkan League of Yugoslavia, Greece and Turkey to provide a second European front.

British aid to Greece had been insufficient to do more than delay the German advance in the Balkans and indirectly assisted the Afrika Korps insofar as the resources thrown into Greece had been taken from North Africa. The entry of the USSR and the United States into the war on Britain's side in June and December 1941, respectively, had done little at first to alter Britain's strategy of closing and tightening the ring round Germany as a means of exerting pressure upon the Third Reich and its allies, not least because the USSR's very survival had appeared to be in the balance until Stalingrad, while it would take time for American military strength to be applied across the Atlantic even if Roosevelt managed to honour his commitment to deal with Germany before Japan. America shared British doubts regarding Soviet resilience which is why provisional plans were drawn up for Operation Sledgehammer: a cross-Channel attack in 1942 if Russian collapse appeared imminent or – more fantastically – if German collapse rendered it possible. Considering the British 'ring' strategy indirect, indecisive and imperial in motivation, the United States also successfully pushed for the concentration of Anglo-American forces in the United Kingdom (Operation Bolero), in preparation for a cross-Channel invasion planned for 1943 (Operation Roundup), if Sledgehammer was not required beforehand. By mid April 1942, the British had accepted the American proposals for offensive action in Europe in 1942 possibly, and in 1943 for certain.

The alacrity with which the British agreed may have had more than a little to do with the desire to cement the 'Germany First' strategy. Certainly on reflection the British felt obliged to communicate the view that Sledgehammer was impracticable. However, Roosevelt was concerned that American forces must be put into a position to fight German ground forces somewhere in 1942 in order to relieve pressure on the Russians and pre-empt any demands for a 'Pacific First' strategy.

This was the context in which Churchill had revived the proposal for Allied landings in Vichy French North Africa: a suggestion which Roosevelt accepted as fulfilling the conditions referred to above, although the practical consequence was to delay Bolero and completely undermine Roundup, as the resources for Operation Torch (the Anglo-American landings in Morocco and Algeria in November 1942) could only be found at such short notice by raiding the forces earmarked for cross-Channel attack. Indeed, once it was admitted that no cross-Channel invasion would occur in 1943, resources which otherwise would have flowed to the United Kingdom were diverted for the Pacific War as much as US resources in the United Kingdom already were channelled into the Mediterranean strategy. Thus by the end of 1942, there were 11 American divisions in the Pacific theatre (including Hawaii) compared to six in North Africa and one in the United Kingdom.

By May 1943, with the surrender of Axis forces in Tunisia, all of North Africa was now in Allied hands. The British pressed for exploiting this success by attacking Sicily: a course of action only accepted by the Americans on the understanding that the Mediterranean theatre was to be regarded as subsidiary to the cross-Channel attack, now renamed Operation Overlord and rescheduled for the summer of 1944. The latter's preeminence was symbolised by the fact that it was agreed that ultimately seven divisions would be withdrawn from the Mediterranean theatre to assist its success.

After Sicily fell, mainland Italy was invaded in order to knock Italy out of the war, acquire valuable airbases and stimulate resistance in the Balkans. However, any thought that Italy represented a 'soft underbelly' which might be attacked with relative impunity was invalidated by Operation Axis, whereby German troops took over Northern and Central Italy.

As 1943 had progressed, and notwithstanding German success in slowing the Allied advance up Italy, Churchill began to urge a greater concentration of Allied resources on the Mediterranean as an alternative to Overlord, which he considered fraught with risks. However, at Tehran, as shown above, the Russians backed the American commitment to cross-Channel attack in favour of pressing on in the Mediterranean. Churchill merely succeeded in getting Overlord postponed, for not more than one month, in order to secure an advance to the Pisa–Rimini line but on the firm condition that Allied resources in the Mediterranean were then to be used in Operation Anvil, a landing on the southern coast of France which would supposedly distract German reserves at a critical point in the battle to establish a bridgehead in Normandy. The British were unconvinced of the strategic value of Anvil but were prepared to go along with the Americans because acquiescence ensured that the Italian campaign could proceed at full strength for the foreseeable future. Indeed, the British were able to persuade the Americans to postpone Anvil until after the fall of Rome. As this did not occur until 4 June, the landings in the south of France, which took place in mid-July, no longer served their original strategic purpose (as was tacitly admitted when the operation was renamed Dragoon), and was instead justified by the Americans on logistic grounds (as Toulon and Marseille would counteract the fact that Cherbourg still had not fallen to the Allies and one of the two Mulberry artificial harbours had been wrecked by bad weather).

Following the fall of Rome, General Alexander optimistically assumed that if he had been left in command of his full force of 27 divisions, he would be able to force the so-called 'Ljubljana Gap' into northern Yugoslavia from whence he might even take Vienna. This fanciful notion appealed to Churchill and all those attracted to the 'might-have-beens' of history. Its appeal largely consisted in the fact that Churchill was becoming increasingly worried about the spread of Soviet influence in Europe and that this scheme, and variations of it, seemingly offered a means of pre-empting what became known as the Iron Curtain, coming down so far to the west. Churchill liked to present himself as a seer, and just as he could claim that World War Two could have been avoided if his words about Germany had been heeded sooner, so he liked to claim that the Cold War was equally unnecessary, and that if he had been listened to then the Soviet domination of Central and Eastern Europe might have been avoided. A patriotic bonus for Churchill was the fact that under this scenario the final blow of the Second World War and the first and decisive blow of the Cold War would have been struck by a force in which British troops predominated.

To sum up, success in the Mediterranean theatre encouraged the British by the end of 1943 to begin to see it as offering opportunities to damage Germany and its allies with far less risk and far greater prospect of success than a cross-Channel attack. Even after D-Day, there were some who considered Italy a more fertile field of military operations than North-West Europe. However, it was the advent of the Cold War which rendered the Mediterranean a historical battleground as the benefit of hindsight and some highly questionable military assumptions allowed armchair strategists to claim that both the Second World War and the Cold War might have been won more quickly and economically if Churchill and Alexander had prevailed over Roosevelt and Eisenhower.

From D-Day to Germany

D-Day eventually came on 6 June 1944. The Allies achieved surprise, not least through a process of disinformation, which made the Germans expect the main thrust would be at the Pas de Calais even after the Normandy landings were underway. They were also assisted by the fact that there were strategic disagreements between Rundstedt, Commander-in-Chief in the West, and Rommel, with overall responsibility for the Atlantic Wall, about how best to repel an attack.

By midnight 130,000 American, British and Canadian troops had come ashore (with an additional force of over 20,000 dropped by parachute or sent in by glider) and by 12 June the five beachheads (Utah, Omaha, Juno, Sword and Gold) had been connected. The port of Cherbourg fell on 30 June but was not capable of unloading supplies for a further six weeks.

The battle to break out of the bridgehead took seven weeks, and led to recriminations between the Allies regarding the campaign to close the Falaise Gap, as the Americans felt that Montgomery's caution allowed many German forces to escape unnecessarily. The main Allied drive was originally going to by-pass the French capital, but as the Germans began to pull out, the resistance forces took to the streets on 19 August, and on 23 August Eisenhower and Patton, the commander of the Third US Army, consented to release the 2nd French Armoured Division, under Leclerc to move towards Paris, which was formally liberated two days later.

By the end of the month, with the Allies firmly across the Seine, it appeared as if the Germans were about to be driven out of France entirely, and that Belgium and Luxemburg would be liberated next. However, the offensive stalled as a consequence of the German consolidation of a cohesive defensive position, the onset of winter and logistical difficulties.

It was partly to solve the latter that the Allies launched in September 1944 what became an 85-day campaign centred upon the Scheldt Estuary and the Belgian port of Antwerp. Montgomery's concentration on Operation Market-Garden as a means of obtaining a bridgehead on the further side of the Rhine led to the battle of the Scheldt Estuary receiving insufficient attention and resources, while the failure of the 12,000 men dropped behind enemy lines to retain control of the bridge at Arnhem, crushed any hope of opening Rotterdam or Amsterdam as alternative supply ports. Antwerp was only finally opened to Allied shipping on 28 November.

Antwerp was the ultimate objective of the campaign Hitler launched in the Ardennes in December 1944 – the so-called Battle of the Bulge. Surprise and poor weather temporarily negating Allied command of the air allowed the Germans to delay the Allied advance for a month but achieved nothing beyond that. The next Allied objective in North-West Europe was crossing the Rhine, which was achieved in March 1945 thanks to the capture of the bridge at Remagen on 7 March. All German resistance west of the Rhine was ended by 25 March. To Churchill's annoyance, Eisenhower decided not to race the Russians to Berlin, preferring instead to capture the Ruhr, although it is questionable whether this could have been achieved even if Eisenhower had decided differently, given that Soviet forces were already within roughly 35 miles (65 kms) of the city on 28 January and were inside the city by mid-April.

The Western Allies made contact with the Red Army at Torgau on the Elbe on 24 April. Hitler having committed suicide on 30 April, his designated successor, Grand Admiral Karl Doenitz surrendered the Netherlands, Denmark, and north-western Germany to Montgomery on 4 May. Eisenhower accepted Germany's unconditional surrender on 7 May, and all German forces in the west terminated military action the following day. Precisely what that meant for Eastern Europe in general and Poland in particular was not yet visible to the cheering crowds on VE Day, otherwise their celebrations might have been more muted.

Wartime tensions (2): Poland

Almost as important to Stalin as the early mounting of a cross-Channel invasion was an Anglo-American acknowledgement of the USSR's vital interests in Eastern Europe. This amounted to ratification of the gains made under the Nazi–Soviet Non-Aggression Pact or, to put it another way, restitution of the lands of the Tsarist empire. The key to all this was Poland which, in Churchill's words, was, 'to prove the first of the great causes which led to the breakdown of the Grand Alliance'.[6]

There were two (overlapping) Polish issues, namely, its frontiers and its government. Stalin wished to make Poland's eastern frontier roughly conform with the so-called Curzon Line. That is to say, the line originally agreed by the Allied Supreme Council on 8 December 1919 and subsequently confirmed by the British Foreign Secretary, Lord Curzon, during the Russo-Polish War of 1920–21.

The 1921 Treaty of Riga had instead established Poland's eastern frontier roughly 150 miles east of the Curzon Line, giving Poland roughly 80,000 square miles at Soviet expense. It was roughly this land which was reclaimed by the Red Army in September 1939 in accordance with the 'Molotov–Ribbentrop' line: the dividing line between Nazi- and Soviet-occupied Poland in accordance with the secret provisions of the Nazi–Soviet Non-Aggression Pact of August 1939.

Stalin sought to compensate Poland for this loss at Germany's expense, by moving Poland's western frontier westwards. Such a move would both weaken Germany and render Poland more compliant, as the Poles would require protection from the USSR to prevent Germany reclaiming what it had lost. However, such a demand was unacceptable to the so-called London Poles: the Polish government in exile in London.

Relations between the London Poles and Moscow were irreparably damaged by the mid-1943 German revelation of mass graves of Polish officers at Katyn. The Germans claimed that they had been shot by the KGB. The British and Americans suspected that this was so but could not give comfort to their enemy by admitting that their ally had committed an atrocity. They therefore paid lip service to Soviet claims that the Germans were engaged in a bluff and that they were in fact responsible for the murders. The truth of the matter could be deduced from Stalin's refusal to acknowledge the London Poles after they requested that the Red Cross should be allowed to investigate the matter.

On reaching the Curzon Line on 21–22 July 1944, the Soviets established their own pro-Soviet Polish government (the Polish Committee of National Liberation) at Chelm. Its members became known as the Lublin Poles when they relocated to the larger city of Lublin and on 27 July the Lublin Committee was officially recognised by the USSR and took over the administration of all Polish territory occupied by the Soviets west of the Curzon Line.

With the Red Army approaching the outskirts of Warsaw, on 1 August 1944 the Home Army (the military wing of the London Poles) began the Warsaw Uprising, hoping to liberate the city without Soviet help. They could not, and not only did the Russians refuse to resume their advance until the Home Army had been crushed, they also refused to allow Western requests to use airfields in Soviet-occupied territory to send relief supplies until the uprising had been almost completely liquidated. Nearly 200,000 Poles were killed and roughly 150,000 were deported for forced labour, while much of the city was razed to the ground.

This affair is sometimes represented as a landmark in disabusing Western policymakers regarding Stalin's ruthlessness: the Russians deliberately allowing the Nazis to destroy the Polish resistance so as to make it easier for them to control the country once they had 'liberated' it. Apologists for the USSR defend Soviet inaction by arguing, for example, that the speed of the Soviet advance to the Vistula obliged a period of regrouping during which the uprising was launched. This is all rather disingenuous. Whatever illusions Western policymakers had regarding the nature of the Soviet regime were dispelled by Katyn Wood, if not before, while the whole point of the Warsaw uprising was that it would fail in its fundamental political objective if its military objectives were achieved with Soviet help. The London Poles gambled and they lost. They were bound to lose insofar as Great Powers decide the fate of little powers and while Poland was symbolically important to the West (as Britain and France had entered the war nominally to safeguard Polish independence, while the modern state of Poland owed much to Wilson's Fourteen Points), for the USSR it was strategically vital (as the invasion route into Russia).

Thus Churchill stated that 'it would be difficult not to take cognizance of the fact that the British people had gone to war because of Poland'.[7] and Hopkins averred that 'The question of Poland per se was not so important as the fact that it had become a symbol of our ability to work out problems with the Soviet Union'.[8] The Soviet leadership, by contrast, was determined to block the Polish invasion route or 'gateway' into Russia which had been used by the French in 1812, the Germans in 1914 and

1941 and by the Poles themselves in 1920–21. This was to be achieved by extending Soviet frontiers to their fullest possible extent and by installing 'friendly' (which is to say pro-Soviet) regimes in Poland and elsewhere in Eastern Europe.

At Teheran in November 1943, Stalin secured verbal acceptance from his allies of Poland's western and eastern frontiers as defined by himself, extending Polish territory westwards into Germany territory, to the Oder river and making the Curzon Line Poland's eastern frontier. However, this arrangement was not committed to writing or made public for fear of provoking an adverse reaction among the London Poles or the 5–6 million American voters of Polish extraction: an important consideration for FDR in the light of his standing for re-election in 1944.

Churchill tried to get the London Poles to accept the Oder and Curzon Lines as Poland's post-war frontiers in return for a Soviet guarantee of Polish independence following his October 1944 Moscow conference with Stalin, but this move was undermined by the US ambassador Harriman saying (falsely) that FDR had not agreed to the Curzon Line. American failure to back Churchill in his efforts to disabuse the London Poles of their territorial and political illusions at this point helped undermine their increasingly weak position.

Roosevelt was too confident regarding his personal powers of persuasion regarding Stalin, especially given his rapidly deteriorating health. His fatigue at the Yalta Conference in February 1945 was such that he was reluctant to drag out negotiations, which hastened the granting of concessions from the American side and a willingness to accept formulae which lacked precision. The Declaration on Liberated Europe, for example, called on liberated peoples 'to create democratic institutions of their own choice' stating that it was a principle of the Atlantic Charter that all peoples possessed the right 'to choose the form of government under which they will live' and promising 'the restoration of sovereign rights and self-government to those peoples who have been forcibly deprived of them by the aggressor nations'.[9]

Moreover, instead of sticking to the policy that the Lublin government should be replaced, the West, through the Yalta Declaration on Poland accepted its 'enlargement': a move which in itself went a long way towards legitimising the Lublin government and marginalising the London Poles.

The Hopkins mission to Moscow finally settled the degree of this enlargement before the Potsdam conference opened in July 1945, with four non-Warsaw Poles joining the provisional Polish government. After they took their places, the British and US governments recognised the Polish government on 5 July 1945 (Stalin having in the meantime amused himself by pointing out that the unelected character of de Gaulle's provisional French government had not prevented its having been officially recognised).

On behalf of the United States Hopkins stated that 'we would accept any government in Poland which was desired by the Polish people and was at the same time friendly to the Soviet Union'.[10] Such a statement betrays the fundamental contradiction underlying the American attitude towards Poland insofar as a truly democratic Poland would not be a Poland friendly towards Russia.

In a sense Poland's fate was settled not at Potsdam or Yalta or even in Teheran but in Italy because when Anglo-American forces began its liberation in 1943, the Soviet request for a share in its administration was denied and real power was instead vested in the Western Allied commander of the occupying forces, thereby setting the precedent whereby the disposition of military forces broadly determined territorial and administrative arrangements. As Stalin told Milovan Djilas in early 1945, 'whoever occupies a territory also imposes his own system as far as his army can reach'.[11] Thus when the Big Three met at Yalta (February 1945), the broad framework of territorial arrangements, including Soviet domination of Eastern Europe, had already effectively been determined by the success of the Red Army in pushing back the Wehrmacht.

The situation which Truman inherited following Roosevelt's death on 12 April 1945 was then hardly auspicious. Truman lacked a personal mandate as President and in some senses felt personally inferior to his illustrious predecessor. He had only been Vice-President for 82 days and not been kept fully informed even when he had occupied that office. On the one hand (as was the case with Lyndon Baines Johnson in 1963) he felt the need to honour the vision of his predecessor and see through his plans, on the other hand he also (again like Johnson) felt the need to show himself to be his own man (especially if he were ultimately to seek election in his own right in 1948).

The extent to which Truman appreciated that the pass had already been sold over Poland and Eastern Europe generally is open to question, so too is the extent to which possession of the Bomb emboldened him to think that lost ground might be regained. Certainly Truman talked tough to Molotov regarding alleged Soviet breaches of promises made at Yalta when the Soviet Foreign Minister met the new President. However, just two weeks after this event 16 Polish underground leaders were arrested by the Soviets after having been promised a safe passage.

Stalin got his way insofar as post-war Poland gained 40,000 square miles in the west at Germany's expense, in partial compensation for the 69,000 square miles in the east ceded to the Soviet Union. Moreover, the Polish communists predominated after the January 1947 elections. These were not 'free' but neither were US elections of the time (especially if one considers the black constituency in the South) and at least the notion of an independent Polish state persisted as a marker for the future which was eventually realised with the collapse of Soviet power and the ending of the Cold War.

What was true of Poland was broadly true of Central and Eastern Europe: the lands 'liberated' by the Red Army sooner or later saw the imposition of puppet communist regimes. The only significant exception comprised those parts of Germany assigned to the Western powers for military occupation.

11 The German question

The death toll of World War Two will never be known precisely but the best estimates suggest that over 50 million lost their lives, with civilian dead outnumbering regular combatants. The casualties for the Big Three – Great Britain and the Commonwealth, the United States and the Soviet Union – were of the order of magnitude of 450,000, 480,000 and between 20 and 27 million, respectively, while Germany lost at least 5 million.

Moreover, 11 million ethnic Germans or Volksdeutsch were expelled from areas such as East Prussia (part of nearly 40,000 square miles of Germany which was ceded to Poland), and within Germany proper two-fifths of the population were on the move at the end of the war. But if Germany appeared to be prostrate there were few who shed tears and many who feared its revival, not least the Soviet Union which in addition to the immense human suffering referred to above had lost about one-third of its national wealth.

Thus the question which had haunted the twentieth century – the question of how best to integrate Germany peacefully into a Europe which potentially it could dominate – dominated much of the post-war years just as it had dominated much Allied thinking during the war, with a policy of dividing and debilitating Germany ultimately giving way to a policy of binding Germany economically to her neighbours.

Wartime planning regarding Germany

The historiographical division over the creation of two Germanies and a divided Berlin centres upon the questions of timing and responsibility. Some see the Soviet Union as principally to blame, while others view the Western allies as chiefly culpable. Similarly, while some regard division as implicit in the occupation zones agreed even before the war ended, others would argue that even the creation of the Federal Republic of Germany (FRG) and the German

Democratic Republic (GDR) in 1949 – a division which lasted until reunification in 1990 – might have been forestalled had Stalin's offer of a unified but neutral Germany been accepted in 1952. The one claim not in dispute is that Germany's future was the most divisive issue for the Big Three, which is hardly surprising given that their wartime alliance was a marriage of convenience precipitated by Hitler's actions.

Fearful that Stalin might make a separate peace with Germany, as Lenin had done at Brest–Litovsk in March 1918, Roosevelt had pushed Churchill into accepting that unconditional surrender of the Axis powers was the declared aim of the Allied powers, at Casablanca in January 1943, and from the time of the Teheran Conference in November–December 1943 he increasingly moved the Western allies away from the Mediterranean strategic focus favoured by the British, towards the early opening of the Second Front in Western Europe which had consistently been called for by the Soviets (see Chapter 10). This was part of a general effort by the Americans to court Stalin, borne out of a recognition that the Red Army was engaging the bulk of Germany's forces (80 per cent of the Wehrmacht's divisions, right up until D-Day) and would soon be liberating Eastern and much of Central Europe, and a belief that 'Uncle Joe' was a man with whom one could do business.

With the American 1st Army crossing the German frontier near Eupen and American armoured forces entering Germany north of Trier in the course of the Second Quebec Conference of 12–16 September 1944, Germany's defeat seemed assured (although Arnhem later that month and the Battle of the Bulge before the end of the year both appreciably delayed that event). Thus the future of Germany was at the centre of the discussions between Churchill and Roosevelt. Without consulting their foreign ministers they both endorsed the Morgenthau plan, which was so named because its author was Henry Morgenthau, America's Secretary to the Treasury. He sought to render Germany incapable of making war in the future by 'pastoralising' it. This was to be accomplished by liquidating the war-making industries of the Ruhr and Saar.

However, the United States was obviously less inclined than the USSR, for reasons of both history and geography, to be fearful of German resurgence. Thus while Roosevelt toyed with a punitive

peace he soon reverted to the idea of relative moderation, reassuring his Secretary of State, Cordell Hull, on 29 September 1944
that 'No one wants to make Germany a wholly agricultural nation
again' and telling him that he would like to 'catch and chastise'
whoever it was who 'has handed this out to the press'.[1]

Roosevelt was worried that an impoverished and resentful
Germany would damage Europe economically and destabilise it
politically, as it had done in the aftermath of what had come to be
regarded as an excessively harsh Treaty of Versailles and that the
net result would be that sooner or later the United States would
have to pick up the bill.

Stalin, by contrast, consistently pursued the complementary aims
of gaining massive reparations for the damage wrought by Hitler
and crippling Germany so that she could never again pose a threat
to the Soviet Union. At the Yalta conference in February he successfully proposed that $20 billion should at least form the basis
for discussions regarding German reparations, and that half of the
final amount agreed would go to Russia.

The Potsdam conference

Germany surrendered unconditionally on 7–8 May 1945, and shortly afterwards the four Allied powers formally assumed supreme
authority in Germany. The Potsdam Conference of July–August
1945 saw the Big Three agree that Germany should undergo disarmament, demilitarisation, denazification, democratisation, political decentralisation and the dismantling of its war industries.

However, once this negative programme had been enunciated,
differences soon emerged between the Big Three. For example,
while agreeing that 'During the period of occupation Germany
shall be treated as a single economic unit'[2] there was less unanimity regarding the precise question of reparations until the Soviets
reluctantly accepted the compromise suggested by Secretary of
State Byrnes that the four occupying powers would extract reparations primarily from their own designated occupation zones, and
that the Soviets would additionally receive from the western zones
10 per cent of industrial capital equipment considered unnecessary
for the German peace economy (to offset the fact that the Western
zones contained the bulk of Germany's industrial wealth) and a
further 15 per cent (principally from the metallurgical, chemical

and machine manufacturing industries) in exchange for an equivalent value of food, coal or other commodities from the Soviet occupation zone.

The scale of Soviet despoliation of Germany is illustrated by the fact that by the end of 1946 the equipment of some 1400 industrial enterprises in the Soviet occupation zone had been wholly or partially transported eastwards and over the next 12 months a further 200 firms, which were collectively responsible for producing roughly 25 per cent of the total output of the East German industrial economy, were converted into Soviet-dominated joint stock companies.

Weakening Germany through systematic deindustrialisation and heavy reparations represented just one element of the three-pronged policy pursued by the Soviets in order to achieve their aim of blocking the Polish invasion route or 'gateway' into Russia. The other elements consisted of extending Russian borders to their fullest (pre-revolutionary) extent (for example by absorbing the Baltic States); and installing 'friendly', that is to say, pro-Soviet, regimes in Poland and elsewhere in Eastern Europe. Thus Poland lost land in the east so that the old Curzon Line became roughly its frontier with the Soviet Union but was compensated with land from Germany to its west as far as the Oder–Neisse. The Western allies at Potsdam accepted this redrawing of frontiers as a *fait accompli*, rather than *de jure*.

It was precisely because he had feared that the presence of the Red Army would determine the post-war redrawing of boundaries that Churchill had wanted the deepest possible military penetration of Central Europe by Western forces. He had, however, been overruled by the Americans in his desire to push on to Berlin, Vienna and Prague because they believed that a pre-arranged line of demarcation would both prevent 'friendly fire' between Russian and Western military forces and facilitate the swift redeployment of troops to the Pacific. Moreover, Eisenhower felt that a single Anglo-American thrust would expose his flanks to German counterattacks and saw no reason to risk more American lives than was absolutely necessary, especially given his political masters' earlier agreement to divide Berlin between them, while Roosevelt had been chary of listening to Churchill for fear that his advice, if followed, would only increase Stalin's distrust of the West and might even provoke hostilities. Thus Eisenhower and Zhukov had decided that their two armies would stop about 25 miles short of each other, with the Americans at the Mulde and the Russians at the Elbe river.

The German occupation zones had not been drawn up in line with projected military dispositions but represented rather an attempt to divide Germany equally between the Big Three (later Four) powers, with the Americans having the southern zone (embracing Bavaria, Württemberg–Baden and Hesse), the British the *Länder* of Lower Saxony, North Rhine–Westphalia, Hamburg and Schleswig–Holstein, the Russians the eastern, less industrialised, part of the country.

Fearing eventual American withdrawal, Churchill sought to bolster France as a continental counterweight to the Soviet Union and successfully persuaded the Russians and Americans to accept the proposition that France should participate in the occupation of Berlin and Germany as a whole. Stalin did not mind as long as the French zones did not detract from the Soviet allocation, and the Americans were won round after the *Lände* of Bremen was placed in their zone and they were assured of the right of transit across the British zone, so as not to be dependent upon the French (who took the south-west and the Palatinate from the western part of the original American zone) for their supply lines.

Berlin was similarly divided into four sectors and was administered jointly by an Inter-Allied authority chaired by the Allied military commanders there. The supreme military commanders were to deal jointly with all matters relating to the country as a whole through an Inter-Allied Control Council, with decisions requiring unanimity. Thus the nominal unity of Germany was already fatally compromised insofar as no central German government was established, except for administrative departments in the fields of finance, transport, communications, industry and foreign trade which would form a part of the Allied Control Council. Moreover, as the Potsdam Protocol gave each of the four military governors supreme authority in their respective zones, the *de facto* division of responsibility already threatened to become permanent.

Each occupation power proceeded with the reconstruction of German governmental institutions in its own zone according to its own lights. However, as the Cold War developed this ultimately resulted in the creation of two Germanies which were diametrically opposed images of one another because reflections of their superpower sponsors, with the FRG a beacon of private enterprise and parliamentary democracy on Anglo-American principles, while the GDR embodied the Stalinist variation of Marxist-Leninist principles.

The impact of the Cold War on the two Germanies

Whereas the Soviets were keen to keep Germany weak, the British and Americans came to consider it highly desirable to rebuild Germany economically not only in order to reduce the costs of occupation and to stimulate the European economy but in order to reduce the risk of communist influence expanding. To foster this process, the British and Americans merged their two zones in terms of economics, food and agriculture, transport and finance, to create Bizonia in September 1946. The French, who had not, of course, been a party to the Potsdam Agreements, and who had just as much reason to be fearful of any revived Prussian militarism as the Russians were initially much closer to the Soviet position than the Anglo-American one, wishing to punish and weaken the Germans. Indeed, this led them to adopt the unpopular policy of seeking to obstruct any Anglo-American measures that might contribute to German political, organisational and economic unity or recovery. If they could not permanently detach the Rhineland from the rest of Germany, they wished to create a Germany consisting of a loose federation of states.

The Marshall Plan was designed in part by the Americans to calm French fears about a revived Germany by integrating western Germany into a European-wide system (all three western zones being included in the Marshall Aid Plan). However, Marshall's insistence on German participation in the European Recovery Programme destroyed any remaining prospect of a four-power accord on Germany, and led directly to the acrimonious collapse of the November 1947 meetings of the Council of Foreign Ministers.

In that same month, President Truman had expressed the view that some form of German government would have to be created in order to cope with the reintegration of the German economy into the European economy. Moreover, this would have to evolve indigenously rather than being imposed by the allies. Democratic political activity had indeed already re-emerged in Germany with the encouragement of all four occupying powers, and the political parties which had become active had done so on a regional and zonal and finally on an inter-zonal level.

Initially the Soviet-backed Communist party (KPD) expected to emerge as the strongest party but when it became apparent that it lacked sufficient support to win an outright majority in the forthcoming East German local and regional elections, the Social Democratic party (SPD) came under intense pressure to accept a merger of the two working-class parties. It succumbed, with the result that the Socialist Unity Party (SED) was acclaimed at a joint KPD–SPD meeting on 21–22 April 1946. The new party, with an executive composed equally of representatives of the KPD and SPD, was pledged to work towards realising a special, which is to say a non-Stalinist, road towards socialism. Many working-class Germans certainly welcomed a fusion of the Social Democrats and Communists because they recognised that the divisions on the Left had helped Hitler to achieve and consolidate power. However, many viewed the means by which that fusion was achieved as unfortunate.

However, in the Saxon elections of 20 October 1946, the SED gained 49 per cent of the vote while the LDPD (Liberal Democratic Party of Germany) and the Christian Democratic Union (CDU) took 22 and 21 per cent, respectively, (despite the SED having enjoyed certain advantages over its rivals during the election campaign, such as more favourable allocations of newsprint). The SED similarly disappointed the expectations of its Soviet backers in the local elections in Thuringia and Sachsen–Anhalt. Indeed, the SED narrowly missed gaining an absolute majority in Mecklenburg and Thuringia as well as Saxony.

This precipitated a Stalinist backlash which included the adoption of a centrally planned economy in June 1948 and culminated in January 1949 in the SED formally proclaiming its devotion to the (Stalinist interpretation of the) principles of Marxism-Leninism. The acceleration of the process of nationalisation and the introduction of collectivisation brought eastern Germany into ever closer conformity with the Soviet model of a command economy, complete with its own Two-Year Plan for 1949–50.

This battening down of the hatches in the east was also a response to developments in the west, particularly the conference held in London in February 1948 which was attended by representatives of the United States and five West European nations where it was decided to introduce a new currency into the western zones of Germany. This decision was taken to provide financial stability for economic revival (undermining the flourishing black market) and as a tentative move towards (West) German statehood (French anxieties on this point being largely alleviated by an American commitment to retain some troops in Europe indefinitely).

On 6 March 1948 the French agreed that their zone would join Bizonia to form a single economic unit, prompting the Soviet Marshall Sokolovski to withdraw from the Control Council and on 24 June 1948, the day after the new Deutschmark was introduced, the Soviets' immediate response was to cut the land routes between West Berlin and the western zone. The ensuing blockade of West Berlin was to last nearly a year, only being abandoned on 12 May 1949 after 322 days. During that time West Berlin's three million citizens were supplied with food and fuel by means of an Anglo-American airlift down three air corridors previously agreed with the Soviets.

The attempt to destroy West Berlin as a western enclave deep inside the Soviet zone merely encouraged the West to press ahead with the creation of a sovereign West German state and in July 1948, the three Western Allies invited the German Minister-Presidents to merge their three western zones into one economic and political unit by holding elections for a constituent assembly which would provide West Germany with a constitution turning it into a federal republic with a strong central government (although the occupying powers temporarily retained the capacity to control areas such as foreign policy, trade and reparations). This constitution had then to be approved by the military governors and accepted by two-thirds of the western *Länder*. The constitution was formally adopted in May 1949, and on 20 September 1949 the Western powers formally acknowledged the creation of the FRG.

The communists had taken steps designed to forestall such a development, most notably the SED had called upon all political parties, trade unions and other mass organisations to form an all-German 'People's Congress Movement for Unity and a Just Peace' in order to avert the threat of a permanently divided Germany. This movement had pan-German appeal and the Movement's first congress, held in Berlin on 6–7 December 1947 had numbered 664 from the Western zones among its 2215 delegates, prompting the outlawing of the People's Congress Movement in the Western zones, prior to its second congress, held on 18 March 1948 (the one hundredth anniversary of the 1848 revolution). The second congress nevertheless elected a People's Council of 400 members to act as an all-German representative assembly and created a committee, chaired by Otto Grotewohl, to devise a constitution for an all-GDR.

During the Berlin Blockade, in March 1949, the Movement decided to hold its third congress. On 15 and 16 May 1949, 61.8 per cent of the population in the Soviet zone, and 51.7 per cent of the population of the Soviet sector in Berlin voted in favour of a unified list of candidates and predetermined allocation of seats to the congress which gave the SED the largest single bloc, and on 30 May 1949, the congress accepted the proposed constitution for a GDR, which on 7 October 1949 became the constitution of the newly formed GDR. Thus by October 1949 there were officially two German states. Although the preamble of West Germany's constitution committed them to reunification, this did not take place until 3 October 1990, following the collapse of Soviet bloc communism and the East German revolution of 1989.

Arguably there was a genuine chance of reunification 37 years previously, but the Cold War which had rent Germany asunder also conspired to keep the two Germanies apart at that time. In order to appreciate why, it is necessary to examine the fundamental reassessment of America's strategic objectives which was precipitated in 1949 by the ending of America's nuclear monopoly when the Soviets tested their first atomic bomb and by the 'loss' of China to communism. In the light of these developments and McCarthy's attacks on the Truman administration for being soft on communism, Truman had decided to proceed with a crash programme for developing the hydrogen or thermo-nuclear bomb, and in January 1950 commissioned an extensive security policy review which came to be known as National Security Council Resolution 68 (NSC 68). It was forwarded to Truman in April and its recommendation of a rapid build-up of political, economic and military strength in the 'Free World' was approved in September.

The outbreak of the Korean War was decisive in converting NSC 68 from a blueprint for a substantial arms build-up into a practical policy which was manifested in Western Europe by a quadrupling of military aid; a prolongation of economic assistance beyond the end of the Marshall Plan; and an increase in American troop strength (from one infantry division, three armoured cavalry regiments, and two fighter-bomber groups in June 1950 to five divisions and seven air wings by the end of 1952). However, the most controversial offshoot of NSC 68 was a renewed American determination to rearm West Germany, despite bitter French opposition.

The Stalin Note on the Neutralisation of Germany of 10 March 1952 was designed to avert this development, or at least make mischief within the Western alliance by offering German unification and the withdrawal of foreign troops and military bases in exchange for German neutrality. Although America's preferred solution of the German situation was a unified, democratic Germany, the State Department viewed Stalin's offer as a ploy to hamper the West's efforts to integrate the FRG into the European Defence Community (EDC) and accordingly rejected the proposal. We cannot know how genuine Stalin was in making this offer, although it is worth noting that essentially the same deal was offered – and this time accepted – with regard to Austria in 1955. It is also worth noting that the FRG was still far from being a truly sovereign state up to a decade after the end of the war.

Although West Germany became part of the Organization for European Economic Co-operation (OEEC) in October 1949 and joined the European Parliament in 1951, it was not until that year that the High Commission, which replaced the commanders-in-chief in representing the Allies, granted it the right to conduct its own foreign policy, and the not inconsiderable residual rights enjoyed by the High Commission (including the right to veto changes to the Basic Law and laws passed by the *Bundestag*) lasted until the signing of the Paris Treaties on 23 October 1954. West Germany only became a truly sovereign state in May 1955 after the Paris Treaties had been ratified by all parliaments involved. Its armed forces were only to be used by and for the North Atlantic Treaty Organisation (NATO) and it was West German admission to this body in 1955 that provoked the Soviet creation of the Warsaw Pact.

The division of Germany arose less out of a desire to punish the Germans for the war than as a consequence of Cold War fall out between Germany's principal enemies. With the collapse of communism in the Soviet Union and the ending of the Cold War, Germany was reunified in 1990.

Germany and the drive towards European unity

Two major problems confronted Europe in the aftermath of the Second World War, namely, security and reconstruction. Security was tackled by means of three treaties. The Dunkirk Treaty of 1947 was an Anglo-French agreement to provide mutual assistance in the event of German aggression. The Brussels Treaty of 1948 was a 50-year guarantee of mutual military assistance signed by Great Britain, France and the Benelux countries (Belgium, the Netherlands and Luxemburg). The advent of the Cold War meant that the focus shifted from fear of Germany to fear of the Soviet Union. Thus the Brussels Treaty was later joined by West Germany and Italy (in 1955) and the North Atlantic Treaty of 1949, agreed in the aftermath of the Soviet takeover of Czechoslovakia and the Berlin Blockade, was a mutual military assistance pact signed by the United States, Canada, Great Britain, France, the Benelux countries, Italy, Norway, Denmark, Iceland and Portugal. The original signatories were later joined by Greece and Turkey (in 1952), West Germany (in 1955) and Spain (in 1985).

The more immediately pressing problem of reconstruction was tackled by Marshall Aid, under which 16 Western European nations received $13 billion in grants and loans between 1948 and 1952 (of which Great Britain received $2693 million). US support for Europe, 1945–55, totalled $24.8 billion (of which the United Kingdom received $6.9 billion, France $5.5 billion, the Federal Republic $3.9 billion and Italy $2.9 billion).

It was a condition of Marshall Aid that the European countries should work together to plan the best use of this financial assistance. They did this by setting up the OEEC, which came into operation on 16 April 1948, with a membership of 16 countries. The OEEC set itself three tasks, namely, to distribute Marshall Aid; to encourage and assist investment between countries; and to revive European trade.

It was the hope in the United States that the economic integration arising out of co-operation over Marshall Aid might be translated into closer political integration in Western Europe, in much the same way that the Zollverein or customs union had paved the way for German unification. There was obviously much sentiment in Europe in the aftermath of World War Two in favour of exploring this notion as an antidote to the wars which had plagued the continent. The feeling was especially strong in France, which had suffered most since 1870 at the hands of Germany. The French favoured European integration as a means of binding Germany in a framework where cooperation would replace rivalry. The notion also appealed strongly in Germany among those who felt the need for some form of national self-atonement.

Thus Dean Acheson, as US Secretary of State, recalling a visit to Germany in 1949, recorded that

> Adenauer's great concern was to integrate Germany completely into Western Europe. Indeed, he gave this end priority over the reunification of unhappily divided Germany, and could see why her neighbours might look upon it as almost a precondition to reunification. He wanted Germans to be citizens of Europe, to cooperate, with France especially, in developing common interests and outlook and in burying the rivalries of the past few centuries. Their common heritage had come to them down the Rhine, as the successors of Charlemagne, who guarded European civilization when human sacrifice was still practised in eastern Germany. They must lead in the rebirth of Europe.[3]

It was, of course, the shadow of Auschwitz rather than human sacrifice at the time of Charlemagne that Adenauer wished to expunge.

In May 1948, the Hague Congress on European unity was attended by 800 delegates, including Konrad Adenauer and Churchill but not, significantly, by any official representative of the British government. After five days of discussion the Congress made three recommendations. These were that governments should work towards political and economic union in Europe; that a European Court of Human Rights should be established; and that a European Assembly should be set up to discuss issues of common interest.

A first step towards the implementation of these recommendations came in May 1949 when a Council of Europe was established in Strasbourg by the Brussels Treaty powers and five other states (Denmark, Norway, Sweden, Ireland and Italy). However, even more significant for the future because entailing a genuine pooling of national sovereignty was the Schuman plan announced on 9 May 1950 which united the French and German coal and steel industries under a supranational authority and invited other countries to join this arrangement.

Coal and steel at this time were at the economic heart of European and more especially of Franco-German relations, in a manner which is now difficult to comprehend. Oil accounted for only 8.5 per cent of Western Europe's energy needs in 1950, while coal still met 82 per cent of the primary energy consumption of the six countries that were to comprise the European Coal and Steel Community (ECSC): France, West Germany, Italy, the Netherlands, Belgium and Luxemburg.

By making French and German heavy industry dependent on each other the chances of war between the two countries would effectively be removed. In Schuman's words, 'any war between France and Germany becomes not only unthinkable but materially impossible'.

Ernest Bevin, however, was hostile towards the Schuman plan because he thought that the Americans had been informed of the proposals before the British; that the United States would be encouraged to reduce or even withdraw its commitment to Europe; that despite Franco-German protestations to the contrary, it was intended to exclude Britain, and that even if it was not British membership would jeopardise Labour's nationalisation of the coal and steel industries. Thus on 18 April 1951 the Treaty setting up the ECSC was signed by Germany, France, the Benelux countries and Italy but not by Great Britain. The Treaty came into force in 1952, and by early 1953 there were common markets between the six signatories in coal, iron ore, scrap and most forms of steel.

In the meantime, the outbreak of the Korean War in June 1950 had meant that the United States had wanted to withdraw some of its troops from Germany for redeployment in Korea, and had proposed that West Germany create 12 divisions to take their place (against a possible Soviet attack). However, the prospect of German rearmament alarmed many European nations, especially the French. Thus the French premier Rene Pleven put forward an idea, called the Pleven plan, which would place any new German force under joint European control in a EDC, and link the EDC to a European Political Community.

Britain, however, refused to join this project and this proved fatal to its prospects. Nevertheless, in 1954 the British Foreign Secretary, Anthony Eden, suggested an alternative whereby Germany would contribute to European defence through NATO (thus ensuring that Germany was still denied full control over its army), and Britain would join a EDC called the Western European Union

(WEU). The WEU was accordingly set up by the Paris Agreements of October 1954 and was joined by nine countries.

In June 1955 the Foreign Ministers of the ECSC countries met at Messina in Sicily to see what else could be done to improve European unity. The conference lasted for nine months and was chaired by Paul-Henri Spaak, the Belgian Foreign Minister. The Spaak Report of April 1956 recommended pooling Europe's resources for the development of nuclear energy and creating a common market and customs union as a prelude to full political unity one day in a United States of Europe.

Having accepted the Spaak Report, representatives of the six ECSC governments met in Rome on 25 March 1957 to sign treaties which set up the European Atomic Energy Community (Euratom) and established a common market, the European Economic Community (EEC), which came into being on 1 January 1958. The preamble of the Treaty of Rome famously enunciated the aim of 'ever-closer union'.[4]

As is the case with most preambles it is open to question whether this phrase represents a genuine aspiration or vacuous rhetoric. Those who would argue the latter point out that the 'European Community' only emerged and boomed as the consequence of an unrepeatable combination of factors including the aftermath of the two world wars and the Great Depression, and the advent of the Cold War. Taking the long view certainly allows the West German economic 'miracle' and the general prosperity of the EEC (and its later manifestations) to be placed in an illuminating context.

Experience of total war created a presumption in favour of centralised social and economic organisation, while the stagnation of trade since 1914 meant that there was much slack to be taken up once a common market provided a stable economic environment. By 1980, for example, France and West Germany had only achieved shares of worldwide manufactured goods exports in line with what their previous incarnations had achieved prior to the Wall Street Crash (10.9 per cent and 10 per cent, and 20.5 per cent and 19.9 per cent, respectively). This was, of course, a superior performance to that achieved by Great Britain and other non-EEC countries, which explains their increasing eagerness to join the European club. However, it is also worth remembering that the Cold War also played a decisive role in the creation of 'Europe' both politically, providing a unifying focus in face of the alleged communist threat, and financially, as US economic aid in the form of the Marshall Plan and military assistance in the form of NATO subsidised European reconstruction and development so that the relative burden of their defence spending declined dramatically. Thus in the words of Tony Judt, 'the Cold War forced them into a greater measure of unity and collaboration while sparing them attendant military expenses'.[5] Moreover, the Cold War allowed the two Germanies to be absorbed in the rival power blocs on surprisingly good terms and ensured that there was no problem of absorbing the poorer nations of Eastern Europe (until the 1990s when the Cold War had ended).

Indeed, it is worth remembering that French feelings of fraternity towards the former enemy represented a fallback strategy after the failure of their immediate post-war efforts to reduce Germany's political and military strength to the minimum in order to exploit it economically to the full. In 1946–47, fearful of abandonment by his erstwhile Anglo-American allies, and resentful of recent dependence upon them, de Gaulle even cosied up to Stalin in a bid to dismantle Germany or at least impose the heaviest possible reparations upon her. However, wary of having to foot the bill for feeding the populace in their occupation zones and regarding a revived West German economy as underpinning European economic recovery and acting as a bulwark against the spread of communism, the British and Americans effectively vetoed this option, while the advent of the Cold War obliged France to align with the West and find some other means of ensuring the supply of German coal for the production of French steel. The solution, as has been shown above, was the 'European' solution represented by the Schuman plan and its subsequent offshoots.

But why was West Germany willing to accept incorporation in a Franco-centric community? The answer was that it was considered to be the price worth paying for Germany ceasing to be a pariah state and becoming internationally respectable once again. Thus the initial dynamic behind the European movement was as much psychological as economic: the participants were spurred less by the ideal of creating a brave new world per se than in burying the aggressive, collaborationist and genocidal aspects of the old world. The problems besetting the project are fundamentally twofold. Firstly, some have always been willing to take the preamble of the Treaty of Rome at face value and have actively sought to promote political as well as economic integration (insofar as the latter does not entail the former). Secondly, there is the fear that ultimately the facts of geography, economics and history cannot be denied and that Germany – especially a reunited Germany – will dominate Europe whatever the institutional counterweights unless the European community becomes a truly United States of Europe.

All this, however, is to anticipate future developments. In 1958 Britain was content to enter into talks with the Six, in an attempt to change the EEC into a wider free trade area for industrial goods only. However, this proposal was rejected and Great Britain and Switzerland therefore worked with five other Western European countries (Portugal, Austria, Denmark, Norway and Sweden) to form the European Free Trade Association (EFTA) which came into being in 1959.

EFTA applied only to industrial products (explicitly excluding agricultural goods) and was much looser in institutional terms than the EEC. Between 1958 and 1964 trade between Britain and its EFTA partners rose by 72 per cent but trade between Britain and the EEC increased by 92 per cent. This was chiefly because EFTA offered Britain a market of 38 million people while the EEC offered Britain a market of 300 million people.

Largely for this reason, Harold Macmillan, in 1961, launched a campaign to take Britain into Europe, placing Edward Heath in charge of negotiations in Brussels. On Britain's side there were three main problems centring upon the Commonwealth, agriculture and EFTA. Britain's ties with the Commonwealth were not only sentimental but economic – helping to ensure cheap food (notably from Australia and New Zealand). Moreover, government subsidies to farmers worth about £300 million per year, would be forbidden under EEC regulations. Last and least among Britain's problems – at least in the eyes of Britain's policymakers – was the abandonment of its EFTA partners which membership of the EEC would entail.

In any case, on 29 January 1963 de Gaulle (who had returned to power in France in 1958) vetoed the British application on the grounds that Britain remained too closely linked to the Commonwealth and the United States. His precise words were that

England is, in fact, insular. She is maritime, she is linked to her exchanges, her markets, her supply lines to the most distant countries. She pursues essentially industrial and commercial activities and only slightly agricultural ones. She has, in all her doings, very marked, very original habits and traditions. In short, England's nature, England's structure, England's very situation differs profoundly from those of the continentals.

De Gaulle obviously feared that the Paris–Bonn axis would be destabilised by the admission of Britain and that Britain would challenge certain fundamental elements of the organisation in ways that would damage French interests. De Gaulle was glad that the EEC had been based on a customs union with protectionist external tariffs rather than an 'Anglo-Saxon' free trade area or a free trade zone (Finance Minister Ludwig Erhard's economic preference for a free trade area having succumbed to Adenauer's politically motivated preference for a customs union). Moreover, de Gaulle, like every Frenchman, strongly supported the Common Agricultural Policy, not least because it was so strongly subsidised by the Germans, and recognised that the British would be less willing to bear this burden.

The European integrationist project remains stymied by these rival conceptions of Europe's future. Thus when 55 per cent of the French electorate voted 'no' to the European constitution in May 2005, it was more than merely an expression of dissatisfaction with the policies of President Chirac. It was also a rejection of the 'Anglo-Saxon' vision of Europe.

12 The impact of World War Two on Great Britain and its empire

Wartime foreign policy

During a speech to the Conservative Party conference in 1948, Churchill drew a famous image, arguing that a large part of Britain's strength in international relations derived from the fact that she lay at the centre of three interlocking circles, comprising the United States, the Empire-Commonwealth and continental Europe.

Whether or not Churchill thought in such terms prior to 1948, this image certainly provides a useful analytical tool to facilitate understanding of his wartime strategy. Shortly after he succeeded Chamberlain as Prime Minister in 1940, the fall of France meant that the rest of Europe was either absorbed into the Reich (like Austria and parts of Czechoslovakia and Poland); occupied (like Norway and France); allied (like Italy); friendly (like Spain); or neutral (like Sweden and Switzerland). This meant that Churchill would need to draw increased strength from his other two 'circles', namely, the Empire-Commonwealth and the United States.

The first circle was fairly straightforward. Whereas the Dominions (Canada, Australia, New Zealand and South Africa) had supported Munich and the policy of appeasement they had willingly entered the war on Britain's side in 1939 (with only some reservations on the part of certain Afrikaners), while the colonies were not given any say in the matter. With the exception of Congress in India and the Arabs in Palestine they, nevertheless, largely supported the British war effort.

The second circle – American support – was more problematical because of the strength of American isolationism, which was bolstered by dislike of the British Empire and the feeling that American sacrifices in the First World War had been frittered away by the wily British and French at the Paris Peace Conference. The United States would thus not give any support unless Britain could show that it had the necessary resolve to keep on fighting (rather than negotiating a peace), and it would not be invaded and conquered.

Roosevelt was reassured on these points by Churchill's speeches ('we shall never surrender') and refusal to respond to German peace feelers; the Royal Navy's sinking of the Vichy French fleet; and the victory of the RAF in the Battle of Britain. Churchill thus succeeded in enlisting US aid for the war effort. Landmarks in this process include the bases for destroyers deal of September 1940; lend–lease in March 1941, and the Atlantic Charter of August 1941: a somewhat ambiguous eight-point statement of war aims.

However, these all show that America was determined to drive a hard bargain and that Churchill was prepared to pay a very high – some would say crippling – price to gain US support. For example, America received 99-year leases in return for dated destroyers, while Britain had to liquidate all of its overseas assets as a precondition of receiving lend–lease.

Nevertheless, Congress and the American public remained fundamentally isolationist and it is difficult to imagine how the United States would have become directly involved in World War Two had it not been for the Japanese attack on Pearl Harbor of 7 December 1941 and the German and Italian declarations of war on the United States four days later.

Britain had, of course, acquired an important ally before this when Hitler launched Operation Barbarossa against the USSR on 22 June 1941. Anglo-Soviet relations had been strained since the Bolshevik revolution of October 1917 and British intervention on the side of the Whites in the Russian Civil War, 1918–21.

Relations had improved somewhat in the 1930s given the desire both to increase trade with the USSR after the Great Depression struck and to enlist Soviet support against the growing threat of Nazi Germany, as indicated by the invitation for the USSR to enter the League (with a permanent seat on the Council) in 1934, following Germany's departure from the League in 1933.

However, Moscow interpreted Anglo-French appeasement as meaning that either the western democracies lacked the guts to stand up to Hitler or, even more ominously, were happy to see Germany expand, so long as it did so eastwards.

Stalin had therefore been willing to buy time and land by sign-ing the Nazi–Soviet Non-Aggression Pact of August 1939. How-ever, British suspicion and dislike of the USSR was confirmed by the Molotov–Ribbentrop Pact and the resulting Soviet moves against eastern Poland, the Baltic States, Rumania and Finland.

Indeed, had the Nazis not conquered it so quickly in 1940, British forces might have crossed Norway to assist the Finns and have got involved in war with the USSR. However, Churchill's overwhelming priority was the defeat of Hitler and he therefore showed no hesitation in warning Stalin from April to June 1941 about the impending German attack and in offering aid to the USSR as soon as Operation Barbarossa was launched (22 June 1941).

Moreover, Churchill did not merely offer Stalin verbal support. Arctic convoys took enormous risks to deliver desperately needed military supplies from Britain to the Soviet ports of Archangel and Murmansk. However, Churchill was under no illusions regarding Stalin and Soviet communism, especially given the German revela-tion in 1943 that roughly 4000 Polish officers had been murdered by the KGB at Katyn Wood, and the Russian refusal to assist the Warsaw Rising in 1944.

Churchill's policy towards the USSR was thus based upon the recognition that my enemy's enemy is my friend, and that Eastern Europe under Soviet control was preferable to all of continental Europe under Nazi control. However, having persuaded the Americans to agree that Germany should be defeated before Japan, Churchill managed to persuade them to postpone launch-ing a cross-Channel attack in 1942 or 1943, despite Stalin's plea that the Second Front should be opened as soon as possible, and instead to invade North Africa (in 1942) and Sicily and mainland Italy (1943).

Churchill's motives for this were twofold. He believed that attacking the 'soft underbelly' of the Axis in the Mediterranean would not only result in fewer Allied casualties and enable Britain to protect its imperial interests in the region (including Egypt) but would also offer the best chance of the western allies beating the Red Army into Central Europe and thus ensuring that these countries enjoyed a genuine liberation.

Unfortunately the Americans thought that Britain was primar-ily motivated more by imperial designs, and even after D-Day

(6 June 1944) preferred to consolidate control of the Ruhr rather than follow Churchill's advice to push for Vienna, Prague and Berlin.

American stubbornness on this point was motivated by the desire to minimise casualties, a refusal to confront the facts regarding Soviet aims, and a reluctance to annoy Stalin, given the desire to secure Soviet entry into the war against Japan. Roosevelt's deteriorating health compounded the problem as it rendered him more willing to terminate negotiations by making concessions.

Anglo-American relations improved by the time of Potsdam because Truman increasingly shared Churchill's view of the Soviets and the successful testing of the Bomb simultaneously offered the prospect of America ending the Pacific War without Soviet help and strengthened its bargaining position in relation to the Soviets (threatening them or trading nuclear knowledge with them).

However, British influence at Potsdam had declined compared with Yalta given Churchill's defeat at the July 1945 general election and replacement in mid-conference by Attlee, and Britain's manifest exhaustion after six years of fighting.

To sum up. The direction of British foreign policy first changed during World War Two in 1940 insofar as appeasement of Germany might be thought to have come to an end with the Polish guarantee of March 1939 but was in fact only truly rejected in May 1940 when Churchill succeeded Chamberlain as Prime Minister rather than Halifax and defeated those in the Cabinet led by Halifax who were willing to enter into peace talks. Churchill welcomed working with the USSR from June 1941 to defeat Hitler but tried, as Germany's defeat came closer, to alert the United States to the danger of a Soviet takeover of Central and Eastern Europe.

British foreign policy under Churchill consistently sought to make every effort and employ any means to defeat the Axis powers, and to maintain the British Empire and Britain's position as a Great Power. However, these last two aims were mutually exclusive and the effective cost of defeating Hitler (particularly arising from the need to secure American support) was the virtual bankrupting of Britain (through the sale of overseas assets, massive borrowing and acceptance of the convertibility of sterling) and the liquidation of the British Empire.

Decolonisation

By 1940 the European colonial powers had their grip on their overseas possessions loosened as a result of war with Germany (France, Belgium and the Netherlands having been defeated by Hitler's forces and the British Expeditionary Force being obliged to evacuate the continent without most of its heavy equipment and Britain itself being threatened with invasion).

In 1941–42 Germany's Japanese ally destroyed what little prestige the European colonial powers retained by taking possession of French Indo-China, the Dutch East Indies, Hong Kong, Malaya, Singapore and Burma. Singapore was the largest surrender in British military history with some 85,000 made POWs and the retreat through Burma was the longest ever British retreat. The 'jewel in the Crown' – India itself – was only saved from a full-scale invasion at the eleventh hour by British victories at Kohima and Imphal.

These Japanese victories were so dramatic because they were achieved so quickly (the bulk of British forces being concentrated in Europe and North Africa) and produced shock waves comparable to those of the Russo-Japanese War of 1904–05 because an Asiatic power had triumphed over European powers. The difference was that this time the Japanese had defeated some of the most 'advanced' rather than one of the least industrialised of European nations and this was achieved in full view of those powers' colonial subjects, thereby exploding the myth of the white man's supposed racial superiority.

The success of the Japanese had other consequences for Britain's – and others' – former colonies. Lacking sufficient numbers of skilled personnel to administer their newly conquered lands, they sometimes either set up puppet governments or entrusted relatively high administrative responsibilities to the local native elites whom the former colonial powers had hitherto systematically kept in lower grade jobs, thereby stimulating nationalist pride among native elites and providing them with valuable administrative experience (both enhancing their desire and making them realise that they could govern themselves).

In 1941 Britain entered into partnership with two powerful states – the USSR (in June) and the United States (in December) – which were both paid lip service to anti-imperialist sentiments (despite Moscow seeking to expand the USSR to the boundaries of the former Tsarist empire and America controlling the Philippines and Guam among other territories).

The United States was traditionally anti-imperialist because it had thrown off its own colonial yoke (from the British in the American War of Independence in the eighteenth century and dismantling European empires would weaken competitors and open up new sources of raw materials and markets to American businessmen.

On 14 August 1941, even before the United States had entered the war, Churchill and Roosevelt had signed the Atlantic Charter which included the principle (in paragraph 3) of respecting 'the right of all peoples to choose the form of government under which they will live'. Churchill subsequently claimed that by this he was referring only to those peoples conquered by the Axis powers (Germany, Italy and Japan) but colonial peoples, as was Roosevelt's intention, interpreted this phrase as referring to all those kept under European domination against their will.

When America entered the war in December 1941 (following Pearl Harbor) FDR was particularly keen to be seen as the friend of decolonisation because the American people would be unwilling to make sacrifices merely to prop up the British Empire; he considered the promise of decolonisation to be the best means of motivating the colonial peoples to take an active part in the Allied war effort; and in the event of colonies gaining independence such new countries would presumably feel gratitude and look favourably upon the United States with regard to commercial and security arrangements.

The British reluctantly agreed to make concessions, such as the Cripps Mission of 1942 (which promised Dominion status to India) in an effort to please their American allies and rally both Hindus and Muslims behind the war effort, although Gandhi famously dismissed the offer as akin to a promissory note by a failing bank. Others took more radical steps than civil disobedience to exploit Britain's difficulties and secure independence, notably Subhas Chandra Bose, who created the Indian National Army of Liberation from former Japanese POWs.

The swiftness of Japan's defeat (thanks to the Bomb and the Soviet attack upon Manchuria rather than a D-Day-style invasion of the home islands, which would have seen the war prolonged into 1946 or even beyond) and General MacArthur's insistence that no individual surrenders were to take place before the surrender ceremony on board the *USS Missouri* in Tokyo Bay (on 2 September, 18 days after VJ Day) created a power vacuum which allowed the nationalists in Japanese-occupied territories to seize arms and ammunition stocks and proclaim their independence. In the short term, such nationalist moves might be contained but they represented a marker for a post-colonial future which drew appreciably closer when the 1945 general election replaced the arch-imperialist Churchill with the anti-imperialist Labour party under Clement Attlee.

The stated objective of the Attlee administration was to guide the colonial territories to responsible self-government within the Commonwealth and by the time the Conservatives returned to office under Churchill in 1951 they had adopted the same attitude (except for some right-wing diehards). This consensus was in large part a recognition of hard facts. The war had drained Britain's power to such an extent (depriving it of about 25 per cent of its pre-war wealth and making Britain the world's largest debtor nation) that it could no longer hold on to all of its empire by force.

Moreover, not having experienced defeat and occupation (unlike the French, Belgians and Dutch), Britain was less likely to see decolonisation as involving humiliation or a loss of national face. On the contrary, Britain had ended the war with enhanced prestige, as one of the 'Big Three' at Yalta and Potsdam, with its empire nominally intact and with British troops occupying lands across the globe.

Britain also found it easier than the continental imperial powers to decolonise because she already had experience of this process, having already allowed the white settler colonies (Canada, Australia, New Zealand and South Africa) to become first Dominions, and then independent Commonwealth nations, and she already had experience of 'informal' or 'free-trade Empire' (for example, in Argentina) and thus realised that it was possible to enjoy the economic benefits of empire without necessarily exercising expensive political control.

However, the ambiguous nature of America's attitude towards imperialism became increasingly marked with the advent of the Cold War insofar as its traditional anti-imperialist sentiments clashed with its desire not to give comfort to the Soviet Union in its attempt to use anti-colonialism as a political weapon against the West and its Chiefs- of-Staffs advised retaining as secure naval and air bases some of the Pacific Islands which they had liberated at great cost from the Japanese. The Cold War thus acted as a brake upon decolonisation insofar as America was less inclined to put pressure on Western powers to give up their empires for fear that this would benefit the USSR. Thus at Yalta in 1945, FDR abandoned his idea of transforming all colonial territories into international mandates; at the Inter-American Conference at Bogota in 1948, the United States abstained from the vote condemning colonial regimes; and at the United Nations in 1951, the United States opposed including the right to self-determination in the Declaration of Human Rights.

The Bomb

Britain – thanks in part to refugee scientists from Nazi Germany – was in the forefront of nuclear research in the 1930s and early 1940s. For example, in 1932 Professor James Chadwick discovered the neutron (for which he was awarded a Nobel Prize in 1935), and in 1940 Otto Frisch and Rudolf Peierls (who had both fled to Britain from Germany) recognised the practical possibility of building an atomic bomb based on a fast chain reaction and using a relatively small amount of uranium-235.

A Frisch–Peierls memorandum resulted in the creation of a high-powered committee codenamed MAUD, which in July 1941 produced two reports which helped persuade Churchill to authorise the research and development of an atomic bomb.

This project was entrusted to the Department of Scientific and Industrial Research, which in the autumn of 1941 formed the Directorate of Tube Alloys to oversee research. The project was so secret that the War Cabinet was not consulted but copies of the MAUD reports were officially sent to the United States and were also read in the USSR thanks to the efforts of a Soviet spy.

The United States proposed a pooling of resources but the British responded coolly, saying that they feared a breach of security, and limiting co-operation to a free exchange of information. However, by June 1942 American research (which could draw on enormous resources and which was accelerated following America's December 1941 entry into the war) had already surged ahead of

Britain's and suggestions for a combined Anglo-American effort now began to come from the British side. Roosevelt however, restricted the exchange of information with Britain, when he personally became aware of an agreement Britain had signed with Russia in September 1941 for the exchange of scientific information, despite the fact that this agreement had been signed with America's knowledge and was limited to a list of subjects approved by the United States.

Anglo-American collaboration was impeded because atomic research in America was increasingly controlled by the military, and Congress was worried about post-war British commercial exploitation of atomic energy: a suspicion which was encouraged by the appointment of W.A. Akers, formerly Research Director of ICI, to the key post of Director of the British nuclear project. Obstacles to the resumption of Anglo-American collaboration were only removed in 1943, with a draft agreement in July providing the basis for the Quebec Agreement of 19 August under the terms of which in mid-December 1943 a first contingent of over 40 top British scientists joined the Manhattan Project in America, including James Chadwick, Rudolf Peierls, Klaus Fuchs (another refugee from Nazi Germany) and William Penney. About half of this group worked at Los Alamos, while the others worked in other parts of the project, except at Hanford in Washington State, the site of the production reactor, from which they were specifically excluded. Although small in number, this group was highly talented and made a disproportionate contribution to the success of the Manhattan Project, arguably shortening its successful completion by at least 12 months.

On 19 September 1944, Churchill and Roosevelt signed the Hyde Park Agreement (named after FDR's home in New York State) in which they agreed that knowledge of nuclear weapons research should be restricted to Great Britain and the United States; the Bomb, once developed, might, after 'mature consideration', be used against Japan; and, last but not least, 'Full collaboration between the United States and the British government in developing tube alloys [nuclear energy] for military and commercial purposes should continue after the defeat of Japan unless and until terminated by joint agreement'.

Thus when Attlee succeeded Churchill as Prime Minister following the July 1945 general election, his Labour government fully expected Britain's nuclear partnership with the United States to continue, under the terms of the Quebec and Hyde Park Agreements. The Americans, however, found it difficult to accept the ingratitude of the British public in electing the 'colourless' Attlee in place of the colossus Churchill; were suspicious of a 'socialist' government; and disliked Labour's handling of specific issues, notably Palestine.

Thus in August 1946 the United States passed the Atomic Energy Act, commonly known as the McMahon Act (after Senator Brian McMahon), which established the US Atomic Energy Commission and declared that there would be no sharing of information about nuclear technology with any other nation.

Britain was included under the terms of the McMahon Act because Congress had been kept in the dark about the Quebec and Hyde Park Agreements, and when FDR died the only American copy of the Hyde Park Agreement was mistakenly filed away in the paper's of Roosevelt's naval aide and was not found for some time, while Dr Bush, the only American aware of FDR's intentions regarding continuing post-war collaboration with the British, personally favoured America following a policy of placing nuclear research under international control and therefore made no effort to assist Britain.

When Britain politely reminded America of its obligations, the United States used its economic power to blackmail Britain. Thus in December 1947 the United States threatened to withhold further financial aid unless Great Britain surrendered its share of uranium ore, and its claims under the Quebec and Hyde Park Agreements.

The British had no choice but to agree, although in January 1948 the Americans relented to the extent that they agreed to an arrangement which became known as the *modus vivendi*. It was an informal understanding and therefore did not have to be referred to Congress. It allowed for the joint procurement of uranium supplies and co-operation in nine areas of nuclear research unrelated to weapons. It also confirmed modification of the Quebec Agreement, removing Britain's power of veto over the American use of atomic weapons, and restrictions on Britain's industrial exploitation of atomic energy.

Attlee had been instrumental in creating the UN Atomic Energy Commission, believing that ideally nuclear power should be controlled internationally. However, he and a small ad hoc group of Cabinet ministers had secretly decided in January 1947 that Britain should develop its own independent nuclear weapons given the failure of proposals to control nuclear power internationally; the McMahon Act and the threat of an American return to isolationism; the Soviet threat to Western Europe and its superiority in conventional forces, and Britain's desire to continue to be regarded as a Great Power (Bevin famously saying that he wanted a bomb with a 'Union Jack' on top). Moreover, the British hoped that if they could demonstrate their ability to 'go it alone', the United States would revive the atomic partnership in order to avoid a continuing wasteful duplication of efforts. Within the Ministry of Supply a new Department of Atomic Energy (DATEN) was formed, which took over all the responsibilities of the Directorate of Tube Alloys.

On 29 August 1949, the Soviets tested their first atomic bomb: a fact announced to the world by Truman on 23 September. Given that US intelligence had predicted that the USSR would not have the Bomb before 1953, this came as a shock to the West and crystallised fears of treachery in their midst.

The British were initially blamed because of the exposure of Alan Nunn May, who was sentenced to 10 years' imprisonment for spying on 1 May 1946, and Klaus Fuchs, who was sentenced to 14 years' imprisonment for spying on 10 February 1950. However, it soon emerged that the Americans had their own atom bomb spies, most notably Ethel and Julius Rosenberg, who were arrested in May 1950, brought to trial in March 1951 and executed on 19 June 1953.

When the Conservatives won the 1951 general election Churchill was delighted to learn, upon entering office, that Britain was developing its own Bomb, and endorsed October 1952 as the date for testing it.

At 9.15 am local time on 3 October 1952 a 20-kiloton British Bomb was detonated below the waterline on board *HMS Plym*, which was stationed offshore of the Montebello Islands, 47 miles north-west of the Australian mainland.

The British resented the fact that their requests to use American facilities to conduct the test had initially been fobbed off, despite permission having been given to the United States to base its strategic bombers in Britain. Partly for this reason and partly in order to stress that the programme was an entirely British affair, no American observers were invited to the test.

Three weeks later, however, the United States exploded the first thermonuclear weapon, a hydrogen bomb device that was 1000 times more powerful than the British weapon. The Americans' decision to proceed with its development without delay stemmed in large part from their belief that Klaus Fuchs had also provided the Soviets with information concerning thermonuclear technology. By 1957 Britain, fully committed to becoming a nuclear power, had also tested its own hydrogen bomb at Christmas Island.

By demonstrating its independent expertise in nuclear weapons Britain eventually succeeded in persuading the Americans to accept extensive atomic co-operation. Thus on 17 February 1954 Eisenhower communicated to Congress his desire to amend the McMahon Act and the resulting Atomic Energy Act of 1954 paved the way for Anglo-American agreements in 1955 relating to civilian and military uses of atomic energy, and an agreement of 1956 whereby the United States provided Britain with privileged information on the nuclear submarine '*Nautilus*' which made it easier for her to accept President Kennedy's offer of Polaris missiles to Macmillan at Nassau in December 1962.

The story of nuclear research illuminates both the fruitfulness and the fragility of Anglo-American co-operation, and in particular suggests that the 'special relationship' functions effectively in peacetime only when a personal rapport exists between the two heads of government.

Post-war foreign policy

Great Britain emerged from World War Two territorially strong, with the Empire and Commonwealth covering roughly a quarter of the earth's surface and embracing approximately a quarter of its population. It also enjoyed enormous moral authority, having been at war with Nazi Germany since September 1939 and having fought alone in Europe for the 12 months prior to Hitler's attack on the Soviet Union. Britain was also in a strong position diplomatically, as an acknowledged member of the Big Three and with a permanent seat on the UN Security Council.

However, as has been shown, the war had meant that overseas investments had to be liquidated, debts to the United States were enormous, and Britain lacked both the resources and the will to resist decolonisation (including the Transjordan, 1946; India, 1947; and Ceylon, Burma and Palestine, 1948). Moreover, the 'old Commonwealth' of 'white' Dominions (Canada, Australia, New Zealand and South Africa) changed its character as non-white former colonies joined. Britain felt the need to compensate for the declining importance of the Empire-Commonwealth by achieving closer ties with either the United States or Europe.

In 1945 there was a considerable psychological gulf between Britain and her continental neighbours as they had been under Nazi occupation whereas Britain had escaped that fate. It thus appeared to make more sense that Britain should look to the United States rather than Europe as partners given their common experience as comrades-in-arms since 1941; the so-called 'special relationship' (based upon a common language and culture); and the fact that only the United States appeared capable of countering the supposed communist threat given the devastated state of continental Europe; the size of the Red Army; Stalin's avowed ambition of ensuring that the USSR was protected by 'friendly' states; and the strength of communist parties in countries such as France and Italy (where communists had played a leading role in resistance movements).

It was thus considered vital to overcome traditional American isolationism as continental Europe might easily fall to communism if America withdrew. Moreover, the Bomb – in which the United States enjoyed a monopoly until 1949 – represented a means of offsetting the Soviet Union's massive advantage in terms of conventional forces.

Britain played a leading role in getting the United States to commit to Europe. Firstly, Churchill's 'Iron Curtain' speech at Fulton, Missouri in 1946 did a great deal to alert the American public to the supposed Soviet threat and thus make it easier for the Truman administration to take the steps which privately (through media such as Kennan's 'Long Telegram') it had come to believe were necessary. Secondly, when the Attlee administration informed the United States in 1947 that it would no longer be able to provide aid to Greece and Turkey this led to the announcement of the Truman Doctrine, pledging US aid to those combating communism internally or externally, and Marshall Aid, providing practical economic assistance to European countries so that they would be less likely to fall prey to communism and provide markets for US exports in due course.

The British Foreign Secretary Ernest Bevin, alongside his French counterpart, Georges Bidault, took the lead in organising a positive and concerted European response to the offer of Marshall Aid, and organising the defence of Western Europe through the 1947 Anglo-French Treaty of Dunkirk, and the 1948 Treaty of Brussels, which also included the Benelux countries and which helped pave the way for the North Atlantic Treaty Organization (NATO) in 1949.

It should be noted that the Treaties of Dunkirk and Brussels were primarily aimed at deterring future German aggression but the communist takeover in Czechoslovakia in 1948 and the Berlin Blockade of 1948–49 helped ensure that NATO had the additional purpose of deterring Soviet aggression. In British eyes the purpose of NATO (in its early days) was, as one wag put it, 'to keep the Americans in, the Germans down and the Soviets out'.

The Americans, however, not surprisingly, took a different view of the 'special relationship' from Britain. Firstly, they had rooted objections to the British Empire and in general terms (modified only by Cold War strategic considerations) wished to see British decolonisation extended and accelerated. Secondly, they wanted to see Western Europe, *including* Great Britain, working together because then it would be better able to stand up to the USSR and would be less reliant upon US aid. Thus it was a condition of the European Recovery Programme (set up to administer Marshall Aid) that it be organised and run by representatives of the European countries themselves. Churchill, too, welcomed the creation of 'a kind of United States of Europe' and propagated this message at the 1946 Zurich conference on European unity and the 'Congress of Europe' at the Hague in 1948. However, he made it perfectly clear that he recommended this for the countries of continental Europe and not for Great Britain itself.

In other words, while Britain worked with Europe as a means of securing US aid as a counterbalance to the USSR, and as a counterbalance to continental Europe itself, the United States welcomed the OEEC and the European Economic Community (EEC) as desirable in themselves and wanted to see Britain to play a central role in them rather than holding herself aloof because still clinging to the illusion that she was a world power.

For their part, the continental European nations moved towards greater unity because they believed that a customs union offered commercial benefits and that closer ties would render another European war less likely, especially if coal and steel resources were managed by a supranational body. Having just achieved the nationalisation of coal and steel, however, Attlee's Labour government was unwilling – apart from any other considerations – to pool these resources with the European Coal and Steel Community (ECSC) set up by the 1951 Treaty of Paris.

Although Britain played an important but subsidiary role in the Cold War in the late 1940s and early 1950s, for example assisting the United States in the Berlin Airlift of 1948–49 and the Korean War of 1950–53, the 1956 Suez Crisis revealed the unpalatable truth that Britain was no longer a great imperial power, and could not rely upon the 'special relationship' in a crisis (President Eisenhower forcing a ceasefire and withdrawal of British forces from the Canal Zone by doing nothing to prevent a debilitating run on the British currency). This forced an agonising reappraisal of Britain's foreign policy options. As Secretary of State Dean Acheson said in 1962, 'Britain has lost an empire and has not yet found a role'.

Hitherto, Great Britain had taken a very dismissive view of closer European co-operation. Thus in 1955 when the foreign ministers and other senior diplomats of the ECSC had met in Messina to discuss the scope for establishing a common market, Eden had merely sent a minor official from the Board of Trade, Russell Brotherton, as an observer, who was withdrawn at an early stage of the proceedings.

The British-led European Free Trade Area (EFTA), which came into being under Macmillan in 1960 was a very pale imitation of the EEC which had been established by the 1957 Treaty of Rome. Macmillan also accelerated decolonisation (with Ghana, for example, gaining its independence in 1957, and Nigeria following suit in 1960), as a result of both increasing nationalist demands (the 'wind of change'), and the example of France's rapid – and bloody – decolonisation (in French Indo-China and Algeria).

Most dramatically, Macmillan made a central plank of his policy British membership application for membership of the EEC, in response to shrinking trade with the Commonwealth, the relative failure of EFTA, the economic growth and enhanced political influence of the EEC, and the general belief that this offered the best way of securing continued British influence in the world.

World War Two resulted in the emergence of a bi-polar world, with the United States and the Soviet Union as superpowers. Britain fought a rearguard action which ensured that it remained a Great Power but the undermining of empire obliged Europe to be embraced in a way which had hitherto been eschewed.

13 The impact of World War Two on the United States

Introduction

The United States of America was blessed with a comparatively substantial domestic supply of most important raw materials for modern industry (only really lacking rubber) and possessed a level of gross output which, even prior to the wartime recovery from depression, exceeded the combined output of the Axis powers. It entered World War Two (like World War One) later than any other major power. Unlike many participants it did not suffer invasion or occupation. Moreover, it was almost unique insofar as mainland America was not bombed (unless one counts Japanese incendiary balloons). It placed a smaller percentage of its population in uniform than any other power (12 per cent) and its losses, while high by American standards (only being surpassed by the Civil War) were light by international standards. With 405,000 dead (291,557 in combat) the United States suffered a lower total casualty rate in terms of percentage of population than any other major belligerent. Thus for every American to die, 15 Germans and at least 53 Russians died[1] Looked at another way, the Red Army suffered as many combat deaths in the Battle of Stalingrad as the Americans suffered in the entire war[2] and more women lost their lives in the Soviet armed forces than men in the American military.[3]

However, it would be a mistake to deduce from the above that the impact of the war on the United States was slight. In 1939 there had been fewer than 200,000 men in the Army, 125,200 in the Navy, and less than 20,000 in the Marine Corps but by 1945 it possessed an army of over 8 million – a figure with which only the USSR could compete – together with the world's largest and most powerful navy and air force. Furthermore, by 1945 the United States had atomic weapons and had shown it was not afraid of using them. This transformation had been accomplished by virtue of an enormous expansion of the American economy. United States gross national product (GNP) grew by 52 per cent between 1939 and 1944 and ushered in a boom which lasted until the outbreak of the Korean War in 1950. At the end of 1939 there had still been five million Americans unemployed. It was thus the war rather than the New Deal which decisively ended the Great Depression and ushered in a period of full employment. Indeed, the shortage of manpower on the home front created opportunities for both women and African Americans, with many of the former coming out of their kitchens to work in factories or dockyards, while many of the latter left agricultural employment in the South for the expanding defence industries of the North. But if it was a 'good war' for these groups it was a humiliating and painful experience for Japanese Americans who were interned en masse.

The Arsenal of Democracy

It used to be the orthodox view, and is still the staple fare of most school textbooks, that Roosevelt's alphabet laws spelt out the solution to America's economic problems, as the New Deal anticipated Keynesian economic thinking, allowing the United States to spend its way out of depression.

In scholarly circles explanations of what ended the Great Depression have been radically revised.[4] Margaret Mary Barrett, for example, concedes that FDR's New Deal was not a coherent and consistent programme so much as a series of short-term responses to particular problems and pressure groups. It did not permanently stimulate the economy, increase production, or alleviate unemployment, nor did it proceed smoothly and evenly. Thus the severe cuts in spending ordered by FDR in 1937 contributed to the recession of 1938, which saw the economy fall back to a position that nearly matched that of 1929 (with industrial production falling by one third over the 12 months from the spring of 1937 and the average unemployment rate jumping to 19 per cent).

Barrett, nevertheless, claims that FDR's policies alleviated the impact of the Depression by restoring the American people's confidence in (a reformed) capitalism and by benefiting certain key sections of society.

Thomas E. Woods Jr., on the other hand, argues that the New Deal actually hurt the economy, because it was not so much intended to restore prosperity as designed to protect wages and the rights of workers by imposing regulations on business (notably through the National Industrial Recovery and Wagner Acts). Thus far from accelerating America's recovery from the depression, FDR's New Deal actually tended to prolong it through tax increases, increased labour costs and over-regulation which bred uncertainty and hostility among the business community in general and investors in particular (because redistribution of wealth was given a higher priority than its creation).

Certainly unemployment averaged 18 per cent between 1933 and 1940 and never fell below 14 per cent during FDR's first two administrations. The rate did drop briefly to 14.3 per cent in 1937 but at the time of Pearl Harbor unemployment was still at 18 per cent: the same rate as during Roosevelt's first year as president. Indeed, full employment only returned in 1943, assisted not only by a resurgence in demand but also by the fact that millions of men and women had been drafted into the armed forces.

In 1939 FDR managed to persuade Congress to approve the programme allowing US industries to sell war goods to France and Britain on a cash-and-carry basis, on the basis that America should serve as the arsenal of (European) democracy. Roosevelt's re-election for an unprecedented third term on 5 November 1940, and Hitler's continuing successes meant that Roosevelt felt that he was now able and there was even more need to offer further assistance to Britain. Thus Lend–Lease was proposed in December 1940 and became law in March 1941. After the US freighter *Robin Moore* was sunk on 11 June 1941 Roosevelt reacted by occupying Iceland (relieving the British garrison there) and in October 1941, he further persuaded Congress to allow American merchant vessels to carry goods to British ports. These steps certainly helped ensure that democracy was not extinguished across the Atlantic but they also had the welcome effect of helping to stimulate American economic recovery, as indicated by the fact that the average rate of unemployment which had never fallen below 14.3 per cent prior to the war dropped in 1941 to 9.9 per cent.

World War Two reopened the US economy to international trade and stimulated both existing industries (such as textiles and steel) and newer ones (including aviation and electronics) as the federal government increased its spending and overseas markets expanded. Thus while US exports had averaged below $4.4 billion in the years immediately preceding 1940 they rose by $1.5 billion in 1941. At nearly $13.8 billion (out of total federal expenditure of $16.9 billion) defence spending in 1941 was roughly two and a half times the figure (of below $5.4 billion) for all federal spending in the previous year.

America's industrial potential was enormous and was rapidly realised, so that by 1944 its war production was more than double that of the Axis despite the organisational genius of Albert Speer maximising Germany's efforts by that period. In the course of the war America was responsible for producing nearly two-thirds of all Allied military equipment including 86,000 tanks, 193,000 artillery pieces, 14 million shoulder weapons, 2.4 million trucks and jeeps, 1,200 combat vessels, 82,000 landing craft and ships, and 297,000 aircraft.

Between 1940 and 1944 US industrial output rose by 90 per cent; agricultural production grew by 20 per cent (assisted by rising consumer purchasing power and by federal policies of price supports and controls); and the total national production of goods and services expanded by 60 per cent. The GNP more than doubled from $100 billion in 1940 to $214 billion in 1945: more than half the world's total.

These developments brought unprecedented levels of employment and income. Prosperity, Woods argues, only fully returned, however, when the Republican Congress of 1947 removed some of the more radical features of the New Deal (as symbolised by the Taft–Hartley Act) and when the Eisenhower administration returned the country to what President Warren G. Harding had called "normalcy" – undoing many of the regulations on business imposed by the Democrats in the 1930s.

Mobilisation

The federal government grew enormously in size, power, and cost as a consequence of the war, although Roosevelt took steps to mobilise American industry for war even before the war in Europe began, setting up the War Resources Board to analyse mobilisation options in August 1939, and declaring an unlimited national emergency on 27 May 1941.

James F. Byrnes was a key appointment both as head of the Office of Economic Stabilization from October 1942, and Director of the Office of War Mobilization (OWM) from May 1943. In the former capacity he successfully curbed inflation by imposing comprehensive controls over civilian purchasing power, despite the general public's reluctance to see items like oil rationed and resentment at the extreme youth of many of Byrnes's officials. As Director of the OWM (which became the Office of War Mobilisation and Reconversion or OWMR) he was effectively director of domestic affairs, co-ordinating all federal agencies in maximising the war effort and thereby allowing Roosevelt to concentrate on diplomatic and military affairs.

The Japanese Americans: first mainland American victims of the Pacific War

'High school history books barely mention it. It's been the subject of only a couple of ... movies and novels ... And ... many of the people who lived through it have kept mum for decades' wrote a Japanese American journalist about the internment of Japanese Americans during World War Two.[5]

This policy, which Eugene V. Rostow called 'our worst wartime mistake',[6] which the American Civil Liberties Union later called 'the greatest deprivation of civil liberties ... since slavery'[7] and which is now widely acknowledged as 'one of the darkest moments of America's history'[8] has indeed received surprisingly little attention, at least when compared with the African-American struggle for civil rights. For example, both *The Color Purple* and *Amistad* are Oscar-winning Steven Spielberg films while his 1979 film *1941*, dealing, albeit humorously, with West Coast wartime paranoia regarding the Japanese threat, was one of his few flops both commercially and critically.

It is true that comedies traditionally find it harder to garner recognition than dramas but one cannot help feeling that for the bulk of Spielberg's American audience *1941* was no laughing matter not because they believed that year to be their finest hour but rather because it was a period characterised by humiliation overseas and hysteria at home: the first inflicted by the Japanese and the second directed against those of Japanese ancestry.

The fact that the internment of Japanese Americans still touches a raw nerve was demonstrated recently when Republican

Congressman Howard Coble of Greensboro, North Carolina, the influential Chair of the Judiciary Subcommittee on Crime, Terrorism and Homeland Security, aroused protests when he stated, in the course of a WKZL–FM radio interview that the Japanese Americans had been interned for their own safety: 'They were an endangered species. For many of these Japanese-Americans, it wasn't safe for them to be on the street'.[9]

Coble caused even greater offence when he sought to justify internment by adding that, 'Some [Japanese Americans] probably were intent on doing harm to us ...'.[10]

Coble's controversial comments thus crystallise the question of whether the internment of Japanese Americans was motivated more by fears for national security or fears for their own safety.

US–Japanese relations had deteriorated to such a point by late 1941 that war seemed likely (see Chapter 9 above). In October 1941, President Roosevelt accordingly commissioned Curtis Munson of the State Department to compile a report assessing the loyalty of Japanese Americans.

Munson's report, which was delivered in November but was suppressed until 1946, found that in spite of discrimination against them 'the vast majority were loyal to America ...'.[11]

However, the Japanese attack on Pearl Harbor on 7 December 1941, produced a state of shock comparable to that of 9/11 on the present generation of Americans. The 'sneak' nature of the attack – without a formal declaration of war and undertaken while Japan was still engaged in talks – combined with the success of Japanese Imperial forces in overrunning Hong Kong, Manila, Thailand, Singapore, Midway, Wake and Guam in the following weeks, compounded the racial stereotyping of the Japanese as deceitful and duplicitous. The Congressional Record for 15 December shows Congressman John Rankin declaring that he was in favour of 'catching every Japanese in America, Alaska and Hawaii ... and putting them in concentration camps'.[12] *Time* magazine depicted the national mood as one of intense bitterness: 'What would the people ... say in the face of the mightiest event of their time? What they said – tens of thousands of them – was: "Why, the yellow bastards!"'[13] Feelings ran especially high on the West Coast because 'units of US Marine Reserves and of the National Guard from Arizona, California, Oregon and Washington had been stationed in the Philippines prior to December 7, 1941' and it became 'widely known' that these units 'had been decimated by the Japanese who treated them brutally as prisoners of war'.[14]

The Federal Bureau of Investigation (FBI), the Office of Naval Intelligence and the Military Intelligence Service had already compiled lists of those individuals whose loyalties were considered questionable and on the day following Pearl Harbor the US Attorney General, Francis Biddle, announced that the FBI was in the process of detaining the small number of Japanese regarded as potentially 'dangerous'.[15] On the first day, 736 Japanese immigrant leaders were detained. By 11 December the number arrested in this manner totalled roughly 1200 and by February the number picked up totalled 2192.[16] Precisely because all those identified as potential threats to national security were already in custody, the FBI Director, J. Edgar Hoover, opposed as unnecessary any move for wholesale internment.

Why then did President Roosevelt sign Executive Order 9066 on 18 March 1942 authorising the War Relocation Authority 'to provide for the removal from designated areas ... persons whose removal is necessary in the interests of national security' and why did the WRA ultimately decide to intern all the Japanese on the West Coast?[17] Was fear for national security or fear for the safety of the Japanese Americans at the hands of their fellow Americans uppermost in policymakers' minds?

In a letter of 12 February 1942 to Secretary of War, Henry L. Stimson, the Attorney General, Francis Biddle, distinguished between 'alien enemies' and 'American citizens of Japanese origin', reiterating the point made in his letter of 9 February that 'the proclamations issued by the President directing the Department of Justice to apprehend and evacuate alien enemies' did not include the latter. Biddle nevertheless suggested how the Army might circumvent the legal problem of evacuating both groups if they considered this militarily desirable.[18]

The key point is that Biddle clearly did not regard it as needful for the Japanese Americans to be protected for their own safety, as such protection is the role of the law enforcement agencies rather than that of the military. He nowhere refers to the risk of vigilante violence, referring instead to evacuation as solely 'the responsibility of the Army' because it 'involves a judgment based on military considerations',[19] namely, the perceived threat to national security.

Unfortunately, both Secretary of War Stimson and Lieutenant General John L. DeWitt, in charge of the Western Defense Command, were predisposed to believe that a significant proportion of Japanese were actively or potentially disloyal, and neither of them was disposed to make the necessary expenditure of time or effort to distinguish between the patriotic and the perfidious. Thus Stimson's diary entry for 10 February 1942 damningly records his belief that 'their racial characteristics are such that we cannot ... trust the citizen Japanese'.[20] While DeWitt, candidly told the Attorney General's representative, 'I have no confidence in their loyalty whatsoever'.[21] On 14 February 1942 he stated his belief that there was 'no ground for assuming that any Japanese ... though born and raised in the United States, will not turn against this nation ...'.[22]

Racist sentiments were also voiced by local politicians, the media (especially the Hearst press) and members of the white community who stood to profit from removal of the Japanese (such as the Western Growers Protective Association). Thus the Governor of Arkansas, for example, expressed the view that 'The Japs live like rats, breed like rats and act like rats'.[23] Bert Miller, the Attorney General of Idaho, declared, 'We want to keep this a white man's country. All Japs should be put in concentration camps',[24] while his Californian counterpart, the future State Governor and Chief Justice, Earl Warren, declared, without any evidence to back his claims that, 'there is more potential danger among the group of Japanese who are born in this country than from the alien Japanese who were born in Japan'. Indeed, neither evidence nor logic featured prominently in public pronouncements at this time. Pulitzer prize-winning journalist Walter Lippmann, for example, deduced from the fact that no acts of sabotage had as yet been committed by the West Coast Japanese 'that the blow ... is held back until it can be struck with maximum effect'.[25]

Senator Wallgren, who was a prominent member of the Senate Subcommittee of Military Affairs later speculated that 'with this war going on and with all the bitterness that might be created because of the loss of sons and brothers and relatives ... in the South Pacific, it might not be any too safe to allow some of those people [Japanese Americans] too much freedom, and it might be for their own protection to keep them under strict supervision and under some sort of protection on our part'.[26] Certainly, when

DeWitt authorised Karl R. Bendetsen to act as commanding offi-cer of the Wartime Civil Control Administration, his order stated that internment was 'for the protection of the nation ... and for the protection of the Japanese people themselves'.[27]

However, in the light of DeWitt's earlier comments cited above it is difficult not to feel that he regarded internment as jus-tified primarily in terms of national security and that when he and others referred to relocation as necessary to pre-empt vigilante-style violence this was motivated not by the desire to save them from harm so much as a desire to provide a cover under which their civil rights might be violated with impunity. As Cheryl Greenberg puts it, 'Government's rhetorical reliance on national security as the motivation for evacuation helped minimize' the identification of 'relocation as a civil rights problem ...'.[28]

This is not to deny that the Japanese Americans were threat-ened with and, in some instances, subjected to violence. However, it is worth recording that this violence did not arise spontaneously but was rather whipped up by those in positions of responsibility.

In the immediate aftermath of Pearl Harbor it was natural for the authorities and the media to attempt to explain their humili-ation by reference to a Japanese fifth column. Thus Mississippi Senator John Rankin, for example, told Congress that the Japanese Americans on Hawaii 'were making signs ... guiding the Japanese planes to the objects of their iniquity in order that they might destroy our naval vessels, murder our soldiers and sailors, and blow to pieces the helpless women and children of Hawaii'.[29]

As if such inflammatory remarks were insufficient to spark racist attacks, supposedly reputable newspapers such as the *Los Angeles Times* invoked California's vigilante tradition, calling in an editorial on 8 December for 'alert, keen-eyed civilians' to co-operate with the military authorities 'against spies, saboteurs and fifth columnists' as no one could afford to take a chance on the loyalty of Japanese Americans 'in the light of yesterday's demon-stration that treachery and double-dealing are major Japanese weapons'.[30]

Those who seek to defend internment continue to claim that it was primarily motivated by a desire to save the Japanese-American community from the (understandable) wrath of their neighbours. Thus Tom Clark, in the course of an interview in 1972 stated that 'you have to put it [internment] in the perspective of the time, which was that there was a great hullabaloo about getting them out of California, or something would happen to them'.[31]

In fact, given all the above, it is surprising how little violence was actually visited upon the Japanese Americans prior to 119,803 of them being placed behind barbed wire fences supposedly for their own safety. In total there were just 43 acts of violence, although admittedly seven of these were killings.[32] Nevertheless, when one considers how high feelings were running, stoked by politicians, the military and the media, and how freely lynch law operated in this period, the overall impression is that the risk to the Japanese Americans of leaving them at liberty was not such as to justify their incarceration.

Thus when Roosevelt signed Executive Order 9066 he was bending to the pressure of those who did not have the best interests of the Japanese Americans at heart, such as the Californian Senator Hiram W. Johnson, who six days previously had forwarded to the President the unanimous recommendation of the congressional delegations of California, Oregon and Washington calling for 'The immediate evacuation of all persons of Japanese lineage and all others ... whose presence shall be deemed ... inimical to the defense of the United States ...'.[33]

Keen to prove their patriotism 12,000 young men later enlisted, many straight from the internment camps, for the all-Japanese American 442nd Infantry Regiment, after it was announced in January 1943 that a special combat team would be open to Japanese American volunteers. It became the US unit to suffer the highest casualty rate and to receive the largest number of decorations in World War Two.[34] One volunteer stated that 'The 442nd would rather fight the Japs than the Germans to prove our loyalty'.[35] They were, instead, deployed on the Italian front: a fact symbolising the suspicions which surrounded the Japanese Americans even when there was abundant proof of their willingness to make the supreme sacrifice in the service of Uncle Sam.

No person of Japanese ancestry was ever charged with any subversive act in the United States during World War Two, whereas several Germans were convicted of such acts. But whereas the Japanese Americans were interned en masse, Italian and German Americans were considered on their individual merits. Why was there this disparity of treatment? Was it due to fears for the personal safety of the Japanese Americans or did it rather stem from fear that they posed a unique threat to national security? It is difficult to argue the latter in light of the fact that the Japanese Americans of Hawaii (and Alaska) were not interned en masse.

In part this difference of treatment could be attributed to the fact that the Italian and German Americans had celebrities to plead their cause, including baseball star Joe di Maggio's mother and conductor Bruno Walter, respectively, while no one spoke up for the Japanese Americans.[36] It is thus difficult not to conclude that crude racism supplies a large part of the answer. To put it bluntly, it was easier to pick upon the Japanese than the German or Italian Americans by virtue of the colour of their skin. In terms of the potential threat to national security German and Italian spies and saboteurs posed a much greater threat precisely because they would generally find it easier to blend into their surroundings.

In an interview, Tom Clark wisely remarked that 'Of course your hindsight is much better than your foresight'.[37] Nevertheless, having examined the primary and secondary literature on the subject it is difficult to disagree with Mikiso Hane's judgment that 'In retrospect it is clear that the decision to evacuate and intern all people of Japanese blood from the West Coast was based not on military but on racial ... grounds'.[38] Since the 1980s this has also been the official view of the US government, the final report of the Commission on Wartime Relocation and Internment of Civilians stating that 'the record does not support the claim that military necessity justified the exclusion of the ethnic Japanese from the West Coast'[39] – an admission that has provided the basis for both compensation payments and official apologies to the Japanese American community.

The quotation which opened this investigation bemoaned the lack of attention paid to this shameful episode in America's history. What has followed has shown that while that was once true it is no longer the case. The internet, in particular, has rendered accessible some astonishingly candid primary sources which enable one to determine that internment was motivated more by fears for national security arising out of racial stereotyping rather than out of fears for the safety of the West Coast Japanese Americans. Racial superiority was so widely assumed in the West at that time that 'even ... liberal politicians were not inhibited from expressing their opinions in racial terms'.[40] Ironically, the expression of racist sentiments which made life so difficult for some contemporaries makes life easier for historians of the period, allowing them to establish dishonourable motives which in more politically correct times might remain hidden.

Migration and racial tension

The booming economy, centred upon the defence industry, encouraged many African Americans, Mexican Americans, and Native Americans to migrate in search of employment and better pay.

The US government took a hand in this process, for example in sponsoring the Bracero Programme, which encouraged wartime agricultural employment for Mexican labourers in the Southwest United States. However, the influx of Mexicans and Mexican Americans to the West led to a violent backlash, of which the most notorious example was the so-called Zoot Suit riots (named after the dandyish apparel of the day), of June 1943, in which mobs of white GIs attacked Mexican gang members in Los Angeles, California.

Most African Americans moved from the South to the West and North so that by 1950, for the first time, a third of all black Americans lived outside the South. They were to find, however, that they had not escaped racial bigotry. Whites resented working next to blacks, let alone seeing them get on. Thus in June 1943, 25,000 Packard plant workers in Detroit stopped work in protest of the promotion of three blacks.

By 1943, the number of African Americans in Detroit had doubled since 1933 to 200,000. They arrived in such numbers that it placed enormous strains upon housing, transportation, education and recreational facilities. The housing problem was compounded by the authorities, who badly mishandled the situation.

Already in June 1941 the Detroit Housing Commission had recognised the need for new housing for defence workers, and approved one site for whites and another for African Americans. However, the federal government first chose to place the latter project – which came to be named Sojourner Truth – in a white neighbourhood and then, when hostility from whites kept out blacks, decreed that the project would be for whites and another site would be selected for African-American workers. To complete the catalogue of incompetence, when a suitable site could not be found, Washington allowed African Americans into Sojourner Truth after all. The predictable consequence in February 1942 was violence by a white mob directed against those African Americans who tried to move into their new properties. It was not until April that these families could take up residence, and only then under protection from the police and state troops.

The resentment caused by the Sojourner Truth riots provided the backdrop for even worse disorder. On 20 June 1943, whites and African Americans clashed on Belle Isle. The fighting escalated until about 200 were involved. Moreover, rumours of atrocities on both sides began to fly and led to 36 hours of rioting in which 34 lives were lost, 25 of them black. The city's 2000 police officers and 150 state police troopers were overwhelmed by the numbers of lawbreakers (although at least some police appear to have turned a blind eye to acts of lawlessness directed by whites against African Americans) and order was only restored by the intervention of federal troops. More than 1800 (roughly 85 per cent of them African American) were arrested for a variety of offences including looting, larceny, assault and carrying concealed weapons. The only reason why there was not more arson was because gasoline was rationed.

African Americans and the Civil Rights movement

Notwithstanding the lazy stereotyping which portrayed African Americans as lazy (as shown, for example, by the lyrics of the contemporary hit song, 'Chocolate Soldier from the USA'), it was difficult for increasing numbers of politicians of the time to deny that the contribution to the war effort of African Americans, both in the armed forces and on the home front, entitled them to greater respect and consideration as citizens than they had hitherto enjoyed.

Moreover, the migration referred to above meant that a potentially powerful black constituency now existed in the North. A. Philip Randolph, the President of the Brotherhood of Sleeping Car Porters, sought to flex new-found black muscle even before the United States formally entered the war. Thus in March 1941, he proposed a march on Washington D.C., to demand an end to discrimination in employment and the armed forces.

Alarmed by this proposal, Roosevelt called Randolph to the White House for a meeting, and agreed that in exchange for calling off the march, he would issue Executive Order 8802, stating that federal government hiring practices should not be affected by race, colour, creed, or national origin, and creating the Fair Employment Practices Committee (FEPC) to enforce the order.

In practice the FEPC achieved little, not least because its remit was reactive rather than proactive: only investigating alleged discrimination *after* it received a complaint. However, it symbolised a change in public attitudes and encouraged other initiatives by the African American community, such as the 1942 formation of the Congress of Racial Equality (CORE) on the University of Chicago campus.

World War Two stimulated the demand for better treatment because African Americans from the North witnessed segregation in the training camps of the South, while all blacks serving overseas saw an unsegregated world and appreciated that 'Jim Crow' laws need not be the norm. The 'Double V' campaign for victory against fascism abroad and racism at home illustrates the connection between the war and the demand for reform, while the war also stimulated the civil rights movement by allowing some blacks to experience power and responsibility through their training as officers or specialists.

The GI Bill

All veterans, irrespective of colour and sex, received some consideration for the sacrifices they had made in the service of their nation after the American Legion successfully lobbied for the passage of what it called 'a bill of rights for G.I. Joe and G.I. Jane'.

Kansas lawyer, World War One veteran and former national commander of the Legion, Harry W. Colmery, also helped draft the Servicemen's Readjustment Act which became law on 22 June 1944 (just over a fortnight after D-Day) and was popularly known as the GI Bill or the GI Bill of Rights. It sought to enhance the prospects of those who had served in the armed forces (for a minimum of 90 days and not been dishonourably discharged) by authorising payments for tuition, books and living expenses for up to four years of college or vocational school, low-interest mortgages for homeowners, loans for veterans to buy farms and start businesses, and a "readjustment allowance" of $20 a week for up to 52 weeks while veterans sought employment.

Almost four million veterans received Veterans Administration loans for houses and an even larger number took advantage of the scheme's educational provisions. In the first year of peace over one million veterans enrolled in college: roughly 50 per cent of that year's total enrollment, and by 1956, almost 10 million men and women had benefited from the law's educational and training provisions. The scheme eased the demobilisation process both for individuals and for the economy by ensuring that the labour market was not swamped.

Women

On the face of it, the Second World War represents a watershed in American women's history given the unprecedented job opportunities that arose as a consequence of economic recovery and the military mobilisation of so many men. Thus employment of women increased by 50 per cent, with particularly notable gains in the number and range of blue-collar jobs. Moreover, policies barring married women from white-collar employment were largely removed.

Employment not only brought a degree of financial independence but a widening of horizons and enhanced self-esteem. However, while some men in the workplace came to appreciate that women workers were equal or even superior to their male counterparts, women still suffered from wage discrimination (being paid less than men for doing the same job), job discrimination (being relegated to the less interesting and fulfilling occupations) and were expected to make way for the men on their return home (just as many colleges made places for male veterans under the terms of the GI Bill by turning away qualified women).

Many women themselves willingly resumed their traditional roles as wives and mothers, or at least resumed more traditional female employments after the war because they shared the prevailing stereotyped notion of a woman's place. Thus World War Two did not act as a catalyst for the feminist movement to anything like the same degree as the war promoted the Civil Rights movement.

Post-war prosperity

The military-industrial complex that Eisenhower criticised in his farewell address as President actually had its origins in World War Two rather than the Cold War because it was between 1941 and 1945 that the national economy became bound up with military spending.

As has been argued above, World War Two ended the Great Depression rather than Roosevelt's New Deal policies (which retarded rather than assisted recovery). However, whichever explanation was preferred, Keynesianism was apparently justified by success and thereby justified an enhanced role for federal government in the economic sphere, including a commitment to ensure 'full employment' (although this development also increased fears of socialistic 'big' government in some quarters).

National income more than doubled (GNP rising from $91 billion in 1939 to $214 billion in 1945) and both personal savings and consumer spending reached new heights. Although little income redistribution occurred between classes, the economic diversification experienced by the West allowed it to narrow the gap in standard of living with the rest of the country, while the general rise in living standards produced a renewed sense of optimism. Thus World War Two was a 'good war' for the American people as a whole, with many groups – including African Americans, farmers, bureaucrats and union bosses – making substantial gains, while only the Japanese Americans and grieving families appeared net losers. Women made gains which were mostly only for the duration.

Epilogue

America's booming economy provided the sinews for the superpower status, which enabled her to bestride the world, once she had overcome her vestigial isolationism (see Chapter 10). Indeed, although the United States remained – and remains – anti-imperialistic in rhetoric, World War Two was instrumental in the process whereby she finally displaced the British Empire as the world's economic powerhouse and policeman. Even today, the United States remains in denial regarding its imperial status. despite much to be proud of, not least in its rebuilding of post-war Germany and Japan.[41]

If the irony surrounding World War One centres in its origins – railway timetables dictating to Emperors and Britain defending the honour of a small nation which itself acted atrociously against the peoples of the Congo – World Wars Two's is to be found in its aftermath, including a Poland freed from Nazi rule only to enjoy Soviet tyranny, and Hitler's efforts to create a Jew-free Reich providing a compelling case for the creation of a Jewish state in Palestine. Such is the unpredictability of the past.

Notes

Chapter 1 The Paris peace conference

1. Clemenceau quoted in Margaret Macmillan, *Peacemakers. The Paris Conference of 1919 and Its Attempt to End War*, John Murray, London, 2001, p. 35.
2. Anthony Lentin, *Guilt at Versailles: Lloyd George the Pre-history of Appeasement*, London, Methuen, 1985, pp. 132–3.
3. C.S. Maier, *Recasting Bourgeois Europe. Stabilization in France, Germany and Italy in the Decade after World War I*, Princeton, Princeton University Press, 1977; M. Trachtenberg, 'Reparation at the Paris Peace Conference', *Journal of Modern History*, 51(1) March 1979; and S. Schuker, American 'Reparations' to Germany, 1919–1933: Implications for the Third-World Debt Crisis, *Princeton Studies in International Finance*, no. 61, July 1988.

Chapter 2 Nazi foreign policy

1. J. Noakes and G. Pridham, *Nazism 1919–1945, Vol. 3. Foreign Policy, War and Racial Extermination*, Exeter University Publications, Exeter, p. 629.
2. The Text of the Hossbach Memorandum is available at: http://www.yale.edu/lawweb/avalon/imt/hossbach.htm
3. Noakes and Pridham, op. cit., p. 681.
4. Ibid., p. 685.
5. Ibid., p. 685.
6. Ibid., p. 685.
7. Ibid., p. 683.
8. Ibid., p. 701.
9. Ibid., p. 702.
10. Ibid., p. 703.
11. Ibid., p. 708.
12. Ibid., p. 709.
13. Ibid., p. 712.

14. Ibid., pp. 720–1.
15. Ibid., p. 721.
16. See, for example, T.W. Mason, 'The Domestic Dynamics of Nazi Conquest', in T. Childers and Caplan, J. eds, *Reevaluating the Third Reich*, Holmes & Meier, New York, 1993.

Chapter 3 Appeasement

1. Quoted in Frank McDonough, *Hitler, Chamberlain and Appeasement*, Cambridge University Press, Cambridge, 2002, p. 5.
2. Cato (M. Foot et al.), *Guilty Men*, Victor Gollancz, London, 1940.
3. Churchill, W., *The Gathering Storm*, Houghton Mifflin, Boston, 1948.
4. Charmley, J., *Chamberlain and the Lost Peace*, Hodder & Stoughton, London, 1989.
5. Op. cit.
6. Parker, R.A.C., *Churchill and Appeasement*, Macmillan, London, 2000.
7. Quoted in J. Noakes and G. Pridham, *Nazism 1919–1945, Vol. 3. Foreign Policy, War and Racial Extermination*, Exeter University Publications, Exeter, 1988, p. 720.
8. A. Lentin, *Lloyd George and the Lost Peace: From Versailles to Hitler, 1919–1940*, Palgrave, 2001, p. 126.
9. Myths and Memories of World War Two, BBC TV programme.

Chapter 4 The fall of France

1. William, D.I., 'Domestic Politics and the Fall of France in 1940', *Historical Reflections/Réflexions Historiques*, 1996, as cited in *The French Defeat of 1940: Reassessments*, Blatt, J. ed., Berghahn, Providence and Oxford, 1998, p. 99.
2. Ibid.
3. In his 'Finest Hour' speech on 18th June, Waterloo Day.
4. Quoted in Julian Jackson, *The Fall of France*, Oxford University Press, Oxford, p. 238.
5. Quoted in The Second World War in Colour DVD 1.23.

Chapter 5 Great Britain alone

1. Overy, R., *The Battle*, Penguin Books, London, 2000, p. 41.
2. Ibid., p. 41.
3. Ibid., p. 35.
4. Ibid., p. 57.
5. Ibid., p. xiii.
6. Ibid., p. 121.
7. Churchill quoted in Reynolds, D., *In Command of History. Churchill Fighting and Writing the Second World War*, Penguin Books, London, 2005, p. 231.
8. Keegan, J. *The Second World War*, Pimlico, London, 1989, pp. 93–4.

Chapter 6 The Eastern Front

1. Quoted in Walter Laqueur, *Russia and Germany. A Century of Conflict*, Weidenfeld and Nicolson, London, 1965, p. 20.
2. Quoted in ibid., p. 164.
3. Quoted in ibid., p. 21.
4. Adolf Hitler, *Mein Kampf*, quoted in Ruth Henig, 'The Origins of the Second World War', *New Perspective*, 3(1), September, 1997.
5. Hitler quoted in J. Noakes and G. Pridham, *Nazism 1919–1945*, Vol. 3, *Foreign Policy, War and Racial Extermination*, Exeter University Publications, Exeter, p. 809.
6. See Gerhard Weinberg, *Germany and the Soviet Union, 1939–1941*, E.J. Brill, Leiden, 1954; Edward, E. Ericson III, *Feeding the German Eagle. Soviet Economic Aid to Nazi Germany, 1933–1941*, Praeger, London, 1999; and Samantha Carl, *The Buildup of the German War Economy: The Importance of the Nazi–Soviet Economic Agreements of 1939 and 1940* at: http://muweb.millersville.edu/~holo-con/Carl-1999.html
7. Quoted in Laurence Rees, *War of the Century*, BBC, London, 1999, p. 19.
8. Quoted in ibid., p. 30.
9. Quoted in Michael Wright, *The World At Arms*, Readers Digest Association Ltd., London, 1989, p. 108.
10. Viktor Suvorov, *Icebreaker: Who Started the Second World War?*, Hamish Hamilton, London, 1990.

11. V.I. Semidetko, 'Istoki porazcheniia v Belorussii', *Military-Historical Journal (Voenno-istoricheskii zhurnal)*, 4, 1989.

Chapter 7 The strategic bombing offensive against Germany

1. Siebert Detlef, 'British Bombing Strategy in World War Two', www.bbc.co.uk/history/war/wwtwo/area_bombing_01. shtml (August 2001).
2. Sven Lindqvist, *A History of Bombing*, Granta Books, London, 2002, p. 206. Lindqvist describes his book as 'a labyrinth' by which he means it largely disregards chronology and scholarly convention. Thus while Lindqvist often eschews page references in his own footnotes, he makes it impossible, or at least very difficult, for another to cite his own work other than by reference to section numbers, as his book lacks page numbers. On the one hand Lindqvist argues that the strategic bombing offensive was ineffective yet on the other he makes the bizarre assertion that in 1942 the British could have successfully offered to stop bombing German cities in exchange for a halt in the Holocaust and Germany's adoption of the Geneva Convention with regard to Soviet POWs. Lundqvist, p. 193.
3. Peter Englund, *Brev fran nollpunkten*, 1996, Stockholm, p. 196, quoted approvingly by Lindqvist, op. cit., p. 206.
4. Jörg Friedrich, *Der Brand. Deutschland im Bombenkrieg 1940–1945*, Propyläen Verlag, Berlin, 2002.
5. Lindqvist, op. cit., p. 145, argues that total war emerged before the twentieth century insofar as 'Colonial wars were total for the tribes and peoples fighting for their lives ...'.
6. Lindqvist, ibid., p. 95, quoting Boyle, *Trenchard, Man of Vision*, 1962, Chapter 12.
7. Lindqvist, ibid., p. 96.
8. Malcolm Smith, *Britain and 1940*, Routledge, London, 2000, p. 15.
9. See Lindqvist, ibid., p. 102.
10. R.J. Overy, *Bomber Command, 1939–1945. Reaping the Whirlwind*, Collins, London, 1997.
11. G. Douhet, *The Command of the Air*, Coward–McGann, Inc., New York, 1942, quoted by Lindqvist, p. 176.
12. Douhet quoted by Lindqvist, ibid., p. 104.

13. Lindqvist, ibid., p. 161, quoting Stanley Baldwin, 11/12/1932 from Norman Longmate, *The Bombers: The RAF Offensive against Germany 1939–1945*, Hutchinson, London, 1983.
14. In a speech to the House of Commons in 1932.
15. Lindqvist, op. cit., p. 177, quoting Fuller, 1948, Chapter 7. However, the only Fuller reference in Lindqvist's bibliography is to J.F.C. Fuller, *The Reformation of War*, London, 1923.
16. Although there is no evidence to support Veale's contention that the British bombing of German civilians was intended by Churchill to provoke German reprisals designed to fuel the British will to keep on fighting. F.P.J. Veale, *Advance to Barbarism: How the Reverse to Barbarism in Warfare and War-Trials Menaces Our Future*, Madison, 1953 (republished Mitre, New York, 1968).
17. *The World at War*, Documentary. Reaping the Whirlwind.
18. Ibid.
19. Churchill's statement of 30 October 1940, quoted by Lindqvist, op. cit., p. 181.
20. Ibid., p. 181, quoting 'the official British history of the air war', i.e., Sir Charles Webster and Noble Frankland, *The Strategic Air Offensive against Germany, 1939–1945*, Vol. 1, London, Her Majesty's Stationery Office, 1961.
21. Sinclair letter to Philip Noel–Baker dated 16 December 1946, reproduced as Source 6 at http://learningcurve.pro.gov.uk/heroesvillains/churchill/
22. Harris's official account of Bomber Command, 1946, reproduced as Source 2 at: http://learningcurve.pro.gov.uk/heroesvillains/churchill/
23. Confidential Air Staff Memorandum (C. 28933) on Harris's despatch on Bomber Command's Operations 1942/1945, reproduced as Source 5 at: http://learningcurve.pro.gov.uk/heroesvillains/churchill/
24. Quoted in Lindqvist, op. cit., p. 194.
25. Confidential Air Staff Memorandum (C. 28933) on Harris's despatch on Bomber Command's Operations 1942/1945, reproduced as Source 5 at: http://learningcurve.pro.gov.uk/heroesvillains/churchill/
26. Quoted by Lindqvist, op. cit., p. 196.
27. Quoted in ibid., p. 200.
28. Speer in *The World at War* documentary, Inside the Reich.
29. Ibid.

30. Lundqvist, op. cit., p. 210.
31. Ibid., p. 213.
32. Frederick Taylor, *Dresden. Tuesday, February 13, 1945*, HarperCollins, London, 2004.
David Irving, *The Destruction of Dreseden*, Kimber, London, 1963.
33. Harris's official account of Bomber Command, 1946, reproduced as Source 1 at: http://learningcurve.pro.gov.uk/heroesvillains/churchill/
34. Reproduced as Source http://learningcurve.pro.gov.uk/heroesvillains/churchill/
35. Quoted by Lindqvist, op. cit., p. 217.

Chapter 8 The Holocaust

1. Adolf Hitler, *Mein Kampf*, D.C. Watt, ed., Hutchinson, London, p. 772.
2. Michael Burleigh, *The Third Reich. A New History*, Macmillan, London, 2000, p. 72.
3. Quoted in ibid., p. 316.
4. Quoted in ibid., pp. 339–40 (entry dated 10 January 1939).
5. Prompting the German Supreme Court to produce a definition of sexual intercourse which was as broad as President Clinton's was narrow.
6. Burleigh, op. cit., p. 332.
7. Quoted in J. Noakes and G. Pridham, *Nazism 1919–1945, Vol. 3. Foreign Policy, War and Racial Extermination*, Exeter University Publications, Exeter, 1988, p. 1049.
8. Burleigh, ibid., p. 1661.
9. Quoted in Noakes and Pridham, op. cit., p. 1131.
10. Daniel Jonah Goldhagen, *Hitler's Willing Executioners. Ordinary Germans and the Holocaust*, Alfred A. Knopf, New York: 1996.
11. Noakes and Pridham, op. cit., p. 1199.
12. Melita Maschmann, *Fazit: Mein Weg in der Hitler–Jugend*, Deutscher Taschenbuch Verlag, Munich, 1979.

Chapter 9 The Pacific war

1. Cheryl Greenberg, 'Black and Jewish Responses to Japanese Internment', *Journal of American Ethnic History*, 14(2), 1995.

2. All quotations from: http://www.randomhouse.com/vintage/read/snow

3. Oral History Interview with Karl R. Benedetsen, former General Counsel, Department of the Army, conducted on 24 October 1972. Transcript available at: http://www.trumanlibrary.org/oralhist/bendet1.html#japandocsbendet

4. http://www.ourdocuments.gov/print_friendly.php?page=learn_more&doc=74

5. Tatiana A. Klimova, 'Internment of Japanese Americans: Military Necessity or Racial Prejudice?' Available at: http://www.odu.edu/~hanley/history1/Klimova.htm

6. William Carr, *Poland to Pearl Harbor: The Making of the Second World War*, Edward Arnold, London, 1985, p. 111.

7. Quoted in Richard Overy, and Andrew Wheatcroft, *The Road to War*. Macmillan, London, 1989, p. 288.

8. Quoted in ibid., p. 259.

9. Akira Iriye, *The Significance of the Pearl Harbor Attack: A Fifty-Year Perspective*. Brewster lecture at: http://www.ecu.edu/history/brewster/bl91.htm

10. Quoted in Richard Overy and Andrew Wheatcroft, op. cit.

11. Quoted in William Carr, op. cit., p. 135.

12. Ibid., p. 135.

13. See John L. Harper and Andrew Parlin, *The Polish Question During World War II*, Foreign Policy Institute, Washington, D.C., 1990, p. 79.

14. See Gar Alperovitz, *Atomic Diplomacy: Hiroshima and Potsdam: The Use of the Atomic Bomb and the Confrontation with Soviet Power*, Penguin, London, 1985.

15. MS Harry S. Truman, *Nat. Archives 342*, USAF 13059.

16. Alperovitz, ibid., pp. 103–9.

17. Quoted in Harper and Parlin, op. cit., p. 20.

18. Ibid., p. 20.

19. See the various drafts of this statement at: http://www.trumanlibrary.org/whistlestop/study_collections/bomb/large/documents/fulltext.php?fulltextid=20

Chapter 10 The Second World War and the Cold War

1. Isaac Deutscher, *Stalin*, 1960, p. 479.

2. Harry Butcher,'s *My Three Years with Eisenhower*, Heinemann, 1946.
3. Ralph Ingersoll's *Top Secret*, N. Y. Harcourt, Brace and Company, 1946.
4. Elliott Roosevelt, *As He Saw It*, Duell, Sloan & Pearce, 1946.
5. Richard M. Leighton, 'Overlord Revisited', *The American Historical Review*, July 1963, quoted in Michael Howard, *The Mediterranean Strategy in the Second World War*, Weidenfeld and Nicolson, London, 1968.
6. W.S. Churchill, *Triumph and Tragedy*, Houghton Mifflin Co., Boston, 1953, p. 366.
7. Quoted in John L. Harper and Andrew Parlin, *The Polish Question During World War II*, Foreign Policy Institute, Washington D.C., 1990, p. 13.
8. Quoted in ibid., p. 40.
9. Quoted in ibid., p. 33.
10. Quoted in Ibid., p. 40.
11. Milovan Djilas, *Conversations with Stalin*, Hart-Davis, London, 1962, p. 114.

Chapter 11 The German question

1. Quoted in J.M. Hanhimaki and O.A. Westad, eds, *The Cold War. A History in Documents and Eyewitness Accounts*, Oxford University Press, Oxford, 2003, p. 73.
2. Ibid., The Potsdam Protocol on Germany, August 1945, p. 84.
3. Dean Acheson, *Present at the Creation*, Signet Books, London, 1970, p. 446.
4. http://www.hri.org/MFA/foreign/treaties/Rome57/preamble.txt
5. Tony Judt, *A Grand Illusion? An Essay on Europe*, Penguin, London, 1996, p. 29.

Chapter 13 The impact of World War Two on the United States

1. Stoler, The Second World War in US History and Memory, Diplomatic History, pp. 383–4.
2. Ibid., p. 388.

3. G. Weinberg, World War Two: Comments on the Roundtable, p. 498.
4. For what follows see History in Dispute, World War Two, Thomson Gale.
5. Gil Asakawa, 'Speaking out for the past', *Denver News*, 16 February 2003.
6. Eugene V. Rostow, quoted in Roger Daniels and Spencer C. Olin Jr., 'Racism in California' Macmillan, 1972, p. 167.
7. Quoted in John Dower, *War without Mercy: Race and Power in the Pacific War*, Random House, New York, 1986, p. 110.
8. 'Rep. Howard Coble says WWII internments made sense' available at: http://www.sacbee.com/24hour/politics/story/751093p-5438735c.html (5 Feb. 2003).
9. Congressman Howard Coble, quoted in Congressman Condemns Colleagues Remarks at: http://www.sacbee.com/24hour/politics/story/751093p-5438735c.html
10. Quoted in Pat Morrison, 'Two Republicans draw fire for "outrageous" ethnic comments', *National Catholic Reporter*, 28 February 2003 at: http://www.natcath.com/NCR_Online/archives/022803/022803k.htm
11. Curtis Munson quoted in Eric J. Sundquist, 'The Japanese-American Internment', *American Scholar*, 57, 1988, p. 539.
12. Quoted in Deborah Schiffrin, 'Language and public memorial: America's concentration camps' *Discourse & Society*, 12(4), p. 512.
13. Quoted by Otto Friedrich, 'Day of Infamy', *Time*, 2 December 1991, p. 33.
14. Oral History Interview with Karl R. Benedetsen, former General Counsel, Department of the Army, conducted on 24 October 1972. Transcript available at: http://www.trumanlibrary.org/oralhist/bendet1.html#japandocsbendet
15. Quoted at Truman Library: http://www.trumanlibrary.org/whistlestop/study collections/japanese internment/194
16. Mikiso Hane, 'Wartime internment', *The Journal of American History*, 77(2), September 1990, p. 570.
17. For the text of Executive Order 9066 see, for example: http://historymatters.gmu.edu/d/5154/
18. Francis Biddle, Attorney General to Secretary of War, (Henry Stimson), 12 February 1942. Available at: http://

www.inc.edu/~emuller/isthatlegal/biddle1.jpg and http://
www.inc..edu/~emuller/isthatlegal/biddle2.jpg

19. Ibid.
20. Henry L. Stimson, diary entry for 10 February 1942, quoted
    at: http://www.trumanlibrary.org/whistlestop collections/
    japanese internment/
21. Transcript of a Conference with General de Witt at the Office
    of the Commanding General, Headquarters Western Defence
    Command and Fourth Army, 4 January 1942. Available at:
    http://www.archives.gov/digital_classroom/lessons/
    japanese_relocation_wwii/
22. Quoted in Tatiana A. Klimova, 'Internment of Japanese
    Americans: Military Necessity or Racial Prejudice?' Available
    at: http://www.odu.edu/~hanley/history1/Klimova.htm
23. Quoted in James Weingartner, 'War against Subhumans:
    Comparisons between the German War against the Soviet
    Union and the American War against Japan, 1941–1945',
    Historian, 1996, 58(3), pp. 567.
24. Quoted in America's War, World War II in Colour DVD
    0927-48320-2 Episode 2. Battlefronts: 1942–1944, Track 4:
    Internment of Japanese Americans. It should, however, be
    borne in mind that when this remark was made concentration
    camps did not have the connotations which they were shortly to
    acquire as Nazi-occupied Europe was liberated. The US author-
    ities, initially at least, used the terms concentration camps intern-
    ment camps and relocation camps interchangeably. Miller's views
    are sufficiently odious without presenting them as genocidal.
25. Warren and Lippmann quotations from Mikiso Hane,
    'Wartime Internment', *The Journal of American History*, p. 571.
26. Transcript of the proceedings of the Subcommittee of
    the Committee on Military Affairs considering the War
    Relocation Centers, 28 January 1943. Available at: http://
    www.trumanlibrary.org/whistlestop/study_collections/
    japanese_internment/doc
27. Oral History Interview with Karl R. Bendetsen conducted on
    24 October 1972. Available at: http://www.trumanlibrary.org/
    oralhist/bendet1.htm
28. Cheryl Greenberg, 'Black and Jewish Responses to Japanese
    Internment', *Journal of American Ethnic History*, 14(2),
    1995, p. 34.

29. Senator John Rankin quoted in the Congressional Record 1942, v. 88, pt. 1, p. 1420.
30. *Los Angeles Times*, 8 December 1941 quoted in Roger Daniels, 'Incarcerating Japanese Americans: An Atrocity Revisited', *Peace & Change*, 23(2), April 1998, p. 120.
31. Oral History Interview with Tom Clark conducted on 17 October 1972. Available at: http://www.trumanlibrary.org/oralhist/tomclark.htm
32. Figures from Mikiso Hane, 'Wartime Internment', *The Journal of American History*, p. 570.
33. Quoted in Roger Daniels, 'Incarcerating Japanese Americans: An Atrocity Revisited', *Peace & Change*, 23(2), April 1998, p. 121.
34. Including 52 Distinguished Service Crosses, 560 Silver Stars and 1 Medal of Honor. On 21 June 2000 President Clinton awarded the Medal of Honor to 20 additional Nisei for their actions during World War Two. The Nisei during World War Two sustained 9,486 wounded and more than 600 killed. Source: Robert Davenport, *Alpha Teach Yourself American History in 24 Hours*, Alpha Books, 2003, p. 224.
35. America's War, World War II in Colour DVD 0927–48320–2 Episode 2 Battlefronts: 1942–1944, Track 12: The Japanese American 442nd Infantry Regiment.
36. The World at War, Part One, On Our Way–America Enters the War–1939–1942, DVD PTDVD8011.
37. Oral History Interview with Tom Clark conducted on 17 October 1972. Available at: http://www.trumanlibrary.org/oralhist/tomclark.htm
38. Mikiso Hane, 'Wartime Internment', *The Journal of American History*, p. 572.
39. Quoted in Tatiana A. Klimova, 'Internment of Japanese Americans: Military Necessity or Racial Prejudice?', Available at: http://www.odu.edu/~hanley/history1/Klimova.htm
40. Richard Overy and Andrew Wheatcroft, *The Road to War*, 2nd edn, Penguin, p. 350.
41. See Niall Ferguson, Colossus. *The Rise and Fall of the American Empire*, Penguin, Harmondsworth, 2005.

Select Bibliography

This highly selective bibliography does not include texts cited in the 'Notes' section.

General histories

Keegan, John, *The Second World War*, Hutchinson, London, 1989.
Weinberg, G.L., *A World At Arms*, Cambridge University Press, Cambridge, 1994.
Calvocoressi, Peter, Wint, Guy and Pritchard, John, *Total War*. rev. 2nd edn., Pantheon Books, London, 1989.

Chapter 1

Boemke, M.F., Feldman, G., and Glaser, E., eds, *The Treaty of Versailles: A Reassessment*, Cambridge University Press, Cambridge, 1998.
Henig, Ruth, *Versailles and After, 1919–1933*, 2nd edn, Routledge, London, 1995.
Macmillan, Margaret, *Peacemakers. The Paris Conference of 1919 and Its Attempt to End War*, John Murray, London, 2001.

Chapter 2

Carr, William, *Arms, Autarky, and Aggression: A Study in German Foreign Policy, 1933–1939*, Edward Arnold, London, 1972.
Hitler, Adolf, *Mein Kampf* (with an introduction by D.C. Watt), Pimlico, London, 1992.
Overy, R.J., *War and Economy in the Third Reich*, Oxford University Press, Oxford, 1994.

Chapter 3

Louis, W. Roger, ed., *The Origins of the Second World War. A.J.P. Taylor and His Critics*, Wiley, New York, 1972.

Martel, Gordon, ed., *The Origins of the Second World War Reconsidered: The A.J.P. Taylor Debate after Twenty-Five Years*, George Allen and Unwin, Boston, 1986.

Taylor, A.J.P., *Origins of the Second World War*, Hamish Hamilton, London, 1961.

Chapter 4

Bond, Brian, *Britain, France and Belgium 1939–1940*, 2nd edn, Brassey/Maxwell Pergamon, London, 1990.

Horne, Alistair, *To Lose a Battle: France, 1940*, Papermac, London, 1990.

Kemp, Anthony, *The Maginot Line: Myth and Reality*, Stein and Day, New York, 1981.

Chapter 5

Ray, J.P., *The Battle of Britain: New Perspectives: Behind the Scenes of the Great Air War*, Arms and Armour, London, 1991.

Winterbotham, F.W., *The Ultra Secret*, Harper and Row, New York, 1974.

Chapter 6

Clark, Alan, *Barbarossa: The Russian-German Conflict 1941–45*, William Morrow, New York, 1966.

Erickson, John, *The Road to Stalingrad*, Weidenfeld and Nicolson, London, 1975.

Erickson, John, *The Road to Berlin*, Weidenfeld and Nicolson, London, 1999.

Hitler quoted in J. Noakes and G. Pridham, *Nazism 1919–1945, Vol.3. Foreign Policy, War and Racial Extermination*, Exeter University Publications, Exeter, p. 809.

Chapter 7

Frankland, Noble, *The Bombing Offensive against Germany: Outlines and Perspective*, Faber and Faber, London, 1965.

Hastings, Max, *Bomber Command*, Papermac, London, 1993.

Overy, R.J., *The Air War 1939–1945*, Papermac, London, 1987.

Chapter 8

Dawidowicz, Lucy, *The War against the Jews, 1933–1945*, Bantam, New York, 1976.

Hilberg, Raul, ed., *The Destruction of the European Jews*, 3 vols, Holmes and Meier, New York, 1984.

Marrus, Michael, *The Holocaust in History*, University of New England, Hanover, 1987.

Chapter 9

Alperovitz, Gar, *The Decision to Use the Atomic Bomb*, Knopf, New York, 1995.

Bernstein, B.J., ed., *The Atomic Bomb: The Critical Issues*, Little, Brown, Boston, 1976.

Iriye, Akira, *The Origins of the Second World War in Asia and the Pacific*, Longman, London, 1987.

Nish, Ian, *Anglo-Japanese Alienation 1919–52: Papers of the Anglo-Japanese Conference on the History of the Second World War*, Cambridge University Press, Cambridge, 1982.

Chapter 10

Brands, H.W., *The Devil We Knew: Americans and the Cold War*, Oxford University Press, Oxford, 1993.

Levering, Ralph B., *The Cold War: A Post-Cold War History*, Harlan Davidson, Arlington Heights, Illinois, 1994.

Walker, Martin, *The Cold War: A History*, Henry Holt and Co., New York, 1993.

Chapter 11

Ardagh, John, *Germany and the Germans*, rev. edn, Penguin Books, New York, 1991.

Deighton, Anne, *The Impossible Peace: Britain, the Division of Germany and the Origins of the Cold War*, The Clarendon Press, Oxford, 1990.

Milward, A.S., *The Reconstruction of Western Europe 1945–51*, Routledge, London, 1984.

Willis, R.F., *France, Germany and the New Europe 1945–1967*, Oxford University Press, Oxford, 1965.

Chapter 12

Barnett, C., *The Collapse of the British Power*, Eyre Methuen, London, 1972.

Darwin, J., *The End of the British Empire: The Historical Debate*, Basil Blackwell, Oxford, 1991.

Northedge, F.S., Chapman, B., *British Foreign Policy: The Process of Readjustment 1945–1961*, George Allen and Unwin, London, 1962.

Chapter 13

Blum, J. Morton, *V Was For Victory: Politics and American Culture During World War II*, Harcourt Brace Jovanovich, New York, 1976.

Cashman, S. Dennis, *America, Roosevelt, and World War II*, NYU Press, New York, 1989.

O'Neill, W.L., *A Democracy At War: America's Fight at Home and Abroad in World War II*, Free Press, New York, 1993.

Index